Second Edition

Small Group Instruction in Higher Education
Lessons from the Past, Visions of the Future

James L. Cooper, Pamela Robinson & David Ball, Editors

NEW FORUMS
Stillwater, Oklahoma
U.S.A.

NEW FORUMS PRESS INC.

Published in the United States of America
by New Forums Press, Inc.
1018 S. Lewis St.
Stillwater, OK 74074
www.newforums.com

Copyright © 2003, 2009 by New Forums Press, Inc.

All rights reserved. No part of this publication may be reproduced or transmitted in any form or by any means, electronic or mechanical, including photocopy, or any information storage or retrieval system, without permission in writing from the publisher.

Library of Congress Cataloging-in-Publication Data Pending

This book may be ordered in bulk quantities at discount from New Forums Press, Inc., P.O. Box 876, Stillwater, OK 74076 [Federal I.D. No. 73 1123239]. Printed in the United States of America.

ISBN 10: 1-58107-165-5
ISBN 13: 978-1-581071-65-8

Cover photo by Susan Johnston.

Contents

A Note from Jim Cooper vii
Organization of Book ix

Section 1. Group Learning: Definitions and Distinctions 1
  1. What is Cooperative Learning? 3
     Jim Cooper
  2. Building Bridges Between Cooperative
    and Collaborative Learning 6
     Roberta S. Matthews, James L. Cooper, Neil Davidson,
     and Peter Hawkes
  3. Collaborative & Cooperative Learning in Higher
    Education: A Proposed Taxonomy 18
     Joe Cuseo

Section 2. Why Use Cooperative Strategies?
Research and Theory 27
  4. FIPSE-Sponsored CL Research at Dominguez
    Hills and Community Colleges 29
     Jim Cooper and Pamela Robinson
  5. Research on Cooperative Learning in College
    Science, Mathematics, Engineering,
    and Technology 33
     Leonard Springer
  6. How Cooperative Learning Can Fullfill the Promises
    of the "Seven Principles" 39
     Barbara Millis
  7. What Matters in College? Implications for Cooperative
    Learning of a New National Study 44
     Alexander W. Astin
  8. Critical Thinking and Cooperative Learning: A
    Natural Marriage 63
     Joseph B. Cuseo

9. Cooperative Learning: A Pedagogy for Diversity 75
   Joseph B. Cuseo
10. Ten Reasons College Administrators Should
    Support Cooperative Learning 90
    Jim Cooper

Section 3: Informal Small-group Procedures 97
11. A Cooperative Learning Structure for Large
    Classes: Think-Pair-Share 99
    Barbara J. Millis and Philip G. Cottell Jr.
12. Think-Pair-Square Applied to a Review Session 106
    Joy Ollen
13. Guided Peer Questioning: A Cooperative Learning
    Approach to Critical Thinking 112
    Alison King
14. Quick-thinks: Active-thinking Tasks in Lecture
    Classes and Televised Instruction 122
    Susan Johnston and Jim Cooper
15. Supporting Student Success Through Scaffolding 135
    Susan Johnston and Jim Cooper
16. The Use of Pairs in Cooperative Learning 146
    Mel Silberman

Section 4: Formal Cooperative-learning Strategies 153
17. More Tips for Getting Started in Cooperative
    Learning (CL) 155
    Susan Prescott-Johnston
18. Getting Started with Cooperative Learning 161
    Susan Prescott-Johnston
19. Using Small-Group Development to Facilitate
    Cooperative Learning Base Groups 166
    Nancy E. Stetson
20. College Classrooms' Lost Gold Mine: The
    Cooperative Base Group 171
    Susan E. Gruber and Darlene Vanselow Habanek
21. Structured Controversy/Constructive
    Controversy 179
    David W. Johnson, Roger T. Johnson and Karl A. Smith

22. Group Investigation in the University
    Classroom 183
    Shlomo Sharan

Section 5: Implementing Interactive Group
Instruction: Practical Advice 191
23. Faculty and Student Resistance to Cooperative
    Learning 193
    Ted Panitz
24. Building Community One Brick at a Time 201
    Marcy Hamby Towns
25. Group Formation in Cooperative Learning: What
    the Experts Say 207
    Jim Cooper
26. Trouble-Shooting Cooperative Learning 211
    Susan Prescott Johnston
27. Trouble-Shooting Cooperative Learning 216
    Susan Prescott Johnston
28. Trouble-Shooting 222
    Susan Prescott Johnston
29. Peer Revision: Sharing the Power and the Work 231
    Susan Johnston
30. Supporting Student Success in the Classroom 236
    Susan Johnston

Part II: What the Experts Are Thinking 247
    The 21st Century College: The Three Cs 251
        David W. Johnson and Roger T. Johnson
    Cooperative Learning and Service Learning: Soul-mates
        for Reflection in Higher Education 267
        James Mitchell
    Small-group Learning in Higher Education: A Status
        Report and an Agenda for the Future 282
        James L. Cooper, David Ball and Pamela Robinson
    Cooperative-learning Structures for Brain-compatible
        Instruction 292
        Spencer Kagan

Surveys and Cooperative Learning: Using Student
Experiences as the Basis for Small-group Work 311
Mark H. Maier

Using Cooperative Games for Learning and
Assessment 321
Barbara J. Millis

The Interactive Lecture: Reconciling Group and
Active-learning Strategies with Traditional
Instructional Formats 336
James L. Cooper, Pamela Robinson, and David Ball

A Crisis of Clarity 349
Susan Johnston

The Status of Small-group Instruction, 2008:
What the Experts Say 357
Jim Cooper & Pamela Robinson

A Note from Jim Cooper

I was pleased when Doug Dollar asked Pamela Robinson and I do this second edition of our 2003 small-group instruction book. Pamela and I had, (independently) started to write a chapter which was to be an update of an 1996 article written for the *Cooperative Learning and College Teaching* newsletter in which we surveyed national leaders in teaching and learning concerning a series of issues relating to group learning (it is reprinted on pages 207-210 of this second edition). In 2003 Pamela and I updated the 1996 survey in a chapter written for the first edition of this book (see pages 282-291 of this volume). The new survey chapter, which begins on page 357, generally confirms our own impressions regarding the status of cooperative/collaborative learning, that it is the most widely researched and frequently implemented of the "new" pedagogies emerging within the last 30 years in higher education. Having said that, the lecture remains by far the most common technique actually implemented in higher education, despite the lack of a substantial research base.

We hope that this book will provide an impetus for teachers, department chairs and senior administrators to examine teaching and learning and move to greater use of research based active learning. As a guide to approaching this volume, teachers primarily interested in applied issues may wish to initially focus on Section 3 of this book to get a sense of how to implement informal group learning, then move on to Section 4 in which more formal (and effortful) team learning procedures are described. Section 5 includes advice for practitioners, including a number of trouble-shooting works by Susan Prescott Johnston. At some point teachers will want to get a sense of the empirical and theoretical underpinnings for group work provided in Sections 1 and 2 of this book.

Teachers who would like to examine the rationale for using group work may want to start with Sections 1 and 2 of this book, then read the more applied work that is presented in the rest of the volume. Department chairs and senior administrators may wish to begin by reading *Ten Reasons College Administrators Should Support Cooperative Learning* (pages 90-95) and Alexander Astin's article in which he ties his landmark "what matters in college" work with small-group practice. Pamela and I believe that systematic use of small-group work can provide more "bang for the buck" than other interventions which require extra funding and require students to come to college during non-class time, such as summer bridge and tutoring programs. Effective small-group work is a natural ally for those attempting to improve persistence to graduation and other measures of student success and institutional effectiveness. It should also be noted that many accrediting groups endorse research-based group learning in their evaluation guidelines as promoting active listening, team work and the ability to function in diverse settings, skills which are increasingly valued in most professions.

Pamela and I are hardly dispassionate observers of small-group work, but we think that data is clear in identifying carefully-structured small-group instruction as the most powerful intervention developed in the last 30 years in higher education. We hope that readers of this volume will agree with this assessment and help ensure that a healthy dialog continues in higher education regarding the place of active and group learning as alternatives to more traditional and passive instructional approaches.

Organization of Book

This book is organized into two Parts. The first Part consists of reprints from the nine years that Jim and Pamela edited the *Cooperative Learning and College Teaching* newsletter. It contains 30 articles divided into five sections. Each section contains a brief introduction. The first section contains articles that provide definitions and conceptual distinctions that may be of use to the reader (for example, the difference between cooperative and collaborative learning). The second section offers theoretical and empirical support for the use of group learning. The third section describes low risk, informal active and group learning strategies that may be used in conjunction with lectures and other instructional techniques. The fourth section delineates more effortful, formal strategies that typically require greater planning and organization. The last section of Part I offers practical advice for implementing the strategies identified throughout the book.

When we began publishing the newsletter we decided not to include reference sections for most articles. Instead we asked readers to contact authors if they wished to obtain that information. By doing so, we were able to get one additional article in each issue. Readers will note differences in style and form from article to article. The newsletter editors decided to give authors relative freedom on these issues. For example, some articles abbreviate Cooperative Learning as CL. In editing this volume we rarely changed the articles from their original format, except as it affected clarity for readers of this text.

Part II of the volume is a collection of chapters written specifically for this book. We identified a number of leaders in teaching and learning and asked them to pick issues that they were *currently* interested in and to describe it to our readers. This was an attempt to bring readers up to date on present interests and future trends in active and group learning as identified by those who are at the cutting edge of research and practice.

Section 1
Group Learning: Definitions and Distinctions

This section introduces the reader to cooperative learning. When cooperative learning first made an impact in higher education it was often compared to another form of group instruction known as collaborative learning. The article by Jim Cooper (Article 1, pages 3-5) offers a definition of cooperative learning and identifies its critical features. At the time of the article's publication in 1990, there was a sense among some that differences between cooperative learning and other forms of group learning needed to be highlighted.

Over the years, there has been a movement to bring the forces of active- and group-learning together, to present a united front, making the case that any pedagogical approach that moves college teaching from a strict reliance on passive modes of instruction, such as the lecture, was a positive step. In 1995, the newsletter reprinted an article by Roberta Matthews and her colleagues that was first published in *Change* magazine (Article 2, pages 6-17) representing both the cooperative and collaborative "camps" in higher education. This article sought to unite those interested in group learning around central, active learning principles having a research base. Although the authors did not disguise differences between cooperative and collaborative approaches, they sought a rapprochement between them so that, as Roberta and her colleagues noted, instructors would " …have a broader awareness of the variety of approaches that have different pedagogical implications. . ." in order to "…learn from each other and acknowledge each other's accomplishments. Sharing the success of each enriches us all." The article concludes with an unnotated bibliography of resources containing research and practice in small-group instruction.

Ultimately, faculty members need to examine the literature on college teaching effectiveness and use techniques with which they feel most comfortable for their disciplines and students.

In Article 3, beginning on page 18, Joe Cuseo provides a taxonomy of the most popular forms of group learning, including collaboration between students, between instructors, and between students and teachers. He views collaborative learning as a generic process that encompasses cooperative learning and a wide variety of other group procedures.

1 What is Cooperative Learning?

Jim Cooper

Originally published in the Cooperative Learning and College Teaching newsletter, Fall, 1990.

Cooperative learning (CL) may be defined as a structured, systematic instructional strategy in which small groups work together to produce a common product. The following features are commonly associated with cooperative learning:

Positive interdependence.

There must be structures built into teaching to ensure that students within learning groups develop a sense that they are responsible for one another's learning. At times this is done by assigning discrete roles for each team member while at other times this is done by giving each team member different content to teach to all members of the team. All CL teams must realize that their work is not over until all members of the team have mastered the assignment.

Individual accountability.

Although students are expected to help one another learn in CL, it is essential that students be assessed individually concerning their mastery of course content. Thus, group grades are strongly discouraged in most CL techniques. Virtually all of a student's course grade should be based on individually-completed tests, papers and other assignments. When members of a team make individual contributions to a team presentation or paper, the instructor should require that the individual contribution of each team member be assessed. If this is not done, the dominator/sandbagger phenomenon which often characterizes traditional small group instruction can result.

Appropriate grouping.

Most of us using CL at Dominguez Hills have found that four-person learning teams work best. More than four persons in a team diminishes individual student's opportunities to practice and get feedback on oral and written performances. Fewer than four persons lessens the diversity of viewpoint that is another strength of CL. Usually the four are selected by the teacher to ensure diversity in achievement, race, sex and other characteristics. In some circumstances, three and five person teams can be effective.

Student interaction.

High levels of student-student interaction are essential to success in CL. Highly structured, teacher-constructed tasks should be given to students initially. After experiencing success under these circumstances less structure and more student control may be instituted. Most effective CL classrooms are characterized by intense conversations concerning the academic task.

Attention to social skills.

Many students may not have the appropriate social skills to work in small groups most efficiently. Therefore, we stress on our course syllabi the importance of active listening, equal contributions to resolving the task, and respect for others. At times it may be helpful to point to groups who are modeling such skills as a reminder to the entire class. At other times, group processing can be useful. In this procedure each member of the cooperative learning group assesses his/her own performance and that of each teammate on some explicit social skills criteria, then shares that information with the group and/or the teacher.

Teacher as facilitator.

The role of the teacher in CL is different from his/her role in lecture and lecture/discussion classes. The teacher ceases to be the predominant dispenser of in-class information on a variety of topics and becomes a facilitator, structuring learning assignments for the groups and working in a more collegial arrangement with the groups as they attempt to master the assignments presented to them.

Those of us who have been using CL with our college-level students have not given up lecturing and other forms of instruction. Most of us use CL 15-40% of the total class time. For all of us, the experience has been exhilarating, as we worry less about the content that we "cover" in lecture and concern ourselves with the oral and written skills that our students can demonstrate. For those concerned that they will cover less content when using CL, the research indicates that more content is remembered following CL classes than classes using more traditional techniques such as the lecture.

2 Building Bridges Between Cooperative and Collaborative Learning

Roberta S. Matthews, James L. Cooper, Neil Davidson, and Peter Hawkes

> Published in the *Cooperative Learning and College Teaching* newsletter, Fall, 1995.

In comparing collaborative and cooperative learning as they are practiced in college and university classrooms we have two purposes in mind. On the one hand, we wish to assert the commonalities shared by these two approaches, such as using small groups to facilitate learning; on the other, we wish to highlight the differences so that college and university teachers may make informed choices about how to organize their classes and present their materials. Confusion about these similarities and differences leads not only to misconceptions, but occasionally, to strong differences of opinion. In this brief article, we wish to lay the groundwork for a convergence of purpose. Ultimately, we hope to foster the development of an emerging field of research and practice that includes both collaborative and cooperative learning.

Although collaborative and cooperative learning encompass many different activities in themselves, we have limited our focus here to their presence in colleges and universities as varieties of classroom-based small-group activity. This means, for example, with regard to collaborative learning, that we will not discuss the faculty-faculty collaborations that occur in multi- or interdisciplinary learning communities; faculty-faculty collaboration around research; student-faculty collaborative research or teaching initiatives; or institutional forms of collaboration. With regard to cooperative learning, we will not discuss the rich body of practice and research that has surrounded its growth as an international movement of influence in pre-collegiate settings. With regard to both, we will not consider the nuances of group learning and assessment issues, and can merely acknowledge the potentially rich relationship between collaborative and cooperative learning and various forms of electronic learning. This is not an exhaustive survey, but rather an attempt to situate collaborative and cooperative learning and to define a set of attitudes toward an area of increasing interest to college and university teachers. We refer readers to the annotated bibliography at the end of this article for further reading and study.

We begin with an example that suggests the differences between cooperative and collaborative learning. Mary Jones is a college student taking a class in educational principles and practices from Dr. Davidson, a cooperative-learning adherent. She is also enrolled in a composition course with Dr. Hawkes, an English professor who practices collaborative learning. In Dr. Davidson's cooperative-learning class, Mary and her teammates participate in structured group activities as they work together on a set of problems; at times, they are each assigned a specific role within their team. In Dr. Hawkes' collaborative-learning class, Mary and her group members are asked to organize their joint efforts and decide themselves who will perform group roles as the group critiques a student essay.

While the groups work on their tasks in the cooperative-learning class, Dr. Davidson moves from team to team, observes the interactions, listens to the conversations, and intervenes when he feels it is appropriate. In Mary's composition course, Dr. Hawkes does not actively monitor the groups and refers all substantive questions back to them to resolve. At the end of Dr. Davidson's class period, he often conducts a brief summary session; he may ask groups to give a brief oral report of their findings or to submit a copy of their group-activity materials for his comments. Dr. Hawkes' collaborative-learning class always ends with a plenary session; students keep the composition they evaluated and use it "to go to school on" as they work on their own drafts to be submitted in final form the following week.

Earlier in the semester, Mary and her classmates in Dr.

Davidson's class received training in appropriate small-group social skills such as active listening and giving constructive feedback to teammates. Mary did not receive formal training in these techniques in Dr. Hawkes' class because he feels the students already possess the social skills necessary for group work. In Dr. Davidson's class, groups often perform group "processing" tasks in which students assess how the groups are functioning and how group members individually and together could improve levels of participation and performance. In Dr. Hawkes' class no formal group processing sessions occur, since he wants Mary and other students to resolve group conflicts or participation issues on their own.

In the hypothetical classes just described, the procedures of both Dr. Davidson and Dr. Hawkes suggest a commitment to active small-group learning that represents a radical departure from the values and styles of more traditional college classrooms. Both have decided to hand over some of the teacher's traditional authority to the students. And both have made practical decisions based on assumptions about the role of the teacher, the nature of the learner, and the authority of knowledge. But the practices of the two teachers and their assumptions vary because they have adopted different methods of group learning.

As the classroom descriptions suggest, there are areas where collaborative and cooperative learning are markedly dissimilar. Within the context of small-group learning, there is a wide range of views about:

- the style, function, and degree of involvement of the teacher;
- the issue of authority and power relationships between teacher and student;
- the extent to which students need to be trained to work together in groups;
- how knowledge is assimilated or constructed;
- the purpose of groups to emphasize different outcomes such as the mastery of facts, the development of judgment, and/or the construction of knowledge;
- the importance of different aspects of personal, social, and/or cognitive growth among students; and

- a variety of additional implementation concerns including, for example, group formation, task construction, and the degree of individual and/or group accountability necessary to ensure equitable distribution of work and accurate grading.

In some cases, disagreement between collaborative- and cooperative-learning practitioners about a particular issue or practice might stem from differences in the two methods. In other cases, divergence simply reflects teachers' different areas of interest and concern; what is important to one might be a non-issue to the other— a circumstance that results in asymmetrical debate. Nevertheless, each issue represents for practitioners a point at which conscious, informed choices are necessary.

We wish to acknowledge as well the extent to which personal style and values, local or cultural preferences, the mores and language of particular disciplines, and levels of student preparedness all have an impact upon how an individual teacher decides to implement small-group instruction in particular contexts.

There are also areas where collaborative and cooperative learning share a number of assumptions and areas of agreement. Here are a few commonalities we have identified:
- learning in an active mode is more effective than passively receiving information;
- the teacher is a facilitator, coach, or midwife rather than a "sage on the stage";
- teaching and learning are shared experiences between teacher and students;
- balancing lecture and small-group activities is an important part of a teacher's role;
- participating in small-group activities develops higher-order thinking skills and enhances individual abilities to use knowledge;
- accepting responsibility for learning as an individual and as a member of a group enhances intellectual development;
- articulating one's ideas in a small-group setting enhances a student's ability to reflect on his or her own assumptions and thought processes;

- developing social and team skills through the give-and-take of consensus building is a fundamental part of a liberal education;
- belonging to a small and supportive academic community increases student success and retention; and
- appreciating (or at least acknowledging the value of) diversity is essential for the survival of a multicultural democracy.

There is as well a shared concern about the lecture as the sole mode of communication and a shared perception that some public and institutional resistance exists to the changes suggested by the practices of collaborative and cooperative learning. Practitioners share common challenges that may work against the implementation of small-group learning in college classrooms, whether in the collaborative or the cooperative mode.

What are some examples of common resistance to group work? Instructors often find that the move to small-group learning is accompanied by the fear that all of the material in a course will not be covered, a condition that raises a number of hard questions and points of negotiation about the teaching-learning process. Another kind of challenge confronts students who have become accustomed to lecture-based classrooms and resist more active approaches. Finally, institutional mores pose a challenge to the professor whose use of collaborative and cooperative learning may result in hostile peer or student evaluations that can threaten tenure or promotion.

On the other hand, a number of national commissions and disciplinary groups have advocated the introduction of more collaborative- and cooperative-learning strategies in the classroom. In colleges and universities throughout the country, efforts are under way to transform the classroom from a lecture-based experience to a more active and demanding one for students. The initiative, although grounded in the disciplines, also transcends disciplinary boundaries and, in many of its forms, is consciously multi- or interdisciplinary.

Indeed, the diversity of activities found in collaborative and cooperative classrooms reflects several decades of development. The roots and history of each approach have yielded a rich and varied body of literature and wisdom of practice. In addition, within collaborative and cooperative learning themselves, there are significant differences among adherents, while at the boundaries there is a good deal of overlap between the two. Both methods acknowledge the pervasive and fundamental influence of John Dewey and his belief that education should be viewed "as a social enterprise in which all individuals have an opportunity to contribute and to which all feel a responsibility."

Most of the well-known cooperative-learning researchers and theoreticians are educational or social psychologists or sociologists whose original work was intended for application at the K-12 level. Their primary research emphasis is on empirical comparisons of cooperative learning with other forms of instruction. Within the last decade, techniques have been extended and adapted at the college level, and many of the publications in the field offer practical advice. Cooperative learning tends to be more structured in its approach to small-group instruction, to be more detailed in advice to practitioners, and to advocate more direct training of students to function in groups than does collaborative learning.

Collaborative learning theoreticians and practitioners tend to come from the humanities and social sciences. Their work often explores theoretical, political, and philosophical issues such as the nature of knowledge as a social construction and the role of authority in the classroom. Many are concerned with drawing strong connections between collaborative practice and feminist pedagogy. Collaborative learning practitioners are inclined to assume students are responsible participants who already use social skills in undertaking and completing tasks. Therefore students receive less instruction in group skills and roles and perform less structured reflection on group interaction than in cooperative-learning classrooms.

Collaborative and cooperative learning have developed separately. Followers of the two traditions have published in different journals, created bibliographies with few common names, sponsored different conferences, and for many years, had little contact with each other. As a result, among collaborative- and cooperative-learning practitioners there exists a certain amount of ignorance about the other tradition, and about variations within each school of thought. Lack of information and lack of communication among proponents of different viewpoints have sometimes led to a rigid sense of orthodoxy.

This article is one step on the road to sharing our experiences and our expertise. We are calling for new teachers to have a broader awareness of the variety of approaches that have different pedagogical implications; for practitioners of one method to expand their awareness to other types of group practice; for researchers to engage in more studies of research concerning effective practice; for more interaction among scholars with different techniques, philosophies, and theoretical assumptions; and for institutions encouraging active learning to disseminate information about the different methods and to sponsor conferences to bring together collaborative- and cooperative-learning practitioners. We hope to encourage the exchange of ideas so that we may continue to learn from each other and acknowledge each other's accomplishments. Sharing the successes of each enriches us all.

For Further Reading...

Abrami, P. C., et al. *Using Cooperative Learning*, Dubuque, IA: Brown & Benchmark, 1993.
> Gives a balanced description of the theoretical and empirical underpinnings of cooperative learning and describes a number of cooperative learning techniques.

Belenky M., B. Clinchy, N. Goldberger, & J. Tarule. *Women's Ways of Knowing: The Development of Self, Voice, and Mind*, New York: Basic Books, 1986.
> Documents the limitations of traditional approaches to teaching and posits alternative approaches to learning that are central to feminist pedagogy.

Brubacher, M., R. Payne, and K. Rickert. *Perspectives on Small Group Learning: Theory and Practice*, Oakvale, Ontario, Canada: Rubicon Publishing Inc., 1990.

This is an edited collection of 25 articles offering perspectives on small-group learning from both the cooperative and collaborative viewpoint.

Bruffee, Kenneth. *A Short Course in Writing: Practical Rhetoric for Teaching Composition Through Collaborative Learning*, 4th ed., New York: HarperCollins, 1993.

The practical principles of setting up and managing collaborative learning groups are explained in the instructor's manual of this writing textbook. The author is a central figure in the development of collaborative learning.

Bruffee, Kenneth. *Collaborative Learning: Higher Education, Interdependence, and the Authority of Knowledge*, Baltimore: Johns Hopkins University Press, 1993.

The first section discusses practical and theoretical aspects of collaborative work, and the second places collaborative learning within various institutional contexts.

Bruffee, Kenneth. "Social Construction, Language, and the Authority of Knowledge: A Bibliographical Essay," *College English*, Vol. 48, No. 8, December 1986, pp. 773-790.

This essay is especially good at situating collaborative learning in the context of postmodernist social constructionist thought.

Cohen, E. *Designing Groupwork: Strategies for the Heterogeneous Classroom*, 2nd ed., New York: Teachers College Press, 1994.

This book includes Cohen's "complex instruction" program for cooperative learning with attention to such issues as student status and tasks requiring multiple abilities. It includes major issues in designing groups.

Cooper, J. L., P. Robinson, and M. McKinney. "Cooperative Learning in the Classroom," in D. F. Halpern, ed., *Changing College Classrooms: New Teaching and Learning Strategies for an Increasingly Complex World*, San Francisco: Jossey-Bass, 1994, pp. 74-92.

An overview of cooperative learning in higher education. The authors identify the critical features of cooperative learning, briefly trace its history and research base, and outline four specific forms of cooperative learning that may be adapted to the college classroom.

Cooper, J. L., ed. *Cooperative Learning and College Teaching.*

A newsletter containing a variety of useful articles concerning cooperative learning in higher education. About one-third are research-theory and two-thirds are applied in nature.

Cuseo, J. "Collaborative and Cooperative Learning in Higher Education: A Proposed Taxonomy," in *Cooperative Learning and College Teaching*, Vol. 2, No. 2, Winter 1992, pp. 2-5.

Identifies cooperative learning as a subtype of collaborative learning characterized by six specific critical features and describes over 15 forms of collaborative learning. [Editor's note: See Article 3]

Davidson, N. "Cooperative and Collaborative Learning: An Integrative Perspective," in J. S. Thousand, R. A. Villa & A. I. Nevin, eds., *Creativity and Collaborative Learning: A Practical Guide to Empowering Students and Teachers*, Baltimore: Brookes, 1994, pp. 13-30.

An analysis of the ways in which cooperative learning and collaborative learning are similar and dissimilar that identifies five attributes shared by all approaches and nine ways in which the approaches vary.

Davidson, N. and T. Worsham, eds. *Enhancing Thinking Through Cooperative Learning*, New York: Teachers College Press, 1992.

This book is a collection of essays by leaders in critical thinking and cooperative learning, including both theory and practical ideas for enhancing thinking through cooperative learning.

Dewey, J. *Experience in Education*, New York: Collier Books, 1963.

The classic comparison of traditional and progressive educational practice.

Gabelnick, F., J. MacGregor, R. Matthews, and B. L. Smith. *Learning Communities: Creating Connections Among Students, Faculty and Disciplines*, New Directions for Teaching and Learning, Vol. 41, San Francisco: Jossey-Bass, 1990.

An accessible and practical introduction to multi- and interdisciplinary learning communities as they have been implemented on college and university campuses across the country.

Gamson, Z. "Collaborative Learning Comes of Age," *Change*, September/October 1994, Vol. 26, No. 5, pp. 44-49.

Intertwining personal and institutional history, the author traces the growth of collaborative learning and concludes by offering a rich agenda for future action.

Graves, Ted, issue editor; Liana Forest, executive editor. "Cooperative Learning 101: Applications in Higher Education," thematic issue of *Cooperative*

Learning Magazine, Vol. 13, No. 3, Spring 1993.

This entire issue of *Cooperative Learning Magazine* is devoted to cooperative/collaborative learning in higher education. Published by the International Association for the Study of Cooperation in Education, Box 1582, Santa Cruz, CA 95061-1582.

Johnson D. W. and R. T. Johnson. *Cooperation and Competition: Theory and Research*, Edina, MN: Interaction Book Co., 1989.

A research summary of over 600 studies that describes the impact of cooperative learning on a variety of outcome measures. Results are reported separately for subjects of varying ages/grades (first grade through college and adult).

Johnson, David W., Roger T. Johnson, and Karl A. Smith. *Active Learning: Cooperation in the College Classroom*, Edina, MN: Interaction Book Co., 1991.

This workbook, the first to apply the Johnsons' method to the college level, is the best introduction for the college teacher interested in cooperative-learning practice.

Johnson, David W., Roger T. Johnson, Karl A. Smith, and E. Holubec. *Circles of Learning: Cooperation in the Classroom*, Edina, MN: Interaction Book Co., 1993.

The 1993 edition of this book contains some of the material used in *Active Learning* as well as additional material directed toward teachers of K-12 and a new chapter on assessment.

Kadel, S. and J. Keehner, eds. *Collaborative Learning: A Sourcebook for Higher Education*, Vol. 2, National Center on Postsecondary Teaching, Learning, and Assessment (NCTLA), 1994.

Contains articles on different collaborative learning settings and extensive examples of actual classroom practice submitted by college teachers.

Kagan, S. *Cooperative Learning: Resource for Teachers*, San Juan Capistrano, CA: Resources for Teachers, 1992.

This book deals with Kagan's structural approach to cooperative learning, which offers a variety of procedures for organizing group interaction.

Matthews, R. "Collaborative Learning: Creating Knowledge With Students," in R. Menges, *Teaching on Solid Ground: Using Scholarship to Improve Practice*, San Francisco: Jossey-Bass, forthcoming late fall 1995.

An overview of collaborative learning practice in college classrooms.

Matthews, R., ed. *CUE Newsletter.*
>Offers brief articles of interest about programs, workshops, presentations, and publications. The newsletter is supported by the AAHE action community, Collaboration in Undergraduate Education.

Michaelsen, Larry K. "Team Learning: A Comprehensive Approach for Harnessing the Power of Small Groups in Higher Education," *To Improve the Academy, Vol. 11, 1992.*
>A description of team-learning techniques and practice.

Romer, K., and W. Whipple. "Collaboration Across the Power Line," *College Teaching*, Vol. 39, No. 2, 1991, pp. 66-70.
>An exploration of how the use of collaborative learning depends on a conscious revision of traditional power relationships in college settings.

Schmuck, R. and P. Schmuck. *Group Processes in the Classroom*, Dubuque, IA: William C. Brown Company, 1992.
>This book integrates theory and research into a practical guide for developing fundamental properties of a cooperative classroom.

Schniedewind, Nancy. "Feminist Values: Guidelines for Teaching Methodology in Women's Studies," in Ira Shor, ed., *Freire for the Classroom*, Portsmouth, NH: Boynton Cook, Publishers, 1987, pp. 170-179.
>A fine example of how the feminist classroom embodies collaborative practice.

Sharan, S., ed. *Handbook of Cooperative Learning Methods*, Westport, CT: Greenwood, 1994.
>This text contains chapters on cooperative-learning techniques such as STAD, Jigsaw, Learning Together, Complex Instruction, and Group Investigation as used in math, second-language acquisition, literature, science, and computer classes.

Slavin, R. *Cooperative Learning: Theory, Research and Practice*, Prentice-Hall, 1990.
>This book synthesizes research evidence on student achievement and other outcomes of cooperative learning and offers some practical suggestions for implementation.

Smith B. and J. MacGregor. "What Is Collaborative Learning?" in Goodsell, A., M. Maher, and V. Tinto, eds., *Collaborative Learning: A Sourcebook for Higher Education*, University Park, PA: NCTLA, 1992.
>This article provides a comprehensive overview of different methods of collaborative work. The rest of the book contains previously published

essays. Extensive bibliographies and a list of practitioners are also provided.

Trimbur, J. "Consensus and Difference in Collaborative Learning," *College English*, Vol. 51, No. 69, pp. 602-616, 1989.

An attempt to refine the meaning of consensus as a goal in collaborative activities and classes.

Trimbur, J. "Collaborative Learning and Teaching Writing," *Perspectives on Research and Scholarship in Composition*, 1985, pp. 87-109.

An essay that offers an overview of theoretical and practical issues involved in collaborative learning and the teaching of writing.

Wiener, Harvey S. "Collaborative Learning in the Classroom: A Guide to Evaluation," *College English*, January 1986, pp. 52-61.

A helpful guide to evaluating teachers and the learning environment in a collaborative classroom.

Whipple, W. R. "Collaborative Learning: Recognizing It When We See It," *AAHE Bulletin*, Vol. 40, No. 2, pp. 3-7, 1987.

A brief exploration of collaborative learning that is clear, helpful, and global.

3 Collaborative & Cooperative Learning in Higher Education: A Proposed Taxonomy

Joe Cuseo

Originally published in the Cooperative Learning and College Teaching newsletter, Winter, 1992.

The terms Collaborative Learning (CBL) and Cooperative Learning (CL) are now being bandied about in American higher education with great frequency and enthusiasm. Unfortunately, these terms have not been consistently defined, either conceptually or operationally, resulting in their being used interchangeably by some college educators and differentially by others. After reviewing the higher educational literature, Chickering and Gamson (1987) concluded that these terms are far more suggestive than they are precise. However, at the precollegiate level, CL has been precisely defined in terms of six critical features: (1) positive interdependence, (2) individual accountability, (3) appropriate rationale for grouping, (4) structured student interactions, (5) teacher as facilitator, and (6) attention to social skills.

This article will attempt to redress the imprecise usage of Collaborative and Cooperative Learning in higher education and will attempt to rectify the discrepancy between precollege and college terminology. To this end, a taxonomy will be proposed in which CBL is defined as a generic process that encompasses CL and other specific forms of CBL as subtypes. This proposed taxonomy is not intended merely to be an academic exercise; instead, it has been written with two practical objectives in mind: (1) to bring clarity and coherence to the meaning(s) of CBL and CL so that college educators can begin to dialogue in a common language–among themselves and with their precollegiate colleagues, and (2) to catalogue the wide range of collaborative/cooperative strategies which are now being implemented in higher education, so that readers may be apprised of the present "state of the art" and may be encouraged to initiate one or more of these community-building strategies on their own campus.

Etymologically, both collaboration (to labor together) and cooperation (to operate together) stem from almost identical roots. Thus, by semantic definition both CBL and CL involve *social* (*interpersonal*) processes in which two or more people work together to promote learning. Given this conceptual definition, the nature of the *persons* involved in the collaborative/cooperative process will be used as the key criterion for differentiating CBL into three major categories: (I) collaboration between *students*, (II) collaboration between *teachers*, and (III) collaboration between *students and teachers*. Subcategories of collaborative procedures within each of these three generic categories are identified–based on how the procedure attempts to implement CBL between or among the individuals. So, in effect, the general categories represent the *who* of it (i.e., the persons involved in the collaborative process), and the subcategories represent the *how* of it (i.e., the procedural strategies used to promote collaboration among the persons involved).

I. Collaboration Between Students

A. Small-Group Discussion (a.k.a. Buzz Groups). Several students join together to express their views and hear the views of their peers with respect to some class issue.

In one particular form of small-group discussion, the group must reach some consensus with regard to the issue under discussion. This consensus-building component seems to be the essential element of the type of CBL that has been embraced by college educators in the field of English and literature (e.g., Brufee, 1981; Wiener, 1986). Historically, it has its roots in Abercrombie's (1964, 1970) work on medical students who collaborated in small groups to reach a unified diagnostic decision.

B. Group Project. A group of students collaborate on an assigned project which they typically research and discuss outside of class. The group's final work or product is presented in the form of a written report (e.g., term paper) or oral report (e.g., panel discussion) or some combination thereof.

Grades are assigned on either an individual or group basis or some combination (e.g., the performance of the individual and the group may be graded and then averaged to generate each student's grade for the project).

C. Cooperative Learning. This particular subtype of CBL is the focus of the Network for Cooperative Learning in Higher Education and this newsletter. CL probably is the most operationally well-defined and procedurally structured form of collaboration among students. Its six critical, procedural features have been delineated in the first issue of this newsletter [Editor's Note: see Article 1 for more information.]. Its roots lie in the educational philosophy of John Dewey and the social psychology of Kurt Lewin, and its evolution into a systematic instructional procedure probably originated in the work of David and Roger Johnson and Robert Slavin in the early 1960's. At the precollege level, CL (defined in terms of the aforementioned critical features) has been the most researched and empirically well-documented form of CBL in terms of its positive impact on multiple outcome measures. Its overall effectiveness seems to vary commensurately with the actual number of its critical features that are carefully implemented (Slavin, 1990).

Since its conception, a number of different subtypes of CL have been identified and employed at the precollege level–i.e., Jigsaw, STAD, etc. For a comprehensive description of a large number of CL subtypes, see: Kagan, S. (1989). *Cooperative Learning Resources for Teachers*. Laguna Niguel, California: Resources for Teachers

D. Cooperative Dyads. A collaborative reading strategy involving pairs of students in which each member of the pair reads a passage. One member first serves as a recaller and attempts to summarize the essential elements of the reading, while the other member of the pair serves as the listener/facilitator–who attempts to correct errors in the recaller's summary and offers alternative strategies for organizing and storing the just-read material. The two students then reverse roles as recaller and listener/facilitator.

This procedure was developed at the college level by Donald Dansereau at Texas Christian University (Dansereau, 1983). Though the word "cooperative" appears in its title, this procedure is not classified as a subtype of CL because it does not systematically implement its six critical features.

E. Learning Community Models. The Washington Center for Improving the Quality of Undergraduate Education originated and developed a form of CBL which they refer to as Learning Communities. For classification purposes, this form of CBL may best be viewed as an umbrella program, within which are nested all three major forms of educational collaboration in the present taxonomy, i.e., (1) collaboration between students, (2) collaboration between teachers, and (3) collaboration between students and teachers. Those components of learning community models which involve the first form of collaboration (student-student collaboration) will now be discussed within Category I of the taxonomy. (Those components of Learning Community Models which involve teacher-teacher and student-teacher collaboration will be discussed within Categories II and III, respectively.)

1. Course Linking Models. A group of students co-register for a pair of courses during the same semester. (The course instructors may or may not coordinate their individual syllabi, assignments, etc.)
2. Learning Clusters. A group of students register for the same 3-4 courses during a given semester. (Instructors may or may not coordinate their syllabi, assignments, etc.)
3. Freshman Interest Groups (FIGs). A small cohort of freshman register for the same three courses during the same semester and a peer advisor (trained upperclassmen) is assigned to these freshmen and meets with them periodically throughout the term. (Instructors are not expected to coordinate their course syllabi, assignments, etc.)
4. Federated Learning Communities. A small cohort of

students register for the same three courses, which are offered under the rubric of some overarching theme. Instructors are not expected to coordinate their individual course syllabi, assignments, etc.; however, a master learner–i.e., a faculty member who is not trained in any of the academic disciplines being taught, takes the three courses along with the cohort of students, and leads a 3-credit discussion section designed to integrate the material in the three separate courses.

5. Coordinated Studies Programs. A group of 20-25 students take all their courses together in a given semester. The 4-5 courses are organized under an overarching theme and are team-taught by the same group of faculty; typically, the classes are scheduled for a long time block to allow for alternative learning experiences (e.g., extended discussion sessions, field trips).

Note: These subtypes of learning communities have been adapted from Gabelnick, F., et al. (1990). *Learning communities: Creating Connection Among Students, Faculty and Disciplines*. San Francisco: Jossey Bass. This source provides a comprehensive overview and description of learning community models, and discusses strategies for their implementation.

F. Peer Teaching/Learning Programs. Students who are more advanced in their understanding of certain subject matter are enlisted to provide learning assistance to less advanced students (e.g., in a Learning Assistance Center as peer tutors, or via Supplemental Instruction [SI]–in which the more advanced student attends the same class as the novice learners, helping them individually or in group sessions that are regularly scheduled outside of class time).

G. Peer Advising/Mentoring Programs. More experienced students (e.g., juniors/seniors) serve as advisors or mentors to less experienced students (e.g., freshmen/sophomores) for the primary purpose of promoting educational success of the less experienced students and for the secondary purpose of promoting the development of the more experienced students (e.g., counseling or leadership development).

H. Block Scheduling Programs. A cohort of students register for the same group (block) of courses during the same semester for the purpose of promoting a "community of learners." It is expected that these students will be more likely to collaborate because of the shared learning experiences that may result from their shared academic schedules.

I. Cluster Colleges. (a.k.a., "college within a college" programs). Subgroups of students at larger colleges or universities who have similar academic interests (e.g., humanities majors) do their learning in a circumscribed area or subunit of the campus, i.e., they take courses in the same proximally located buildings and, if they are residential students they live in the same or nearby units. The objective is to reduce the "impersonal" nature of the large university experience and encourage shared discourse among learners with similar academic interests. For more detailed information on cluster colleges, consult: Gaff, J. G. (1970). *The Cluster College*. San Francisco: Jossey Bass.

J. Living Learning Communities. Students who live in the same campus residence, take the same courses, seminars, or workshops–which are offered in the students' residential unit.

K. Summer Bridge Programs. A group of academically at-risk students (e.g., low income, first generation minority students) take courses together and reside on campus in the same student residence during the summer before their first full semester of college.

II. Collaboration Between Teachers

A. Team-Taught Courses. Two or more faculty members combine to design and teach a course. If the instructors are from different academic disciplines, the term interdisciplinary teaching/learning would apply.

B. Faculty Research/Scholarship Teams. Two or more faculty combine to conduct research or engage in other forms of scholarship. If the faculty members are from different academic disciplines, the term interdisciplinary research/scholarship would apply.

C. Learning Community Models.
1. Course Linking Models. The instructors involved in teaching a pair of courses may decide to coordinate their syllabi and assignments for the cohort of students who are taking their linked classes.
2. Learning Clusters. Three or four instructors may collaborate to coordinate their syllabi and assignments for those students taking their clustered courses.
3. Coordinated Studies Programs. All instructors involved in the program collaborate to team-teach all courses together. Note: In many learning community models, faculty will: (a) come together for pre-semester, course planning retreats, (b) audit each other's courses before team-teaching together, and/or (c) meet together for weekly seminars during the semester in which they are team-teaching.

D. Faculty Mentoring Programs. An experienced faculty member serves as a mentor for an inexperienced or newly hired faculty member to help the latter (protégé) learn to successfully meet her professional responsibilities and to promote her professional development.

III. Teacher-Student Collaboration

A. Faculty-Student Mentoring Programs. An experienced faculty member serves as a mentor to facilitate an undergraduate student's academic success (e.g., minority faculty member serves as a mentor for a minority undergraduate).

B. Faculty-in-Residence Programs. A teaching faculty member lives in a student residence and provides out-of-class instruction, advising, or mentoring assistance to students who co-occupy the same residence hall.

C. Student-Faculty Research Teams. A faculty member involves an undergraduate student in his/her research or scholarship.

D. Student-Faculty Teaching Teams. A faculty member co-teaches a course with an experienced undergraduate (e.g., an instructor team-teaches a freshman seminar with a college senior).

E. Federated Learning Community (FLC). In this Learning Community model, a faculty member takes the same courses as the cohort of students, and serves as a master learner to help the cohort of students master and integrate concepts taught in different courses.

Final note on the classification scheme: There are some instances where faculty and administrators or staff members have collaborated to team-teach courses (e.g., freshman seminar). Also, faculty have collaborated with student affairs professionals in planning to integrate course content and/or assignments with co-curricular campus events (e.g., Women's History Week). Such activities could be considered to be another distinctive type (category) of CBL in higher education, i.e., collaboration between faculty and staff/administration. However, in the higher education literature, these arrangements have been referred to and classified as partnerships.

This taxonomy is proposed with the intent of lending some coherence to the wide range of higher educational procedures and programs now being loosely referred to as CBL. Also, it is hoped that the classification scheme may serve to "tease out" the key collaborative components nested within, multi-faceted, multi-purpose forms of CBL (e.g., learning community models).

Conclusion

American higher education is now being criticized for its lack of campus community i.e., lack of community among learners, among teachers, and between learners, teachers and student-service professionals. (See Boyer, E. L. [1990]. *Campus Life: In Search of Community*. The Carnegie Foundation for the Advancement of Teaching. Princeton, NJ: Princeton University Press.) CBL activities constitute one general approach to building communities on campus and the wide range of collaborative strategies outlined on this taxonomy suggests that colleges and universities have multiple avenues through which they can promote a sense of community.

Within this broad context of campus wide community building, CL can be viewed as a specific, classroom-centered procedure for building a community of learners. From this perspective, CL represents a well-defined and implementation-ready form of pedagogy which has a potential to systematically infuse a sense of community within all classrooms and across all disciplines. As such, encouraging college faculty to implement CL in their classrooms would appear to be an essential component of any comprehensive institutional plan for building campus community.

Section 2
Why Use Cooperative Strategies? Research and Theory

This section provides theoretical and empirical support for the use of group learning strategies in higher education. The first article (Article 4, pages 29-32) is by Jim Cooper and Pamela Robinson and describes the use of cooperative learning in a number of classes at CSU Dominguez Hills and two feeder community colleges having diverse student populations. The researchers exposed over 1000 students in 30 classes to cooperative strategies in a large number of content areas. They found that students demonstrated highly significant gains in both knowledge level and higher than knowledge level (critical thinking) achievement from pre- to posttests. They also found that student anxiety about course content decreased substantially from pretests to posttests. These data are consistent with a meta-analysis performed by Leonard Springer and his colleagues at the University of Wisconsin (Article 5, pages 33-38) in science and mathematics. They report that students exposed to cooperative strategies demonstrated significantly higher gains in achievement and attitude toward the subject matter and significantly lower course attrition rates than students receiving more traditional instructional approaches such as the lecture.

Leaders in college teaching research and theory have been calling for the use of group learning for two decades. Arthur

Chickering and Zelda Gamson published an influential report in 1987, *Seven Principles for Good Practice in Undergraduate Education*, that made a strong case for the use of group-learning techniques. Barbara Millis uses this report as a basis for her article, beginning on page 39, and describes how group learning incorporates all seven of the research-based principles of effective college instruction. Alexander Astin, in his classic 1993 book, *What Matters in College? Four Critical Years Revisited*, added additional impetus for the use of cooperative group-learning strategies (see Article 7, pages 44-62, for Astin's summary of this work). In his monumental analysis of data from over 25,000 college students, Astin found that student-student and student-faculty interaction variables were the most critical of the college experiences he studied in predicting a multitude of cognitive and attitudinal gains in college students. Astin is a long-time proponent for the use of group-learning strategies in higher education.

Space does not allow for an exhaustive explication of the large body of research and theory which documents the power of small-group instruction. However, the reader may be particularly interested in the research and theory relating to cooperative strategies as they affect two student outcomes at the forefront of higher education interest: critical thinking and appreciation of diversity. Joe Cuseo provides a scholarly and thorough treatment of these issues, in Articles 8 and 9, beginning on page 63.

Ultimately, the choice of how to teach is a private one with which each faculty member has to feel comfortable. In an article originally intended to convince administrators of the pedagogical, economic and practical value of cooperative, small-group instruction, Jim Cooper identifies ten reasons that group learning should be used in higher education (Article 10, pages 90-96). Teachers considering the use of small-group procedures will also be interested in this non-technical summary providing a variety of reasons for using cooperative techniques.

Taken together, the work reported in Section 2 and throughout the book, provides a kind of *convergent validity*, that small-group instruction is among the best-documented instructional strategies available to college instructors interested in fostering a host of cognitive and attitudinal outcomes.

4 FIPSE-Sponsored CL Research at Dominguez Hills and Community Colleges

Jim Cooper and Pamela Robinson

Originally published in the Cooperative Learning and College Teaching newsletter, Fall, 1994.

Cooperative Learning (CL) is among the best-researched pedagogies in the history of American education (Johnson & Johnson, 1991). Unfortunately for college practitioners, most of this research is based on precollegiate populations. A recent CD-ROM search by the present authors revealed that although the number of higher education CL citations in ERIC has increased by several hundred percent in the last seven years, most of these studies are of an applied nature and not empirical studies. Relatively few have collected data even in the most informal manner.

Many in the higher education CL and Collaborative Learning (CBL) communities point to the work of Treismann, Frierson and Dansereau in support of their claims documenting the efficacy of CL and CBL. Treismann (1985) found that black students at Berkeley who studied in a small-group Calculus enrichment program outside of class received higher mean grades relative to similar students studying alone. He also found substantially higher university retention rates for black students, majoring in math or science and enrolled in the enrichment program, relative to comparable students not enrolled in such a program. Frierson (1986) found that black nursing students who studied in cooperative groups for their state licensing exam performed better than students who studied for the exam on their own. Dansereau (1988) has reported on a series of well-controlled, short-term studies which generally indicate that students who study in cooperative dyads achieve more than students who study similar academic content individually.

A study by Jim Cooper and Randall Mueck on over 1000 students, who had been taught using CL, in 46 classes at an urban comprehensive university indicated that students preferred CL-taught classes when compared to lecture and lecture-discussion classes. CSU Dominguez Hills faculty taught a variety of (largely) undergraduate classes for one semester, then asked students to compare the CL classes with other classes they had experienced on 11 outcome measures. Between 70% and 93% of respondents rated CL as superior to more traditional forms of instruction on such issues as higher level reasoning, general academic achievement, amount of time needed to reach mastery and interest in the subject. The highest rated outcome in this study (93%) was the "frequency and quality of interactions with classmates." "Frequency and quality of contact with instructor" in CL-taught classes was rated significantly more effective or somewhat more effective by 70% of students surveyed. Qualitative student responses supported the quantitative measures. Students' narratives cited benefits of CL that included critical thinking, increased ability to take another's perspective, increased time on task and decreased time to achieve mastery of course content.

Student-student and student-teacher interaction outcomes took on particular significance in 1993 when Alexander Astin published his *What Matters in College? Four Critical Years Revisited* text. In this book Astin described his analysis of over 25,000 students examining the value added by the undergraduate experience. He reported that curricular issues played a relatively unimportant role in influencing a variety of undergraduate cognitive and attitudinal measures. Student-student and student-teacher interaction were by far the best predictors of a large number of outcomes of liberal education, including critical thinking, cultural awareness, and writing ability. Astin summarized his findings and their implications for pedagogy in general and CL in particular in Volume 4, Number 1 of this newsletter. [Editor's Note: See Article 7 in this text.]

Cooper (1990) followed the Cooper and Mueck work with a smaller-scale study which attempted to assess whether CL might have a differential effect on identifiable groups of students. There is a suggestion in some precollegiate and collegiate literature that

Section 2. Why Use Cooperative Strategies?

women and some minority group students may prefer and perform better in cooperative, small-group instructional settings rather than competitive, large-lecture formats (Light, 1992; Belenky, Clinchy, Goldberger, & Tarule, 1986). Cooper also assessed student achievement and subject matter anxiety on the first day and again on the last day of a research methods and statistics graduate education class. He found that women were generally more anxious about the prospect of taking the class than men and scored lower on the achievement pretest. However, by the end of the class, women scored at about the same level as men on statistics achievement and anxiety concerning statistics. Similar results were found in comparing black students to white students. The results from this study were based on a relatively small sample and so generalizations should be made with caution.

In 1990, Jim Cooper received a FIPSE grant to study the effects of CL on a number of general education classes (this newsletter was also a result of that same grant, as was the 1992 conference on CL in higher education co-sponsored by the International Society for Exploring Teaching Alternatives and the Network for Cooperative Learning in Higher Education). Cooper and his colleagues at Dominguez Hills, East Los Angeles (community) College and Cerritos (community) College exposed over 1000 students to CL using a One-group Pretest Posttest design. They found that exposure to CL made no difference in gain on Perry's positions of cognitive development. Perry positions are enduring cognitive schemata which distinguish immature, dualistic thinkers from more cognitively mature relativistic thinkers (see Perry, 1970 and Kurfiss, 1988 for more information on Perry's positions).

However, there was a statistically significant ($p < .0001$) increase in students' mean score on course-specific pre- and posttest measures. CL students' performance on both knowledge level (rote) course content and higher-than-knowledge level (critical thinking) content improved by a statistically significant amount ($p < .0001$). Also, CL students' anxiety about mastering course content was reduced from pretest to posttest, and their confidence in expressing views in class rose, both by a statistically significant amount ($p < .0001$).

Retention theorists such as Vince Tinto and Lee Noel have

found that among the best predictors of persistence to graduation is student involvement. They have called for increased use of small group learning as a primary technique for increasing such involvement. Cooper, Robinson and their associates compared the retention rates of CL-taught classes at Dominguez Hills with comparison sections of the same classes where more traditional forms of instruction were used. They found that in-class retention rates from week three to week sixteen was 97% in the CL classes and 94% in the traditional classes. Eleven of the CL-taught classes had 100% retention while none of the 14 comparison classes had 100% retention. Two years after course completion 36% of the students in CL classes were still enrolled at Dominguez Hills, with 26% of students in comparison classes still enrolled. It should be noted this 10% difference may be influenced by student graduation and transfer (variables we were unable to track). Somewhat curiously, 73% of students in both types of classes were still enrolled at Dominguez Hills one year after course completion.

We would welcome additional research examining CL in college, particularly research which more analytically examines quantitative and qualitative differences in CL compared to more traditional forms of instruction. Reviews of the CL higher education literature would be welcome, as would meta-analyses. Although the "main effect" indicating that CL works better for a variety of outcome measures and student populations is substantial in precollegiate settings, the research base at the college level is still very limited. We would also welcome research which examines the effect of specific variations in the critical features of CL. That is, are extrinsic student rewards necessary for improvement in achievement with college populations? Slavin (1983, 1990) strongly indicates that this is true for precollegiate students. Are heterogeneously-formed teams better than homogeneously formed teams? Faye Arnold at Dominguez Hills is examining that issue, in collaboration with the present authors. Are some CL structures (e.g., Jigsaw) better than others (e.g., Group Investigation) for certain outcomes and student populations? We urge our readers and the college teaching research community to examine these and other pedagogy issues, even if the research is small in scale. Let us know what you find and we will disseminate this information.

5 Research on Cooperative Learning in College Science, Mathematics, Engineering, and Technology

Leonard Springer

Originally published in the Cooperative Learning and College Teaching newsletter, Spring, 1998.

Among the myriad reasons for using cooperative learning, perhaps most compelling is that its effectiveness rests on a solid foundation of research. Hundreds of classroom-based studies on cooperative learning have been conducted with students in grades two through nine during the last 25 years. Cooperative-learning investigator Elizabeth Cohen (1994) asserts that this research has been instrumental in establishing cooperative learning as a "legitimate method of instruction that can help students to learn" (p. 30). Reflecting the solid foundation on which cooperative practices are built, analyses of a recent national survey (Puma, Jones, Rock, & Fernandez, 1993) indicate that 79% of elementary school teachers and 62% of middle school teachers report using cooperative learning in their classrooms on a sustained basis. Indeed, links between cooperative-learning research and practice have been characterized by Robert Slavin (1996) as "one of the greatest success stories in the history of educational research" (p. 43).

Despite the volume of supporting studies, a gap in the research foundation is apparent at the postsecondary level. Although research (e.g., Johnson, Johnson, & Smith, 1991) supports the effectiveness of cooperation among adults, including college students, few studies have been conducted exclusively on undergraduates. Most that do have focused on students in the psychology laboratory. Perhaps not coincidentally, college and university faculty have lagged behind their K-12 counterparts in adopting cooperative learning.

Recent reports from professional societies and government agencies increasingly recommend that cooperative learning be employed in college, particularly in science, mathematics, engineering, and technology (SMET) courses and programs. The National Science Foundation (1996), for example, suggests that students have frequent access to cooperative-learning experiences in class and outside the classroom (as through study groups). The American Association for the Advancement of Science (1989) advises that "the collaborative nature of scientific and technological work should be strongly reinforced by frequent group activity in the classroom. Scientists and engineers work mostly in groups and less often as isolated investigators. Similarly, students should gain experience sharing responsibility for learning with each other" (p. 148).

For the most part, college and university educators have yet to respond enthusiastically to calls for greater opportunities for collaboration and cooperation in SMET courses and programs. Regrettably, the unintended consequences of this lack of innovation and change include unfavorable attitudes toward SMET among students, unacceptably high attrition from SMET fields of study, inadequate preparation for teaching science and mathematics at the pre-college level, and graduates who often "go out into the workforce ill-prepared to solve real problems in a cooperative way, lacking the skills and motivation to continue learning" (National Science Foundation, 1996, p. iii).

Beginning in October, 1996, Mary Elizabeth Stanne, Samuel Donovan, and I responded to the numerous calls for instructional innovation and change in undergraduate SMET courses and programs by striving to solidify the foundation of research on which to base policy and practice. Under the auspices of the National Institute for Science Education, sponsored by the National Science Foundation, we began conducting a meta-analysis of research on undergraduate SMET education since 1980. Meta-analysis is a quantitative literature review that integrates statistical results from various studies. The technique has proved particularly effective in informing policy and practice, and was endorsed by the National Research Council in 1992.

Our meta-analysis was informed by James Cooper and Pamela Robinson, who reported in two papers commissioned by the National Institute for Science Education that cooperative and collaborative learning in undergraduate SMET occur in a great variety of forms. We included cohort groups, various types of structured cooperative learning, brief activities for pairs of students during breaks in lectures, and several types of informal collaborative work among students—in short, a range of small-group learning procedures. This inclusive approach follows from our observations of substantial differences in how particular small-group learning practices are implemented as well as similarities among divergent procedures.

Over several months, we found 383 reports related to small-group learning in postsecondary SMET since 1980. Most of the reports, such as workbooks and conceptual papers, did not involve research. Of the research studies, about one-fifth met our rigorous criteria for inclusion in the meta-analysis. We calculated effect sizes based on the difference in standardized means between a pretest and posttest, or a control group and an experimental group.

The meta-analysis shows that small-group learning promotes greater student achievement, increased persistence through courses and programs, and more favorable learning-related attitudes.

These effect sizes are quite large compared with research on most educational innovations (See Figure 1). In fact, the 0.51 effect on achievement would raise a student from the 50th to the 70th percentile on a standardized test. The 0.46 effect on persistence translates to a 22% reduction in attrition from SMET courses and programs. Moreover, the 0.55 effect on students' attitudes (in-

Figure 1

Meta-analysis Results			
Outcome	Studies	Students	Effect Size
Achievement	49	3,472	0.51
Persistence	10	2,014	0.46
Attitudes	12	1,293	0.55

cluding self-esteem and attitudes toward learning SMET material) far exceeds the average effect of 0.28 for classroom-based educational interventions on comparable attitudinal measures.

Not only are these effects quite large, but they remain positive and statistically significant across all SMET fields of study investigated and pass several rigorous tests of potential sources of bias in the meta-analysis method. In addition, the positive effects of small-group learning extend across differences in gender and race/ethnicity. Small-group learning has particularly large effects on the achievement of African Americans and Latinos and the learning-related attitudes of women and preservice teachers. These results are especially important given widespread efforts among policymakers and practitioners to promote inclusivity and diversity in postsecondary SMET education.

The effects of small-group learning also remain positive and statistically significant across a wide range of settings and procedures. Student learning is enhanced in both out-of-class study groups and in-class interactions—from short discussions during breaks in lectures to group work on semester-long projects. The meta-analysis results also suggest that greater time spent working in groups leads to more favorable attitudes among students in general and that even minimal group work can have significant effects on student achievement. Moreover, the significant and positive effects on achievement persist whether measured by instructor-made exams or standardized tests.

Clearly the meta-analysis results support broader implementation of small-group learning in postsecondary SMET courses and programs. Still, a great deal of work remains for researchers in this area. One important next step is to forge stronger links between learning theory and practice. Although research indicates that small-group learning has significant and positive effects, we do not have a unified theoretical basis for understanding how and why that is the case. Much work remains to move beyond a "black box" approach and to gain a greater understanding of how and why small-group learning is effective. The necessity for a theoretical foundation for practice is supported by research suggesting that faculty are likely to abandon instructional innovations when initial problems occur if they are not familiar with the theories behind their implementation. Yet knowledge of theory alone is not enough to inform practice. Practitioners must be adept at understanding nuances of situations to determine when a principle is applicable.

From the viewpoint of the meta-analysis authors, work toward improving teaching and learning in postsecondary SMET should increasingly involve researchers and practitioners sharing diverse perspectives and comparing data collected and analyzed through various methods. We hope for bridges between practitioners of different small-group learning procedures and links among researchers who work with quantitative and qualitative methods. Perhaps the most important component of future analyses is the need for more detailed descriptions of small-group procedures by investigators or instructors who report research on the effects of their work. What was done that can be replicated? A second important component is the need for more detailed descriptions of the type of task in which students were involved. Was the task well-structured, with predefined procedures leading to a single answer; or ill-structured, with several possible paths toward more than one acceptable outcome? A third factor is the need for more assessment of higher-order thinking and problem solving. Fourth, comparisons of the effects of various forms of small-group learning are needed. Fifth, reporting grading procedures would help future analyses a great deal. Were students graded on a curve or through criterion-based measures? Sixth, more research on the conditional effects of small-group learning on college students based on achievement level is needed. Is small-group learning effective in general (as suggested by the meta-analysis) or could it have different effects on high- or low-achieving students? Seventh, what are potential barriers to more widespread implementation of small-group learning and how might they be surmounted?

The primary challenge, however, is in moving from analysis to action. Small-group learning is clearly successful in a great variety of forms and settings and holds considerable promise for improving postsecondary SMET education. As recommended by the National Research Council (1996), "Innovations and successes in education need to spread with the speed and efficiency of new research results" (pp. 5-6). Effective action will require bridges among policymakers at national, state, institutional, and departmental levels, and practitioners and scholars across the disciplines. Through collaboration among representatives of these diverse groups, progress can be made toward promoting broader implementation of small-group learning.

6 How Cooperative Learning Can Fullfill the Promises of the "Seven Principles"

Barbara Millis

Originally published in the Cooperative Learning and College Teaching newsletter, Winter, 1992.

Led by Arthur Chickering and Zelda Garrison, a task force of prominent higher education researchers, meeting initially at Wingspread in July 1986, produced a set of "Seven Principles for Good Practice in Undergraduate Education." Based on research but emphasizing practical examples, the "Seven Principles" and the accompanying faculty and institutional inventories have been widely distributed throughout American colleges and universities. Over 100,000 copies of a special June 1987 issue of *The Wingspread Journal*, a Johnson Foundations publication featuring the "Seven Principles," have been mailed. Faculty wanting to incorporate these principles into their teaching have looked for action plans compatible with their other, often discipline-related, educational goals.

As the following examples illustrate, Cooperative Learning (CL) can provide both the theoretical framework and the "action plan" to fulfill the promise of the "Seven Principles."

1. Good Practice Encourages Student-Faculty Contact. In traditional classrooms, faculty frequently stand behind podiums, distanced from their students. Even when discussion occurs, it is frequently teacher directed and teacher focused. In classrooms using cooperative small-group work, the emphasis changes, and the instructor becomes not the "sage on stage," but the "guide on the side." Faculty constantly monitor groups' progress by sitting with students. An accounting professor using these methods, Dr. Philip

Cottell of Miami University, Oxford, Ohio, has identified five desirable outcomes associated with CL: (1) He has become more aware of the kind of learning going on. He can, for example, observe which students are struggling. Often, in listening to explanations couched in peer terminology, as opposed to what he calls "professorese," he can learn the source of student confusion and ways to alleviate it. (2) His presence demonstrates to students that he cares about them and their learning. (3) His students usually come to class prepared because they know that he will be an occasional group member. Students cannot hide their lack of preparation when the instructor is sitting next to their blank sheets of paper. (4) He has far more opportunity to interact with students–and hence get to know them in a positive setting–than with his former "see me after class" approach. Students feel more comfortable about him, and he learns quickly that the "sea of faces" formerly glimpsed from the podium is really composed of unique individuals. (5) He gathers information while sitting with students that enables him to help them with the group processing so important to effective CL.

2. Good Practice Encourages Cooperation Among Students. Grounded in theory, research, and practice, CL is a highly structured, systematic instructional strategy usually using heterogeneous small groups working toward common goals. Teams composed of four students work effectively because they are small enough to promote interaction, large enough to tolerate an occasional absence, and balanced enough to permit focused activities in pairs. Two features, positive interdependence and individual accountability, distinguish CL from other collaborative group work. Positive interdependence means that students–often because of carefully structured mutual goals, division of tasks, role interdependence, or group rewards–have a vested interest in working cooperatively together. Additionally, students are individually accountable for their own academic achievements and are usually tested separately under a noncompetitive, criterion-referenced grading system. Cooperation is also enhanced through appropriate grouping so that students can work in pairs (sometimes called dyads) or in larger groups, depending on the academic task. Many faculty also focus on social skills, routinely modeling them, and at times discussing their value directly so that students know how to interact in a group, particularly as they give constructive feedback or ask probing questions.

3. Good Practice Encourages Active Learning. By its very nature, CL engenders active learning. Students engage in animated discussions as they carry out various structured class assignments. As Kurfiss (1988) notes, courses that are assignment centered rather than text or lecture centered, can promote critical thinking. Such courses emphasize using course content, not just acquiring it. Often students perform various roles such as group coordinator, spokesperson, or recorder. CL structures, such as "think-pair-share," can promote active learning even in large auditoriums. With this structure, faculty ask students to contemplate a problem or issue for about 30 seconds (think); students then turn to a partner and discuss their ideas (pair); then, students within a group or within a classroom share the results of their consultation. If sharing is done as a whole-class discussion, to avoid repetition, the instructor should limit the responses to six or less. In another structure, "send-a-problem," each group of students analyzes a different problem related to a single topic. A recorder writes down the group's solution and places it in a file folder. The folders are rotated to the next group who, without looking inside, brainstorms and record its solutions before forwarding the folder again. In the final round, the last group opens the folder, reads the contributions from the previous groups, and selects the top two solutions. Many other structures, such as the "three-step interview" and "Jigsaw II" encourage higher order thinking skills as well as student involvement with learning. Some, such as "value lines" and "corners," where students indicate choices by moving to designated locations, even get students up on their feet, making them physically as well as mentally active.

4. Good Practice Gives Prompt Feedback. With structured small group work, students have ample opportunity to receive continuous and immediate feedback from their peers. The instructor also is accessible as he or she moves among the various groups. Many CL structures, including "think-pair-share," allow "rehearsal" time before students respond in class. Because students are individually responsible for their own learning, most faculty return exams promptly, giving individual feedback to supplement the group learning.

5. Good Practice Emphasizes Time on Task. Faculty unfamiliar with CL may mistakenly believe that small group work is time-consuming. This is not necessarily true if the tasks are timed and structured and the desired outcome is student learning tied to course objectives. Many CL practitioners use a timer or a bell to signal shifts in the task. In the "three-step interview," for example, the instructor can quickly form groups of four while students are discussing a focus question. The instructor might ask students to find a partner they do not know well and interview that person for two minutes, ascertaining his or her opinion on a class-related topic; at the sound of the bell, the two switch roles and the other person is interviewed for two minutes. The partners then join with another set of partners to form a group of four. For the next four minutes, each group member succinctly shares his or her partner's ideas. After this eight-minute exercise the newly formed learning teams can engage in another efficient exercise such as "roundtable," a two minute brainstorming technique where one sheet of paper is passed rapidly from student to student. To eliminate a common off-task problem associated with group work, faculty can build into every activity an extra topic, assignment, or step for groups that work more rapidly than others. In a "three-step interview," for instance, groups finishing early can discuss an extra interview question.

6. Good Practice Communicates High Expectations. Because CL emphasizes peer tutoring, Collaborative Learning, and interactive social skills, students feel that their abilities are valued and respected. The structured tasks, resulting in positive interdependence, build self-esteem because the contributions of all students are valuable. In "Jigsaw II," for example, students typically divide a task into four parts, each student assuming responsibility for a quarter of the project or material to be mastered. Students then leave their original home teams/groups to meet in newly formed expert teams with members of other groups assigned the same task component. In expert teams, students discuss not only the content of their portion of the task, but they also rehearse teaching strategies they will use in the home team to make certain that fellow teammates master the same material. Expectations, in fact, are consistently higher in such CL environments than in the typical lecture-oriented, teacher-centered classrooms.

7. Good Practice Respects Diverse Talents and Ways of Learning. CL supplements, but does not replace, other methods of classroom delivery such as lecture and whole-class discussion. Students with different learning styles can, in structured small groups, teach each other, as Redding (1990) notes, "from their special and particular perspectives" (p. 47). Psychologists such as Tennant (1988) and adult education scholars such as Brookfield (1991) agree that exposure to a variety of teaching approaches broadens and challenges students, ultimately leading them to greater developmental growth, particularly in the area of critical thinking. CL's positive effects on minority students' self-esteem and student retention have been well documented. The work of Uri Treisman, for example, is widely known and respected. Heterogeneous grouping–with mixed teams of high and low achievers, males and females, and younger and older students from various ethnic and cultural backgrounds–helps education become a vital reality for all students, including those at risk. This positive exposure to the ideas of diverse classmates encourages students to step outside of their own frames of reference and appreciate multifaceted issues. As Robert Slavin (1989-1990) concludes: "When students of different racial or ethnic backgrounds work together on a common goal, they gain in liking and respect for one another" (p. 52).

With the current cries for educational reform, faculty have an urgent responsibility to explore innovative teaching methods. CL is a valuable tool, one well-researched and well-documented, to enhance classroom interactions which promote teaming. The "Seven Principles for Good Practice in Undergraduate Education" printed in *The Wingspread Journal* can now figuratively take wing through CL techniques. (A longer version of this article appeared in the *Journal on Excellence in College Teaching,* Vol. 2, 1991.)

7 What Matters in College? Implications for Cooperative Learning of a New National Study

Alexander W. Astin

> *Originally published in the Cooperative Learning and College Teaching newsletter, Spring, 1993.*

*K*eynote address presented at the first national conference on Cooperative Learning and higher education sponsored by the Network for Cooperative Learning in Higher Education and the International Society for Exploring Teaching Alternatives, San Pedro, California, October 1, 1992. This talk is based in part upon the author's book, What Matters in College? Four Critical Years Revisited *(Jossey-Bass, 1993).*

It is a real pleasure to be here tonight to share some findings from our most recent research. I've devoted most of my professional life to studying our higher education system, and it is particularly gratifying to realize that Cooperative Learning is finally beginning to make some significant inroads into our pedagogical practice. The fact that this is just the first such conference focusing on the postsecondary level is perhaps the best evidence of higher education's reluctance to embrace pedagogical innovation, and I want to take this opportunity to express my personal appreciation to Jim Cooper for making the conference a reality.

While the research I will report on tonight was not specifically designed to examine Cooperative Learning, the more I reflect on the results, the more apparent it becomes to me that the findings not only offer a lot of empirical support for the efficacy of Cooperative Learning, but also provide us with some important clues as to how Cooperative Learning actually works and how we might strengthen and extend it in the future.

Design of the Study

The study involved a national sample of more than 200 four-year colleges and universities that have been participating in our Cooperative Institutional Research Program for a number of years. This longitudinal study involved some 25,000 students who entered these institutions as freshmen in the fall of 1985 and were followed up four years later in 1989. Our data included extensive questionnaires completed by these students in 1985 and 1989, data on academic performance and retention obtained from each institution, college admissions test scores from 1985, and graduate and professional school admission test scores obtained in 1989. In addition, in 1989 we were able to generate "faculty environment" scores for each institution by surveying the entire teaching faculty with an extensive personal questionnaire.

In our study we are primarily interested in student outcomes and in how they are affected by college **environments**. The environment includes not only the type of educational program and faculty to which the student is exposed, but also many other aspects of the undergraduate experience, such as the peer group. However, we also need input data on these same students at the time they first enter college, not only to be able to measure student change over time, but also to control for the fact that different types of students are exposed to different types of environments.

To give you some idea of the scope and complexity of this longitudinal study, we employed some 82 different outcome measures, more than 150 student input measures, and nearly 200 different environmental measures.

For those of you who are methodologically inclined, I might say a word here about the methodology we are using in analyzing the data. The basic challenge in doing longitudinal research of this kind is to compensate for the fact that students who are exposed to different types of educational programs may already differ from each other in important respects when they first enter college. Unless these initial differences are somehow taken into account, differences in outcomes four years later may lead us to conclude incorrectly that student outcome differences by program have been caused by the differential environmental experiences. To adjust for these initial entering student input differences we utilized a series of complex multivariate analyses which allowed us to control for the more than 150 characteristics of the entering student which might bias the outcome results. The net effect of these analyses is to allow us to estimate how student outcomes might have differed across programs if the students enrolling in different programs had been comparable in their input characteristics at the point when they first entered college.

Because of the scope and complexity of this study, there is no way I can do justice to the entire spectrum of findings in a brief presentation such as this. Instead let me try to give you a broad overview of some of the key findings. For convenience I have divided them into three broad categories: academic development, personal development, and satisfaction. The first four measures within academic development reflect the students' self-assessments, obtained at the time of the follow-up study, of how much they have increased their general knowledge, critical thinking ability, analytical and problem solving skills, and writing ability. The fifth measure tries to capture their overall academic development simply by summing responses to the first four measures. The next set of measures of academic development includes the Verbal, Quantitative, and Analytical scores on the GRE, the LSAT, the MCAT, and the NTE tests. As you might expect, the student's freshman SAT or ACT scores turn out to be an excellent "pretest" for most of these measures, especially the GRE. Next we have undergraduate retention. The final measure under academic development is a simple dichotomy indicating whether or not the student had enrolled in postgraduate study by the fall of 1989.

Under "personal development" outcomes we have included a measure called "cultural awareness." This reflects the students' self-estimates of how much their undergraduate experience has contributed to their cultural awareness and acceptance of different races or cultures. Leadership is a measure of the extent to which students give themselves high self-ratings on traits such as leadership ability, popularity, social self-confidence, and public speaking ability. Social activism reflects the extent to which students value such things as participating in community action programs, helping others, and influencing the political structure. Both leadership and social activism were measured longitudinally, first at the time of freshman entry and again four years later in the 1989-90 follow-up. Social activism and the next measure, whether or not the student voted in the 1988 presidential election, are included as indicators of citizenship and social responsibility. Leadership, of course, is another frequently-mentioned goal of general education programs. Attending recitals or concerts is included as an indicator of interest in art and culture. The next outcome item–the importance the student attaches to developing a meaningful philosophy of life–is intended to reflect still another value that one frequently encounters in discussions of general education. The next item–the belief that the principal value of a college education is monetary–is intended to be a negative indicator, i.e., a successful general education program would presumably weaken a student's tendency to equate the value of a liberal education with monetary outcomes.

The last category of outcomes includes four items from the follow-up questionnaire measuring the students' satisfaction with various aspects of their undergraduate experience.

Results

Let's now look at some of the findings that seem especially germane to the issue of Cooperative Learning.

Effects of Student Involvement

The first set of findings concerns something that I like to call "student involvement." In a number of early studies we have found that student involvement has generally beneficial effects on a wide range of developmental outcomes. Basically, student involvement reflects the amount of physical and psychological time and energy the student invests in the educational process. It is somewhat similar to the Freudian notion of "cathexis," or to what the learning theorists like to call "time on task." Like earlier research, our study shows that almost any form of student involvement has beneficial effects on learning and student development. Let me briefly summarize just a handful of these findings. The follow-up questionnaire asked each student to indicate how many hours per week, on the average, he/she spent on various activities.

One statistic computed in our analyses is the "Beta" coefficient which can be interpreted like a correlation coefficient. Basically what it indicates is the strength of the effect of student-student interaction on each outcome, *after* we had controlled for more than 150 characteristics of the student at the point of entry, the type of institution attended, the student peer environment, the curriculum, and the faculty environment. While these and other coefficients that I will discuss are relatively small, please keep in mind that we are using relatively crude measures of both the environmental characteristics as well as the student outcomes. With more reliable measures we would no doubt find substantially larger coefficients.

This form of involvement had significant effects on more than two-thirds of the 82 outcome measures. Basically, hours spent studying is positively related to nearly *all* academic outcomes: retention, graduating with honors, enrollment in graduate school, standardized test scores, and all self-reported increases in cognitive and affective skills. The strongest effects are on overall academic development and preparation for graduate school. This measure also has significant associations with all measures of satisfaction and with the personality characteristics of Scholarship and Social Activism. It also has positive correlations with commitment to the goals of promoting racial understanding, cleaning up the environment, and making a theoretical contribution to science and increases the student's chances of choosing careers in science, engineering, and college teaching. The only outcomes that are negatively associated with hours per week spent studying are Hedonism, alcohol consumption, smoking cigarettes, the view that the chief benefit of a college education is to increase one's earning power, and the goal of being very well off financially.

Other forms of academic involvement that had generally beneficial effects on student learning and personal development include taking honors courses, taking interdisciplinary courses, participating in study abroad programs or in college internship programs, participating in racial/culture awareness workshops, doing independent research projects, making class presentations, and taking essay exams. Academic development turns out to be negatively affected by frequent use of multiple choice exams.

The pervasive positive effects of hours per week spent studying and doing homework may well have significant implications for Cooperative Learning. My best hunch about Cooperative Learning is that it works because at least two things happen during the process. First, students are held **accountable** by their peers to achieve certain learning outcomes. Second, students assume a certain degree of **responsibility** for assisting their peers to achieve the same learning goals. These two peer group phenomena may well serve to motivate students to invest additional time and energy in the learning process. In this connection, it would be interesting to conduct studies to show just what happens to students' out-of-class investment of time and energy when they participate in Cooperative Learning.

Student-Student Interaction

This brings us to what turns out to be the most pervasive and interesting set of findings. The single most powerful source of influence on the undergraduate student's academic and personal development is the peer group. In particular, *we find that the sheer amount of interaction among peers has far reaching effects on nearly all areas of student learning and development.* Let me briefly summarize some of these effects. Keep in mind that our composite measure of student-student interaction includes items such as discussing course content with other students, working on group projects for classes, tutoring other students, participating in intramural sports, being a member of a social fraternity or sorority, participating in a campus protest, being elected to a student office, and hours per week spent in socializing or in student clubs or organizations.

Student-student interaction has its strongest positive effects on Leadership development, overall academic development, self-reported growth in problem-solving skills, critical thinking skills, and cultural awareness.

Student-student interaction also has positive correlations with all satisfaction outcomes except facilities. It also has positive effects on self-concept as well as on attending recitals or concerts. Student-student interaction has negative effects on feeling depressed and on the beliefs that the principal value of college is to increase one's earning power and that the individual cannot change society.

Peer Group Effects

In certain respects, Cooperative Learning can be viewed as an effort to capitalize on the power of the peer group to enhance student learning. Our study incorporated several dozen measures of each student's peer "environment" by aggregating certain characteristics of the students at each institution. Every aspect of the student's development–cognitive and affective, psychological and behavioral–is affected in some way by these peer group characteristics, and usually by several peer characteristics. Generally speaking, students tend to change their values, behavior, and academic plans in the direction of the dominant orientation of their peer group. In addition, the values, attitudes, self concept, and socioeconomic status of the peer group are much more important determinants of how the individual student will develop than are the peer group's abilities, religious orientation, or racial composition.

One of the most interesting aspects of our findings concerns the effect of "input" variables (i.e., characteristics of the individual student at the point of freshman entry). We found that certain student input characteristics such as gender, race, and socioeconomic status were significant predictors of a great many student outcomes. After reflecting on the possible meaning of these input effects, it occurred to us that many of them may actually reflect **peer groups** effects! What are these input effects and how might they reflect the differential impact of peer groups?

Let's start with gender. There are significant gender effects on nearly two-thirds of the 82 outcome measures. Some of the most interesting gender differences are in the area of political views: women become more politically liberal during the undergraduate years, whereas men become more conservative. This actually *reverses* the gender effect noted in research we did 20 years ago, when the men changed more in a liberal direction than the women during the undergraduate years (Astin, 1977). In all likelihood this reversal has something to do with the Women's Movement: women's rights and equality for women in the United States have come to be identified with the left side of the political spectrum. (The Equal Rights Amendment, for example, was strongly supported by most liberals and Democrats and strongly opposed by many conservatives and Republicans.) Such an interpretation is supported by the fact that women also show greater increases in **feminism** than men do during the undergraduate years.

Some of the strongest gender differences occur in the area of psychological well-being: the declines in psychological well-being that occur during college (feeling depressed, feeling overwhelmed, low self-rating on emotional health) are all stronger among women than among men during the undergraduate years. In other areas of personality development (e.g., Hedonism, Status Striving, and Leadership), men show larger increases than women do. They also become more committed than women to several life goals (developing a meaningful philosophy of life, becoming involved in programs to clean up the environment, making a theoretical contribution to science) and more committed to the views that racial discrimination is no longer a problem and that the individual can do little to change society. In the behavioral area, men also show greater increases in alcohol consumption and are more likely to become involved in tutoring other students.

There are also many gender differences in cognitive development. Men become relatively more proficient test takers during college. Women, on the other hand, get better grades in college (even after controlling for their better high school grades) and are more likely to complete the bachelor's degree and to graduate with honors. Since men have higher SAT scores and women higher secondary school grades at the point of entry to college, these differential changes during college serve to widen gender gaps that exist at the point of college entry.

The college experience also seems to exaggerate many other freshman gender differences: during college women are more likely than men are to remain in the fields of school teaching, nursing, and psychology and more likely to drop out of the fields of medicine, law, and engineering. During the undergraduate years women also report relatively stronger increases in interpersonal skills, job-related skills, cultural awareness, knowledge of a particular field, and foreign language ability, whereas men report relatively stronger gains in public speaking ability.

In summary, it seems clear that colleges do not serve to eliminate or even reduce many of the stereotypic differences between the sexes. That is, women enter college already differing considerably in self-rated emotional and psychological health, standardized test scores, GPAs, political attitudes, personality characteristics, and career plans, and most of these differences widen during the undergraduate years. Thus, even though men and women are presumably exposed to a common liberal arts curriculum and to other common environmental experiences during the undergraduate years, it would seem that their educational programs appear to preserve and strengthen, rather than to reduce or weaken, stereotypic differences between men and women in behavior, personality, aspirations, and achievement.

How, then, can these gender effects be attributable to peer group effects? Very simply, women are more likely to affiliate with women during college and men are more likely to affiliate with men. These different peer affiliation patterns are created in part by structural factors–single sex colleges, student housing, and so on–but there are also powerful self-selection factors at work: students tend to form same-sex friendships and to affiliate with same-sex clubs and organizations during the undergraduate years. As a consequence, women are more likely to be influenced by the values and behavior of other women, and men are more likely to be influenced by the values and behavior of other men.

This "peer group effect" interpretation also helps to explain why the changes in political views by gender are different today than was the case with the findings reported 20 years ago (Astin, 1977). Whereas male freshmen were more liberal at college entry than female freshmen were during the late 1960s, today the women freshmen are more liberal than the men. Thus, the college women of today are exposed to more liberal same-sex peers than college men are.

Section 2. Why Use Cooperative Strategies? 53

A similar "peer group" interpretation accounts for the differential effects of race. White and African American students show contrasting patterns of change on a number of affective variables. In particular, white students tend to become more politically conservative during the undergraduate years, whereas black students tend to become more politically liberal. The two groups also grow much farther apart in their agreement with the proposition that racial discrimination is no longer a problem and in their commitment to the goal of promoting racial understanding. Consistent with these trends is the finding that African American students become more likely to engage in campus protests during college, whereas white students become less likely to become campus activists. As is the case with gender, this pattern of differential change indicates that the college experience, rather than narrowing political differences between the two major racial groups in this country, actually serves to exacerbate already-existing differences observed at the point of college entry. That these differential changes by race are attributable to peer group effects is suggested by the tendency for the races to segregate themselves during the undergraduate years (either institutionally or via student clubs and organizations). Part of this segregation is voluntary (students choose their own associates and their own organizations), but it is also caused in part by the structure of the American higher education system: not only do we have many colleges that enroll almost exclusively white students and many others that enroll primarily African American students (the historically black colleges, for example), but there are also demographic and geographic factors that tend to concentrate African American and other minority students in certain institutions.

Finally, we come to the effects of the student's socioeconomic status. SES has its strongest effect on completion of the bachelor's degree. It is important to emphasize that this and all other effects of SES are *over and above* the effects of all ability measures and other input characteristics. The student's SES is also related to satisfaction with most aspects of the undergraduate experience. It has positive effects on GPA, entry to graduate school, and willingness to reenroll in the same college. SES also has significant effects on self-reported growth in critical thinking ability, knowledge of a field or discipline, analytical and problem solving skills, interpersonal skills, and overall academic development. In short, these findings show that students from high SES families, compared to low SES students, can look forward to more positive outcomes in college, regardless of their abilities, academic preparation, or other characteristics.

That these effects may be largely attributable to the peer group is suggested by the fact that American college students are substantially segregated by SES during the undergraduate years. Unlike the situation with race and gender, where self-selection of peers **within** the institution plays an important part, this segregation is largely structural in origin: the great institutional variation in selectivity (which is strongly correlated with SES) means that many high SES students attend colleges populated mainly by other high SES students, and that many lower SES students attend colleges where there is a much greater mix of students in terms of SES (Astin, 1985).

These findings raise some very important issues concerning Cooperative Learning. In particular, they suggest that the **composition** of the student's peer group has very important implications for how students will be affected by their peers. Most models of Cooperative Learning clearly recognize the importance of peer group composition by attempting to distribute the highest and lowest achieving students proportionately across all learning groups. But our findings raise some important questions that clearly merit further analysis in the study of Cooperative Learning. For example, if you look simply at a single trait such as ability or achievement, what is the optimal distribution of such a trait that will produce the most effective learning groups? I'm reminded here of some recent research by Rosebeth Moss Kantor, who has shown that simply adding some women to traditionally male corporate peer groups does not necessarily break down male prejudice toward women executives. Kantor argues that a "critical mass" of women must first be reached before the addition of women has any observable effect on male behavior. Similar findings have been reported by people who have studied the integration of women into U.S. military academies: male prejudice toward women cadets apparently does not begin to break down until sufficient numbers of women have joined the student body.

These studies suggest that merely adding a particular type of student to a Cooperative Learning group may not necessarily produce the desired effect until sufficient numbers of such students have been included to constitute a "critical mass." To me this issue is a wide open area for future research which might pay tremendous dividends if those of us who study the Cooperative Learning process can see fit to incorporate such problems in our research.

The Effects of Faculty

Our study also showed that, next to the peer group, the faculty represents the most significant aspect of the student's undergraduate development. Among other things, we found that the sheer amount of interaction between the individual student and the faculty had widespread effects on student development. Our composite measure of student-faculty interaction includes being a guest in a professor's home, working on a professor's research project, assisting faculty in teaching a class, and talking with faculty outside of class. As would be expected, overall student-faculty interaction has its strongest positive correlations (after controlling for entering student characteristics, environmental variables, and number of years completed) with satisfaction with faculty. It also has positive effects on all other areas of student satisfaction, but especially with the quality of instruction and the overall college experience (Beta = .16). Student-faculty interaction also has significant positive correlations with *every* academic attainment outcome: college GPA, degree attainment (Beta = .16), graduating with honors (Beta = .12), and enrollment in graduate or professional school (Beta = .11).

Student-faculty interaction also has positive correlations with *every* self-reported area of intellectual and personal growth, as well as with three life goals: promoting racial understanding, participating in programs to clean up the environment, and making a theoretical contribution to science. Student-faculty interaction also has positive effects on all self-rated abilities except physical health. By contrast, this involvement measure has negative effects on the belief that the principal value of a college education is to increase one's earning power.

Student-faculty interaction also has a number of positive correlations with behavioral outcomes. Especially notable is the substantial positive effect on tutoring other students (Beta = .25). The most obvious explanation for this effect, of course, is that students who are involved in tutoring other students must necessarily have some additional contact with faculty. Other behavioral outcomes that are positively affected by student-faculty interaction include being elected to a student office, attending recitals or concerts, and participating in campus demonstrations. Student-faculty interaction also has significant positive effects on two perceptual outcomes: Diversity Orientation and Social Change Orientation.

Finally, student-faculty interaction has a number of fascinating effects on career outcomes. Most notable, perhaps, is the positive effect on choosing a career in college teaching. Clearly, this result suggests that interacting frequently with faculty produces in students a greater sense of identification with their faculty mentors. Student-faculty interaction also has positive effects on both career choices and major field choices in all fields of science (but not in engineering, it should be stressed), and negative effects on choice of a career or major in business.

Although I am no expert on the literature of Cooperative Learning, my impression is that our systematic knowledge of how faculty-student interaction is affected by Cooperative Learning is meager. While it is possible to argue that student exposure to faculty is reduced because students spend more time with each other instead of listening to faculty, it could also be argued that the amount of **direct contact** between individual students and their professors can be increased by virtue of the fact that faculty members typically serve as "consultants" to the individual learning groups. You might also say that the amount of student-faculty "quality time" is increased under most Cooperative Learning models.

Just as we developed student peer group measures, we also developed several dozen faculty environmental measures by ag-

Section 2. Why Use Cooperative Strategies?

gregating, by institutions, the faculty's responses to certain questionnaire items. Two of these measures–Research Orientation and Student Orientation–produced especially interesting and contrasting patterns of effects on student outcomes. Research Orientation is defined primarily in terms of the faculty's publication rate, time spent conducting research, and personal commitment to research and scholarship. The Student Orientation of the Faculty, on the other hand, is a perceptual factor reflecting the extent to which faculty believe that their colleagues are interested in and focused on student development.

The Research Orientation of the Faculty had a substantial negative effect on student satisfaction with faculty. It also had negative effects on satisfaction with the overall quality of instruction, on leadership development, on growth in interpersonal skills, on college GPA, and on completion of Bachelor's degree.

The Student Orientation of the Faculty produces a very different pattern of effects. In fact, it has more substantial direct effects on student outcomes than almost any other environmental variable. Its strongest positive effects are satisfaction with faculty (Beta = .32), with the quality of instruction, and with the overall college experience.

The Student Orientation of the Faculty also has positive effects on bachelor's degree attainment, intellectual self-esteem, overall academic development and leadership. It has a negative effect on the view that the principal purpose of college is to increase one's earning power.

In short, this pattern of effects suggests that having a strongly student-oriented faculty pays rich dividends in terms of the affective and cognitive development of the undergraduate.

Even though Research Orientation and Student Orientation are substantially correlated in a negative direction ($r = -.69$) and have opposite patterns of effects on student development, it is important to realize that it is possible for some institutions to score high on both factors and for others to score low on both factors. A weak emphasis on research, in other words, is not an *inevitable* consequence of having a student oriented faculty, nor is a weak commitment to student development an inevitable consequence of having a strongly research-oriented faculty.

It should also be emphasized that this strong negative association between Research Orientation and Student Orientation reflects *institutional* characteristics. When we look at individual faculty *within* a single institution, we find little correlation, or even a very weak positive correlation, between research productivity and teaching effectiveness (Centra, 1981; Feldman, 1987; Pascarella and Terenzini, 1991). These single-institution studies suggest that there is no inherent contradiction in a faculty member's being both research-oriented and effective in teaching. The problem would seem to reside in *institutional* policies: most institutions that hire large numbers of research-oriented faculty apparently give little priority to effective undergraduate teaching.

The institutions that personify the combination of strong research orientation and weak emphasis on student development are, of course, the major public universities. Institutions that personify the reverse pattern include primarily small private colleges with limited resources. Those rare institutions that combine strong orientations toward both research and students include a number of affluent and selective private colleges and a few of the smaller private research universities.

Are there any institutions that combine a low emphasis on research with a weak orientation toward students? Perhaps the closest approximation to this particular configuration would be some of the four-year public colleges, although it should be kept in mind that this is a highly heterogeneous category of institutions that is difficult to stereotype.

In short, this discussion suggests that, while a low priority on undergraduate teaching and student development *tends* to be one of the consequences of a strong research orientation, it is not a *necessary* consequence of assigning a high priority to research.

Implications for Educational Practice

Our study also showed that the form and content of the general education curriculum makes little difference. Since the manner in which curriculum is implemented seems to be much more important than its actual form or content, it would appear that we need to rethink radically our traditional institutional approach to curriculum development. Curricular discussions, it seems, are focused far too much on issues of form and content. We academics love to discuss and debate content. Since most of us are strongly identified with our disciplines and fancy ourselves as experts in specific content areas, we are inclined to lobby hard to have our favorite content be represented in the general education curriculum. These competitive instincts very often consume a disproportionate share of the institutional energy that goes into planning and designing our general education programs, and what results is more likely to be a sort of political compromise rather than an integrated and coherent educational experience.

Our research findings, as well as research on Cooperative Learning, suggest that curricular planning efforts will reap much greater payoffs in terms of student outcomes if we focus less on formal structure and content and put much more emphasis on pedagogy and other features of the *delivery system.* Clearly, Cooperative Learning represents one very effective powerful delivery system whose efficacy has already been demonstrated. Our findings suggest that Cooperative Learning may be more potent than traditional competitive methods of pedagogy because it motivates students to become more active and more involved participants in the learning process. This greater involvement could come in at least two different ways. First, students may be motivated to expend more effort if they know that their work is going to be scrutinized by peers, and second, they may learn course material in greater depth if they are involved in helping teach it to fellow students.

It's easy to understand why we academics put so much emphasis on curricular content and why we worry so much about the *form* of our general education programs. Most of us discovered very early in school that we were skilled at mastering curricular content and we were well rewarded for demonstrating this skill in class and on exams and standardized tests. Moreover, what professional success we might be able to achieve in our disciplines is often dependent on our ability to master highly specialized content in our field or subfield. So when we get appointed to the general education committee, our natural instinct is to battle on behalf of our particular field or discipline or specialized knowledge for a piece of the action. The knowledge explosion and the proliferation of specialized fields and subfields in recent years has served only to exacerbate these competitive exchanges that inevitably occur when we set out to review our general education programs.

The real question, I suppose, is whether we and our faculty colleagues are willing to consider the possibility that the student's "general education" consists of something more than the content of what is taught and the particular form in which this content is packaged.

When I was concluding work on a similar study 16 years ago it occurred to me that many of the policies that seemed to govern the expansion of public higher education during the years following the end of the Second World War were really at variance with what was suggested by the research. Our educational policies seemed to be based more on **economic** than on **educational** considerations. As I have reflected on these dilemmas since that book was originally published, it has become increasingly clear that the problems of strengthening and reforming American higher education are fundamentally problems of *values*. Research universities, for example, can continue shortchanging undergraduate education as long as they value the acquisition of resources and the enhancement of reputation more than they do the educational and personal development of the undergraduate (what I have come to call the "talent development" conception of institutional excellence).

Values are fundamental to just about everything we do in undergraduate education: whom we admit and on what basis, *what* we teach them and *how* we teach it, what *rules* and *requirements* will govern our students' conduct, how to *test* and *certify* our students, *whom* to hire and the *criteria* for hiring, tenuring, and promoting them, the manner in which we treat each other as professional colleagues, the *topics* we choose for our research and scholarship, and how we faculty use our discretionary time. What is especially important about American higher education is that most of our institutions, despite complaints about external threats to institutional autonomy, retain an enormous amount of autonomy over all of these decisions. We are, in other words, relatively free to modify or reform any or all of these activities according to whatever set of values we choose to pursue.

Institutions espouse high-sounding values, of course, in their mission statements, college catalogues, and public pronouncements by institutional leaders. The problem here is that these explicitly stated values–which always include a strong commitment to undergraduate education–are often at variance with the real values that drive our decisions and policies. The real issue in reforming undergraduate education, it seems to me, is to effect a better rapprochement between our explicitly stated values and the values that really drive our institutional policies and decisions.

Value debates in higher education, however, focus far too much on *means* and far too little on *ends.* Nowhere is this misplaced emphasis better illustrated than in the case of the curriculum. Practically all of the current debate over "political correctness" in the curriculum is a debate about *content.* If we really mean it when we say that we are educational institutions, these debates would be much more productive if they were reformulated more in terms of *outcomes.* Thus, our new study clearly suggests that, when viewed in terms of educational *outcomes,* an institutional emphasis on "diversity" issues has widespread beneficial effects

I would like to add a footnote here about our findings concerning factors that affect student commitment to the goal of "developing a meaningful philosophy of life." To me this value has always symbolized the existential dilemmas that college students have traditionally confronted in their studies, readings, and peer group bull sessions: What is the meaning of life? What am I doing here? What is my purpose in life? How can I lead a meaningful and satisfying existence during my time on earth? What intrigues me is that this "philosophy of life" value is strengthened by exposure to a college environment that stresses social activism and a strong sense of concern for others and for community. Is it possible that social activism and concern for the plight of others and for community heightens young people's awareness of these existential dilemmas?

In pursuing an economic or materialistic view of education

we tend to forget the basic values that always lead us to recommend a "liberal education" for undergraduates. The real meaning of a liberal education, in other words, goes far beyond just teaching the student how to be a doctor, a lawyer, a diplomat, or a business executive. What a liberal education is really about is encouraging the student to come to grapple with some of life's most fundamental questions. What do I think and feel about life, death, God, religion, love, art, music, history, and science? What kinds of friends and associates do I want in my life? What kinds of peer groups do I want to affiliate with?

In many ways the philosophy underlying a liberal education, like that underlying Cooperative Learning, is a testimony to the value of the peer group. In other words, a liberal education assumes that a little bit of serendipity is a good thing. Create opportunities for students to interact and learn together in an academic environment, and some good things will happen. Give these young people a good deal of freedom coupled with some new challenges and new responsibilities and some good things will happen. While it is not always possible to know beforehand just what these good things will be, the students will seldom disappoint us.

8 Critical Thinking and Cooperative Learning: A Natural Marriage

Joseph B. Cuseo

Originally published in the Cooperative Learning and College Teaching newsletter, Winter 1994.

Introduction

During the last decade, critical thinking (CT) has emerged as a national issue at all levels of American education (Paul, 1994). There has also been a surge of interest in Cooperative Learning (CL), particularly during the last five years (Conrad & Smith, 1992; Robinson & Cooper, 1994). The goal of this article is to explore areas of confluence between these two growing movements and will embrace the following objectives: (a) To highlight the major developments and arguments that have fueled national interest in CT; (b) To identify the key elements that define and describe the process of CT; and (c) To demonstrate how the characteristic features of CL represent effective vehicles for activating the CT process and realizing its positive outcomes.

National Interest in Critical Thinking

Reports from the National Assessment of Educational Progress have warned that, compared to students in other countries, American elementary and secondary students do poorly on test items requiring higher-level thinking skills (Marzano, 1991). It has also been reported that the decline in performance of American high school and college students on standardized tests is due, at least in part, to students' ineffective use of higher-level thinking and problem-solving skills (A Nation at Risk, 1983; Adelman, 1986;

Applebee, Langer, & Mullis, 1989). Two blue-ribbon reports on the status of American higher education have called for more emphasis on, and development of CT skills among college students (Association of American Colleges, 1984; National Institute of Education, 1985).

Research points to the importance of developing CT skills by revealing that factual material learned in an academic context is soon forgotten (Blunt & Blizzard, 1975; Brethower, 1977; Gustav, 1969; Mc Leish, 1968). Commenting on these findings in their comprehensive 20-year review of more than 2500 studies on how college affects students, Pascarella and Terenzini (1991) conclude that,

> Abundant evidence suggests that factual material is forgotten rather soon after it is presented in educational settings. Thus . . . beyond imparting specific subject matter knowledge, claims for the enduring influence of postsecondary education on learning must be based . . . on the fostering of a repertoire of general intellectual or cognitive competencies and skills. (p. 114)

This conclusion is particularly apropos when viewed in light of the contemporary "information explosion" which has resulted in an estimated doubling of technical information between the time students begin college and the time they graduate. As John Naisbitt (1982) argues in *Megatrends*, "Running out of [information] is not a problem, but drowning in it is" (p. 24). This phenomenon underscores the importance of instructors' moving away from "information-loaded" or "content-loaded" teaching and toward the development of students' lifelong learning skills, such as higher-order thinking (Cross, 1993).

Moreover, it has been argued that instructors in all academic disciplines need to promote CT skills because specialized courses designed to teach CT have not been found to be effective (Kurfiss, 1988). Such courses and programs that teach generic thinking skills do not result in students' transferring these skills across different subject matter; instead, CT skills need to be connected directly to the specific subject matter about which the student is thinking (McKeachie et al., 1986). Thus, analogous to the teaching of writ-

Section 2. Why Use Cooperative Strategies?   65

ing skills, it has been argued that the teaching of thinking skills must occur "across the curriculum" (Ruggiero, 1988).

Definition & Description of Critical Thinking

Although the call for CT has been consistent since the early '80s, there has been much less consistency in how CT has been defined. Following his review of the 1950-1985 CT literature, Mc Millan (1987) concluded that, "What is lacking in the research is a common definition of critical thinking... and a clear definition of the nature of an experience that should enhance critical thinking" (p. 37).

My interpretation of the literature is that differences in how CT has been defined seem to revolve around whether it is conceived of as a thought process which (a) specifically entails a well-reasoned evaluative judgement (Young, 1980; Furedy & Furedy, 1985), or (b) generally embraces all forms of higher-order thinking that are more complex or deeper than mere acquisition of knowledge or factual recall (Bloom, 1956; Greeno, 1989).

The latter, more inclusive definition subsumes a wide variety of specific cognitive processes that have been cited under the rubric of CT, including: application, analysis, synthesis, evaluation, deduction, induction, refutation, interpretation, extrapolation, hypothetical reasoning and perspective taking.

In addition to being defined in terms of a variety of specific cognitive processes, CT has also been described in terms of different attitudinal qualities, including: (a) willingness and courage to engage in intellectual risk-taking (Paul, 1992-b), (b) tolerance for ambiguity or uncertainty (Meyers, 1986), (c) openness or receptivity to new ideas (Brookfield, 1987), and (d) willingness to give up personally-held beliefs when viewed in light of contradictory evidence (Tavris, 1990).

Given such variety of descriptors, it may be best to conceive of CT as a multi-dimensional phenomenon that embraces a cluster of specific cognitive skills and related epistemological attitudes. This conception of CT will be adopted for the purposes of this article.

Critical Thinking & Cooperative Learning

Several key features of CL appear to be ideal vehicles for promoting CT, particularly: (a) face-to-face peer interaction; (b) intentional group formation; (c) promoting positive interdependence by assigning complementary roles to group members; (d) designing an active-learning task for students to perform; (e) instructor serving as facilitator of the learning experience; and (f) processing (reflecting on) the group-learning experience. The effectiveness of each of these CL features for promoting CT will be discussed in turn.

Face-To-Face Peer Interaction

Research has consistently revealed that, when college students are required to engage in face-to-face discussion of course concepts, they are more likely to develop CT skills than by merely listening to lectures and recording course notes. For example, Kulik and Kulik (1979) conducted a comprehensive review of research that was designed to assess the effectiveness of different college teaching strategies and found that, relative to processing information individually, student discussion groups were significantly more effective for promoting students' problem-solving skills than the traditional lecture method. Similarly, Beach (1968) conducted a research review under the aegis of the U.S. Department of Education and reported that peer interaction in class had a significant positive impact on students' higher-order, problem-solving skills.

More recently, Kurfiss (1988) completed an extensive review of the literature on critical thinking and concluded that one of the key teaching practices that supports CT is the use of peers as resources in the development of thinking skills. In his book, *Developing Critical Thinkers*, Brookfield (1987) reaches a similar conclusion,

> When we develop critical thinkers, helping them form resource networks with others who are involved in this activity may make a crucial difference. Because identifying and challenging assumptions, and exploring alternatives, involve elements of

threat and risk taking, the peer support provided by a group of others also trying to do this is a powerful psychological ballast to critical thinking efforts. Where such a network does not already exist, one of the most important tasks of those trying to facilitate critical thinking is to encourage its development (p. 79).

Two particular features of CL may be especially effective for promoting the development of these peer-support networks: (a) Attention to team-building exercises during the initial stages of group interaction—which can work to build trust among group members and reduce emotional defensiveness that can interfere with the development of such important CT attitudes as openness and receptivity to new ideas. (b) Continuity of interaction among group members throughout the semester—which may provide teammates with the time needed to emotionally bond and evolve into a tightly-knit social network that supports CT.

Intentional Group Formation

Rather than leave group formation to chance or student self-selection, one characteristic feature of CL is for the instructor to construct learning groups in a fashion that can maximize the realization of certain educational objectives. If one objective of the group experience is the development of CT skills, the research literature strongly suggests the formation of heterogeneous learning groups comprised of individuals who may bring diverse perspectives or cognitive styles to the learning task.

The positive impact of mixing students with different levels of academic ability or prior academic achievement may be due to the fact that less-advanced students often learn more effectively from peer teachers who are closer to them in age and familiarity with course concepts than they do from college professors who are farther beyond them with respect to mastery of such concepts (Vygotsky, 1978; Whitman, 1988). Also, more advanced-peers who explain or teach concepts to their less-advanced peers have been found to learn concepts more deeply than they do when those concepts are merely taught to them by instructors or when they learn alone, particularly when the to-be-learned concepts require the utilization of higher-order cognitive skills (Webb, 1982).

For example, Annis (1983) found that college students in a history course who prepared to teach, and then proceeded to actually teach course material to peers, evidenced more learning than students who only prepared to teach but did not actually teach the material; both of these groups achieved higher learning scores than students who were taught by the instructor or who learned the material on their own. Similarly, in an experimental study conducted by Durling and Shick (1976), it was found that students who discussed material with a peer (a confederate of the experimenter who allegedly was trying to learn the material) performed better than students who discussed the material with the experimenter (who had already mastered it).

Also supporting the value of heterogeneous groups for promoting higher-order thinking is the epistemological theory of social constructivism which presently is fueling national interest in collaborative approaches to the teaching of college writing (Bruffee, 1981, 1993). According to this theory, human thinking is shaped by social interaction and conversation, with an individual's thought processes representing an internalization of these external dialogues (Vygotsky, 1978). Thus, conversing and thinking are held to be causally related, with thought being a product of verbal interaction. Consequently, to think well is to converse well and conversation characterized by a diversity of perspectives leads to richer, deeper, more comprehensive and more complex thinking. Conversely, to restrict the diversity of perspectives an individual experiences is to restrict the complexity and quality of thought—by restricting the range of conceptual angles, lenses, or frameworks from which the individual can think.

Heterogeneously-formed CL groups would appear to be an ideal vehicle for converting the theory of social constructivism into pedagogical practice. For instance, individual students could be exposed to diverse perspectives when placed in heterogenous groups of students who differ in terms of such demographic characteristics as: (a) ethnicity, (b) national citizenship and (c) age. Heterogeneous groups could also be formed with respect to students' learning styles; for example, the Myers-Briggs Type Indicator (MBTI)

Section 2. Why Use Cooperative Strategies?

may be used to identify students with one of four different learning styles: concrete-active, concrete-reflective, abstract-active, and abstract-reflective (Schroeder, 1993). Students could then be placed in heterogeneous groups to engage in a CL task.

Heterogeneous CL groups, formed on the basis of differing demographic characteristics (in which students experience diverse perspectives), or on the basis of differing learning styles (in which students experience diverse approaches to thinking and information processing) could effectively implement two common recommendations in the literature on teaching for CT: (a) Have students "collaborate to 'stretch' their understanding by encountering divergent views" (Kurfiss, 1988, p. 2), and (b) Intentionally create an "atmosphere of disequilibrium so that students can change, rework, or reconstruct their thinking processes" (Meyers, 1986, p. 14).

Promoting Positive Interdependence by Assigning Complementary Roles to Group Members

A characteristic feature of CL is creating positive interdependence among group members by structuring the learning task in such a way that each member feels that she is an integral part of a team and is responsible to/for other teammates. A common CL strategy for encouraging this feeling is **positive role interdependence**, i.e., assigning complementary roles to different team members (Johnson, Johnson, & Smith, 1991). Typically, these roles have involved the performance of some functional duty (e.g., recorder, spokesperson) or the provision of some informational resource (e.g., contributing one section of a chapter or one unit of instruction to the group's final product).

However, if a major objective of the CL experience to is to promote CT, it might be useful to consider assigning higher-order thinking roles to group members, with each member being responsible for contributing one version or form of CT (e.g., analysis, synthesis, evaluation, application) to the group's final product. To depict these roles visually, a graphic representation (Jones et al.,

1988-89) or graphic organizer (Prescott, 1993) could be constructed, such as a content-by-process matrix (see Figure 1) which juxtaposes key CT processes with key course concepts.

Figure 1

Content/Process Matrix			
CT PROCESS (Student Roles)	COURSE CONTENT (Learning Task)		
	Concept 1	Concept 2	Concept 3
Analysis			
Application			
Evaluation			
Synthesis			

This content-by process matrix serves to structure not only the content of the students' group-learning task but also the type of cognitive process students are to engage in during that task, thus enabling the instructor to gain some control of students' thought processes in the classroom, ensuring that students will spend at least a portion of valuable class time involved in higher-order thinking. Such assurance cannot be attained if students are left entirely to their own devices. For example, students have been found to spend significant amounts of time "off task" during lectures, thinking about topics unrelated to course content (Bligh, 1972).

In addition to visually highlighting what CT processes students are to engage in, the content-by-process matrix could also benefit instructors by: (a) raising their conscious awareness of the importance of promoting specific CT skills, and (b) encouraging them to identify core concepts in their courses—ideas or issues students should think most deeply about or concepts that have the most explanatory power, generalizability, transferability, and long-term value.

Designing an Active-Learning Task for Students to Perform

A cardinal feature of CL is that students actively engage in a learning task; rather than passively receiving information about something, students actually do something—they act on the material to be learned. This is also a cardinal recommendation in the CT literature: If higher-order thinking is to be developed, instruction must involve methods that require students to use content, not simply acquire it (Kurfiss, 1988). CT encourages the student to "act as a practitioner rather than as an observer . . . . These are active processes and they can be fostered only if learners are required to use them" (Young, 1980, pp. 93-94).

The scholarly literature on the teaching of CT also resonates with the recommendation of striking a balance between providing students with a challenging task that demands higher-order thinking and a supportive structure for meeting this challenge (Kurfiss, 1988; Young, 1980). CL readily accommodates the second recommendation by providing a peer group to serve as a supportive structure for learning. The first recommendation, providing a challenging learning task, is a consideration that has received relatively little attention in the CL literature. What type or nature of tasks should be reserved for group-learning experiences? If the objective is to promote higher-level cognitive skills among group members, the CT literature strongly suggests that the CL task be centered on: (a) ill-structured problems that may not be readily resolved, (b) issues to be discussed or debated, or (c) decision-making tasks that require exploration of, and determination from equally appealing alternatives.

These problem-based, issue-centered, and decision-oriented tasks are more likely to promote CT than information-based lectures or textbooks. As Ward (1989) puts it, "One can be quizzed about a textbook (or an expository lecture), but it is next to impossible to discuss it" (p. 29).

Instructor Serving as Facilitator of the Learning Experience

A critical feature of CL is that it is a learner-centered process that encourages students to work independent of the instructor—who, in turn, adopts the role of facilitator or coach. This feature is consistent with an oft-cited tenet in the CT literature: Higher-level thinking can only occur when students experience some independence from the teacher (Brookfield, 1987). CT scholars also argue that instructors can foster higher-level thinking more effectively when they adopt the role of listener in the learning process. As Brookfield (1987) expresses it,

> Listening well is as important to critical thinking as is contributing brilliantly. Unless facilitators listen attentively so that they gain a sense of participants' backgrounds, past experiences, frameworks for understanding, and habitual learning styles, how can they make informed judgments about what exercises, methods, and materials will be most likely to prompt critical thinking? (p. 239)

In the CT literature, a strong case is also made for instructors to assume the role of questioner—one who effectively prods students to come to terms not only with the content of what is being learned but also with the thought processes they bring to bear on this content (Paul, 1992-b).

Both of these recommended roles for CT instructors, that of listener and questioner, are consistent with the role of instructor as facilitator in CL. Instead of grading papers or leaving the room, the CL instructor is expected to circulate among learning groups, listening to their thought processes and issuing timely questions designed to promote students' elaboration and higher-order thinking (Cuseo, 1992).

Processing (Reflecting On) the Group-Learning Experience

A common feature of CL is building some time into the group-learning experience for team members to reflect on the quality of their social interaction. Empirical support for the value of this practice in promoting higher-order thinking has been provided by Johnson, et al. (1990) in their comparative study of the performance of African-American freshmen who learned problem-solving skills in one of three learning formats: (a) individually, (b) in CL

Section 2. Why Use Cooperative Strategies? 73

groups accompanied by instructor processing (i.e., cooperative skills were specified, observed, and then feedback was provided to groups on how effectively they implemented these skills), or (c) in CL groups accompanied by both instructor processing and student processing. Following completion of the learning experience, a complex problem-solving test was administered. It was found that students in CL groups outperformed those who learned individually, and those students who experienced CL accompanied by both instructor processing and student processing displayed the highest levels of test performance.

In addition to reflecting on the social aspects of the group experience, CL advocates have also argued for reflective processing on the cognitive aspects of group learning, i.e., meta-cognitive awareness (Cooper et al., 1990). Such meta-cognitive processing involves student reflection on: (a) individual steps involved in their thinking or problem-solving, (b) specific strategies or approaches they used in the process of reaching problem solutions, and (c) underlying rationales for their ideas.

Incorporating such cognitive processing into the CL experience is consistent with the literature on promoting CT. For instance, in her comprehensive review of CT research, Kurfiss (1988) concluded that one key teaching practice for developing higher-order thinking is requiring students to explicitly formulate and justify their ideas. Also, research on cognitive psychology and problem-solving has revealed that if college students are required to explain why they take the steps they do during problem-solving tasks, they evince higher levels of problem-solving performance—particularly during initial stages of learning and skill development (Ahlum-Heather & DiVesta, 1986).

These empirical findings lend support to philosopher John Dewey's classic assertion that, "We do not learn from our experience, we learn from processing our experience." By incorporating such processing (social and cognitive) into the group experience, CL effectively embraces this important condition for learning and critical thinking.

Conclusion

When taking a retrospective look at this article following its completion, I was struck by the number of fortuitous relationships that emerged between CT and CL. I undertook this project with the hope that I might discover just enough information to justify a short newsletter article. By the time the project was concluded, I ended up with an article of excessive length which still failed to incorporate all the ideas I had hoped to include (e.g., promoting CT via reciprocal peer-questioning in CL groups; delineation of CT perspective-taking roles for CL members).

My experience with this project leads me to conclude that there is great confluence between these two growing movements in higher education which has yet to be even partially tapped. The pedagogical practices embedded within CL and the learning conditions that give rise to CT are strikingly congruent and mutually reinforcing. This suggests that integration of these two educational processes holds promise for producing powerful, synergistic effects on student learning and cognitive development.

9 Cooperative Learning: A Pedagogy for Diversity

Joseph B. Cuseo

Originally published in the Cooperative Learning and College Teaching newsletter, Fall, 1992.

Student Diversity

Arguably, the most pressing issue facing higher education today and in the immediate future is the issue of student diversity. Never in the history of American higher education has there been such a diverse and rapidly changing student body (Hodgkinson, 1985; Levine, 1989). The objective of this article is to provide an up-to-date synthesis of the demographic trends that are contributing to student diversity and illustrate how Cooperative Learning (CL) can serve as an effective pedagogy for enhancing the college achievement and retention of today's "new students."

Described below are: a) the demographic conditions and trends that are contributing to student diversity in higher education, b) the key subgroups of students who comprise this increasingly diverse student body, and c) the potential benefits of CL for meeting the needs and promoting the success of these different student subgroups.

Adult (Re-entry) Students

The average age of today's college student is 26 years, and by the year 2000, the traditional 18-22 year-old student will comprise only 16% of the American college population (Levitz, 1989).

The relevance of CL for this growing number of adult learners is highlighted by research which indicates that, relative to traditional-age students, adult learners are more likely to display the following characteristics: a) lower levels of competitiveness toward other students, b) more interest in participating with others, c) more inclination to assume personal responsibility for their learning, and d) more willingness to work independent of instructor supervision (Eison & Moore, 1980; Fuhrmann & Jacobs, 1980; Kraft, 1976).

Also, the key features of CL are very consistent with the basic tenets of adult learning theory (andragogy), namely: Adults learn best through active, experiential techniques involving discussion and problem solving which allows them to draw on their backlog of personal and professional experiences (Knowles, 1984). After reviewing research and theory on adult learners, Gaff and Gaff (1981) offered the following recommendation, "In most educational systems the teacher is the main actor, who typically holds forth from center stage. Adults may well be less interested in what the teacher knows, however, than in what use that knowledge is to them. The interests and needs of the adult learner may become more central than the interests and competencies of the teacher; rather than being the principal actor, the teacher might better play the role of stage manager, arranging the conditions in which the learners can best perform" (pp. 651-652).

CL would place the teacher in this facilitative position enabling adults to draw upon their diverse life histories by providing them with a support group for discussing and applying academic concepts to their personal and professional lives. Furthermore, CL groups comprised of adult learners and traditional-aged students could provide the latter with a different perspective on course issues—such as: a) a different **developmental** perspective (e.g., a view from the stage of early, middle, or late adulthood), b) a different **historical** perspective (e.g., older students may have personally witnessed historical events that traditional-age student can only discuss vicariously, and c) a **real world** perspective (e.g., attained from experience raising a family and from full-time employment in work settings). Experiential learning theorist David Kolb (1981) eloquently illustrates the educational advantage of such cross-age interaction, "Discussions of human values and the quality of life are very different with high school graduates than they are with managers of an oil refinery. Quality patient care has one connotation to the idealistic pre-med student and quite another to the har-

Commuter Students

In 1989, an estimated 69% of all entering freshmen were commuters (Rice, 1989) and by the fall of 1992 only about 20% of the college population will be residential students (Levine, 1989). Commuters are considered to be "high risk" students because their college attrition rate is significantly higher than that of residential students (Astin, 1977; Chickering, 1974). Research on commuter students suggests that a key factor contributing to their high rate of attrition is their tendency to continue associating primarily with high school friends or coworkers who are not attending college and their related propensity for not becoming actively involved with members of the college community; for example, compared to residential students, commuters are less involved in co-curricular activities and are more likely to perceive college as unfriendly (Astin, 1977; Chickering, 1974; Wilmes & Quade, 1986).

CL may serve as an effective antidote to commuter students' lack of involvement in the college community and can attenuate their perceived lack of campus friendliness by allowing commuters the opportunity to become actively involved with their peers in the classroom. Such in-class social interaction may serve to increase commuter students' involvement in the college experience, permitting them the opportunity to bond with other students and to develop collegial associations with their classmates (which commuters may not have the time or inclination to do outside of class). This potential advantage of CL for commuters was alluded to by Arthur Chickering almost 20 years ago, "The master teacher, or mentor, also helps his students work together with others. By helping each student connect with others, he not only enriches their ongoing academic study and learning, but also helps the student begin to shift his identification to others associated with the institution who may be more identified with his aspirations and his current problems than the friends and reference groups that are part of his home community" (1974, p. 130).

Part-Time Students

From 1976 to 1987, there was a 25.5% increase in the number of part-time students in higher education—a rate of increase which was five times higher than that of full-time students (Carnegie Foundation, 1989). Part-time students now constitute about 43% of all college students; at public 4-year institutions, they comprise almost one-half of the student body and, at public 2-year colleges, they make up two-thirds of the student population (National Center for Education Statistics, 1989). The vast majority of part-time students are adults and commuters (U.S. Department of Education, 1989), so when these three demographic trends are combined (i.e., part-timers, adults, and commuters), it results in a very telling statistic: In 1992, only about 20% of the total college population will be comprised of the traditional full-time, 18-22 year old, residential student (Levine, 1989). The implication of this demographic reality for promoting collaborative activities among students in the college classroom is poignantly captured by Gabelnick, MacGregor, Matthews, and Smith (1990), "As the number of full-time and residential students declines, community-creating activities such as late-night dorm sessions, hours spent lingering in a favorite coffee shop, or study break arguments in a library lounge also decline. For many students, the time and spaces for trying out new ideas in the company of peers no longer exists. The college experience is sandwiched between work and family, and the set of classes taken during any given term constitutes the only sustained contact students have with their colleges. *In this environment, the curriculum must now assume responsibilities for building community formerly assumed by the college as a whole*" (p.10).

Female Students

Since 1978, women have outnumbered men among first-time college freshmen (Astin & Green, 1987) and today the majority of American college students are women. Between 1976 and 1987, the male-female ratio of college students reversed itself from 53:47 to 47:53. During this time period, women accounted for 100% of the growth in graduate and professional school enrollment (Carnegie

Foundation, 1987). By 1999-2000, women are expected to be awarded the majority of associate, bachelor's, master's, and doctoral degrees, as well as 40% of all first-time professional degrees (Levine, 1989).

The implications of this demographic trend for CL is suggested by research on female college students, which strongly suggests that they favor learning experiences that are participatory and collaborative (Fuhrmann & Jacobs, 1980; Kraft, 1976). Such collaborative forms of learning would also be very congruent with women's epistemological style (Belenky, Clinchy, Goldberger, and Tarule, 1986) and their style of moral reasoning (Gilligan, 1982).

Empirical evidence gathered by Cooper and Mueck (1990) suggests that CL has positive effects on college women's academic achievement in and attitude toward math-related subject matter. This finding is particularly noteworthy because women are grossly under-represented in careers that require substantial math and science preparation—e.g., women comprise only 13% of working scientists and engineers (Tobias, 1990). In two recent studies it was discovered that women who enter fields of science are more likely to perceive the classroom situation as unfriendly and feel uncomfortable working in its "intensely competitive environment." The authors of both studies concluded that women would respond better to science if its pedagogy included more "cooperative and interactive modes of learning" (Tobias, 1990, p. 24).

African American (Black) Students

In 1991, the National Center for Education Statistics reported that 45% of African American students enrolled in higher education within a year after receiving their high school diploma (Mow & Nettles, 1990). Though the absolute numbers of African American students attending college is higher than ever before, the actual proportion of Black high school graduates who enroll in college has been decreasing (American Council on Education, 1988). Thus, African Americans are underrepresented in higher education, particularly Black males–who comprise only 3.5% of the national college population (University of California Task Force, 1988). Also, African American students who do enroll in college are at-risk for attrition; only 25-30% are retained to graduation (National Institute of Independent Colleges & Universities, 1990)–an attrition rate which is more than twice that of White students (U.S. Bureau of Census, 1987; Educational Testing Service, 1988).

Research on African American college students suggests that, relative to White students, they are less participative in traditional academic settings–such as the lecture class (Astin, et al., 1971; Heilman, 1981). Their verbal reticence in the college-classroom setting has been attributed to feelings of being isolated from and scrutinized by majority students (Melendez, 1988; Levits, 1992).

The potential value of CL for promoting the involvement, retention, and achievement of African American students is supported empirically by Frierson (1984, 1986) who found that Black nursing students scored higher on a state board exam when they were instructed to engage in CL while studying–relative to a comparable group of African American students who were not instructed to engage in such interdependent learning. The beneficial effects of CL for Black students in science and math has been empirically demonstrated by Treisman (1985), who found that students participating in his cooperatively taught tutorial sessions received a mean grade-point average of 2.6 in freshman calculus, whereas a comparable group of Black students who did not attend these sessions had a 1.5 grade-point average. More recently, these findings have been replicated in a 5-year longitudinal study of 320 African American students at California State Polytechnic University-Pomona which revealed that: a) only 4% of Black students who participated in collaborative taught workshops eventually withdrew from college–compared to a 42% attrition rate among non-participants, and b) collaborative techniques used by Black students in math and science classes resulted in a greater likelihood that these students would join together to study collaboratively outside of class (Wheeler, 1992). This latter finding is particularly noteworthy when considered together with recent research on Harvard students, which indicates that academic achievement is enhanced appreciably when students engage in collaborative study-group sessions outside of class (Light, 1991, 1992).

Hispanic (Latino) Students

American Hispanics are comprised of numerous subgroups, including: Mexican Americans or Chicanos (60.6%), Puerto Ricans (15.1%), South or Central Americans (10.2%), Cubans (6.1%), and others of Spanish ancestry or descent (8%) (Nieves-Squires, 1991).

The number of Hispanic students in higher education has been on the rise since the mid-1970's and in 1991 the National Center for Education Statistics reported that 57% of Hispanic high school graduates enrolled in postsecondary education within a year after receiving their high school diploma (Mow & Nettles, 1990). The increase in the absolute number of Hispanic students on college campuses is due primarily to higher than average birth rates in the 1960's and 1970's which have resulted in a sizable increase in the number of Hispanics of college-going age (Estrada, 1988). Unfortunately, the actual percentage of Hispanic high school students who go on to college has been decreasing in recent years (Barr, 1991) so Hispanics are still under-represented in American higher education–particularly Mexican Americans and Puerto Ricans (Nieves-Squires, 1991). Those Hispanic students who do enroll in college are at risk for attrition–approximately 70-75% do not complete their baccalaureate degree (National Institute of Colleges & Universities, 1990).

Research on Hispanic college students indicates that, relative to White students, they are less participative in class (Astin, et al., 1971; Heilman, 1981) due to feelings of alienation (Melendez, 1988) and due to the fact that silence in the presence of an authority figure (such as a teacher) is a sign of courtesy and respect in Hispanic culture (Cortes, 1978; Melendez & Petrovich, 1989).

CL could be especially effective with Hispanic students because: a) it would provide them with a social-learning context that is free of a silence-inducing authority figure, and b) its features are consistent with two very important values in Hispanic culture–cooperation and group cohesiveness (Nieves-Squires, 1991).

Empirical support for the benefits of CL for Hispanic students is provided by Kagan (1986), who reports precollegiate research indicating that Hispanic students evince higher levels of academic achievement when taught via CL rather than by traditional instructional methods.

American Indian (Native American) Students

Though often considered to be a single minority group, American Indians are comprised of approximately 300 different tribes in the continental United States and Alaska and almost 200 different languages are spoken (Henderson, 1991). Native American enrollment in higher education increased by 19% between 1978 and 1988, with the greatest growth occurring at 2-year colleges (Evangelauf, 1988). Nevertheless, American Indians are under-represented in higher education–only 8% have completed four or more years of college (O'Brien, 1990) and the attrition rate among those who attend college is extremely high–estimated to be over 80% (Guzette & Heath, 1983; Noel & Levitz, 1989).

The positive implications of CL for promoting the learning and retention of American Indian students is succinctly summarized by Swisher (1990) after comprehensively reviewing the research literature: "In both learning style and interactional style preference, it is apparent from the literature that [American] Indian students from different tribal groups are predisposed to cooperative versus competitive styles of acquiring and demonstrating knowledge" (p. 43).

Asian American Students

Constituting 60% of the world population, Asian Americans are comprised of numerous subgroups, including: Chinese, Japanese, Koreans, Filipinos, Southeastern Asians (e.g., Vietnamese, Cambodians, Hmong, Laotians) and Pacific Islanders (e.g., native Hawaiians, Samoans) (Hsia, 1988). Between 1970 and 1980, the Asian American population increased from 1.5 to 3.5 million, making them the nation's fastest-growing minority group. Since 1980, the Asian American population has doubled its size, reaching 7.3 million in 1990 (Escueta & O'Brien, 1991). The number of Asian

Americans enrolled in college more than doubled between 1976 and 1988, and given the increasingly high college-going rate of Asian Americans (O'Hare & Felt, 1991), the total number of Asian American college students should continue to increase dramatically throughout the 1990's.

Though Asian Americans, in general, are well represented in higher education, it should be noted that Southeast Asians are under represented (Escueta & O'Brien, 1991) and tend to come from families who are disproportionately below the poverty line (Suzuki, 1989). Those Southeast Asians who do enroll in college are considered to be at-risk for attrition (Bagasao, 1989).

While remaining cognizant of the fact that there is a large variety of subgroups within the Asian American population, a relatively safe generalization can be made that, compared to White students, they are less likely to verbalize questions or opinions in class–particularly Asian American females (Meredith, 1988). This reticence to speak out in classroom settings may reflect their cultural view that silence reflects respect for an authority figure–the teacher (Minatoya & Sedlaceck, 1981; Sue & Kirk, 1975; Sue, 1981). Other research suggests that Asian American students prefer college teachers who provide structured learning experiences rather than open-ended discussions (Meredith, 1988).

CL may be able to provide Asian American students with this learning structure (e.g., via specific role assignments, individual accountability, and construction of a final product) while, at the same time, promote their verbal involvement in the learning process by providing them with a small, student-centered discussion format which is not led by a teacher–thus removing the authority figure who should be revered with silence.

International (Foreign) Students

Between 1980 and 1990, the number of international students in American higher education increased by approximately 25%, resulting in a total enrollment of over 400,000 foreign students; this number is expected to grow to over 425,000 by the year 2000. The majority of international students are from Asian countries

(56%)–China (9.7%), Japan (9.0%), Taiwan (8.2%), Korea (5.7%), Malaysia (3.3%), Hong Kong (3.1 %), followed by European countries (12.1 %), Latin-America (11.7%), the Middle East (11.3%)–India (7.8%), Indonesia (2.3%) and Pakistan (1.9%), then Canada (4.5%) (Institute of International Education, 1992).

Given that many international students are also ESL (English as a Second Language) students, the smallness, intimacy, and longevity of CL groups may provide a less threatening social context for ESL students to practice their English-speaking skills than would whole-class discussions and center-stage oral reports.

Via heterogeneous grouping of international and American students, CL could effectively capitalize on the rich reservoir of cultural differences which international students bring to the classroom. Cooperative interaction and positive interdependence between international and American students would promote cross-cultural dialogue that could reduce students' ethnocentrism as well as provide students with a comparative perspective that could contribute significantly to the realization of two oft-cited student outcomes of general education: global awareness (Gaff, 1992) and self-awareness (Cross, 1982).

It is also interesting to speculate on how CL experiences in American college classrooms could affect international students' perceptions of our country, and how such cooperative experiences might influence the political attitudes and negotiatory styles they bring back to their home countries–and share with their compatriots. Favorable educational experiences in American classrooms, involving collaboration and interdependence among students of different nations, may have the potential for improving international relations.

Diversity-Related Issues

Embedded within the contemporary issue of student diversity are two important sub-issues: a) multicultural education, and b) interracial relations. I will conclude this article with a brief discussion of these two diversity-related issues and their implications for CL.

Multicultural Education

Discussions of multicultural education at the postsecondary level have almost exclusively focused on course and curricular **content**–for example, whether the general-education curriculum should be "politically correct" (i.e., include third-world, racial/ethnic, and women's studies) or whether it should remain focused on the canon of Western tradition. In contrast, comparatively little attention has been paid to classroom **pedagogy** and the **learning process** as they relate to multicultural and general education (Gaff, 1989). Reflecting on his survey of over 300 colleges and universities which have attempted to strengthen their general education programs, Gaff (1992) argues that, "Multicultural general education courses cry out for more personal, experiential, interactive, and collaborative kinds of instruction. Pedagogical 'business as usual' in any general education program...will not allow students to learn what even the most fervently argued courses have to teach" (p. 35).

The need for greater attention to the learning process in general education is further supported by a recent 4-year, longitudinal study of students at 159 colleges which revealed that the form and content of the general education curriculum had no significant effect on a wide range of student outcomes related to general education; what did have the most significant impact on students' achievement and development was **student-student interaction** (Astin, 1991). This empirical finding suggests that classroom pedagogical practices that promote meaningful student-student interaction (e.g., CL) could make a significant contribution to student achievement in general education.

The implication of Astin's recent empirical findings for CL and general education is consistent with an articulate epistemological argument for collaborative classroom experiences, posited over 100 years ago by the German philosopher, Nietzsche, "The more affects we allow to speak about one thing, the more eyes, different eyes we can use to observe one thing, the more complete will our concept of this thing, our objectivity, be" (cited in Hill, 1991, p. 41).

Moreover, the multicultural and general education implications of CL for our nation's future political leadership has been underscored by Supreme Court Justice, William J. Brennan in 1967, "The classroom is peculiarly the 'marketplace of ideas.' The nation's future depends upon leaders trained through wide exposure to that robust exchange of ideas which discovers truth out of a multitude of tongues, rather than through any kind of authoritative selection" (cited in Weimer, 1991, p. 6).

Research on learners in higher education suggests that they would be very receptive to the use of CL in general education courses because college students: a) report significantly higher levels of course satisfaction in classes that allow for regular small-group discussion (Bligh, 1972), b) are more likely to experience attitudinal change in classes that involve small group discussion (Kulik & Kulik, 1979), and c) prefer student-discussion groups that are diverse in composition (Feichtner & Davis, 1991). These findings imply that the use of ethnically- and culturally-diverse CL groups could have several advantages for general and multicultural education, including: a) increasing students' level of satisfaction in general-education courses–courses which traditionally receive lower student ratings than electives (Braskamp, Brandenburg, and Ory, 1984), b) increase students' retention in general education courses–because student satisfaction and student retention are highly correlated (Noel, 1985), and c) increase students' potential for positive attitudinal change (e.g., increased multicultural appreciation).

The potential of collaborative experiences for enriching students' multicultural appreciation and cognitive development is poignantly illustrated by the following comment from a student at La Guardia Community College who was part of a diverse Collaborative Learning group, "We were seventeen to seventy years old, all different races and religions, and had lived in this country all our lives or for only a few months. We shared what we knew. Our seventy-year-old [co-learner] lived through the Great Depression in the 1930's, and he told us about that. It helped us understand what happened to the Grand Army of Starvation" (Gabelnick, et al., 1990, p. 69).

By creating positive interdependence among culturally heterogeneous groups of learners, CL and Collaborative Learning have the potential to capitalize on the contemporary wave of student diversity–converting it from a pedagogical liability (which instructors must somehow adapt to or accommodate)–into a pedagogical asset to be used by faculty as an instructional vehicle for reaching and realizing the goals of multicultural education.

Interracial Relations

Discussion of higher education's role in promoting positive race relations has focused mostly on access, i.e., effective recruitment of under-represented minority students (as well as minority faculty and staff) in an attempt to increase campus diversity. A tacit objective and assumption of this strategy is that access should result in more contact between minority- and majority-group members, thereby reducing racial prejudice and promoting interracial harmony.

However, judging from the sizable and reportedly increasing number of "racial incidents" on American college campuses (Thomas, 1991), it appears that increased college access and exposure to minority-group members has not been particularly effective in promoting interracial harmony. This should not come as a surprise when viewed in light of school-integration research at the precollege level which strongly indicates that mere exposure to, or incidental contact with minority students does not improve interracial relations (Stephan, 1978), nor does it even promote interracial interaction–minority and majority students still manage to segregate themselves within the school setting (Gerard & Miller, 1975; Rogers, et al., 1984). In fact, one comprehensive review of all school-desegregation research, covering a span of 30 years, revealed that racial prejudice in some desegregated schools actually increased rather than decreased (Stephan, 1986).

Such findings suggest that something more than mere exposure to minority-group members must occur in order to enhance interracial and subcultural appreciation. As Hill (1991) trenchantly expresses it, "Meaningful multiculturalism transforms the curriculum. While the presence of persons of other cultures and subcultures is a virtual prerequisite to that transformation, their 'mere presence' is primarily a political achievement, not an intellectual or educational achievement. Real educational progress will be made when multi-culturalism becomes interculturalism" (p. 45).

The relevance of CL for promoting this interculturalism and improving race relations is suggested by experimental research in social psychology, which indicates that continued exposure to an initially-disliked person under conditions of **competition and conflict** will intensify the dislike of that person (Burgess & Sales, 1977; Swap, 1977). In contrast, there is empirical evidence that intergroup contact in the context of CL activities will decrease racial prejudice and increase interracial friendships among: a) elementary and secondary school students (Aronson, 1978; Slavin, 1980), b) college students (Worchel, 1979), and c) workers in industrial organizations (Blake & Mouton, 1979).

In particular, the most dramatic gains in promoting positive race relations have been achieved when each of the following conditions stipulated by the "contact hypothesis" (Allport, 1954; Amir, 1969) is met: a) Participants have equal status (e.g., having each student assigned an equally important role in the completion of a CL task); b) There is cooperation that produces a successful outcome (e.g., by structuring positive interdependence and requiring a well-defined final product); c) Social norms and authorities promote positive relationships and friendship formation (e.g., via team-building exercises and monitoring of social processing in CL groups by the roving instructor); and d) The situation encourages participants to generalize changed attitudes to other people and situations (e.g., by occasional changes in the membership of CL groups and the assignment of a number of different CL tasks to be completed during the semester).

When these conditions of the contact hypothesis are met, the empirical evidence supporting its positive impact on race relations is extremely impressive. The author of a comprehensive review of the research literature on race relations in schools concluded, "The concept of interracial work groups as a means for reducing prejudice and improving race relations has a great deal of empirical support. It is rare in social science to find such robust results across a wide range of techniques, empirical evaluation methodologies, grade levels, [and] regions of the country. The importance of contact under the conditions specified by the contact hypothesis is truly impressive" (McConahay, 1981, pp. 50-51).

CL has the potential for meeting all the conditions stipulated by this contact hypothesis and, in so doing, has the potential for reducing racial prejudice and improving the quality of race relations in higher education.

10 Ten Reasons College Administrators Should Support Cooperative Learning

Jim Cooper

Originally published in the Cooperative Learning and College Teaching newsletter, Fall, 1995.

It is no secret that resources available to colleges and universities in 1995 are very limited, with little prospect for relief in sight. It is equally true that the demands made on these institutions by the unique composition of our student populations are straining our capacity to cope. Faculty are graying and most were never trained in pedagogy, particularly the pedagogy most effective for the diverse students who have come to us in the last 15 years. Administrators are attempting to address a myriad of faculty, community and student concerns in an era of downsizing.

Cooperative learning is a relatively cost-effective method for dealing with a substantial number of issues confronting college administrators and faculty. Unlike many of the interventions already in place for dealing with the ten issues described below, there is a firm empirical and theoretical base which indicates that cooperative learning can have an impact on these issues.

Reason 1. Increasing student retention. Why students leave school has been studied by Vince Tinto, Lee Noel and others for at least twenty years. The most powerful predictor of student retention is the nature of his/her involvement with the institution. Students who report positive interactions with other students and with faculty are much more likely to continue in college, particularly in the first few months when most attrition occurs. Well structured cooperative learning builds in the kind of positive interactions that Tinto, Noel and others have argued for during the last two decades.

Reason 2. Appreciating diversity. This issue continues to confound college administrators and faculty. We would like to create an environment in which tolerance, if not appreciation of diversity, is the norm. Racist and sexist incidences continue to plague our institutions of higher learning as they do society at large. Most administrators and faculty want to foster appreciation of diversity. But what can faculty and administrators do that is both effective and within their comfort levels? Many faculty are uneasy speaking directly in class about issues relating to diversity. Cooperative learning is a relatively straightforward teaching technique that all or most faculty can manage and which holds great promise for fostering positive attitude change toward women, minorities and others. And it doesn't require the major shifts in curricular content implied in some interventions designed to foster appreciation of diversity. Research by Light, Tobias, Kagan, Triesman, and others suggests that women and some minorities prefer and may perform better with cooperatively-structured small group tasks. These findings extend from elite institutions to colleges with open enrollment.

Reason 3. Using technology in the classroom. Researchers at San Diego State and Cal Poly Pomona completed two syntheses of the impact of television and two-way interactive video in the classroom. Based on hundreds of comparisons they found that these technologies were about the same as more traditional instructional formats in fostering achievement among students. In cases where televised instruction surpassed more traditional forms of instruction, Witherspoon (1994) found that it was the frequency and quality of student-student and student-teacher interaction that distinguished the more effective from the less effective televised classrooms. For example, students in more effective televised classes were required to interact with one another and the professor outside of class in small groups or by E-mail. Those who look to technology to solve the cost problems of traditional instructional approaches need to take a close look at the pedagogical underpinnings of the change they are examining. Simply televising a lecture to 1000+ students is not a means for fostering quality instruction, whatever the cost. It is encouraging that the American Association for Higher Education's Technology Exchange group is making cooperative/collaborative learning a major focus as a way of humanizing and enlivening many technology applications to the classroom and to the governance of institutions.

Reason 4. Developing critical thinking. There is a difference of opinion in the professional literature regarding the specific definition of critical thinking (Kurfiss, 1988). But such diverse theorists as Kurfiss, Paul, Halpern, Martuza, Palincsar and King all agree that small group problem solving is a powerful way to foster critical thinking. Cooperative learning requires students to actively engage with academic content and to manipulate information in a social setting. Pupils are challenged by peers who stimulate cognitive processes such as problem clarification, justification, elaboration, and evaluation. Researchers and practitioners interested in the cognitive development theories of Perry, Belenky and Vygostky have also called for small group instruction (Cuseo, 1993; Gabelnick, MacGregor, Matthews, & Smith, 1990; Kurfiss, 1988).

Reason 5. Fostering the goals of liberal education. In 1993 Alexander Astin completed a landmark study of what makes a difference in undergraduate education. He published the work in an influential book entitled *What Matters in College: Four Critical Years Revisited*. Astin's research and complimentary work by Terenzini and Pascarella have provided cooperative learning with significant empirical support for the power of student-student and student-teacher interaction. Astin found that curricular issues were not significantly predictive of most goals of liberal education. Instead, student-student and student-teacher interactions were the best predictors of a host of liberal education goals including commitment to helping others, interest in cultural events, appreciation of diversity, problem solving and leadership development. These interactions were also positively related to higher scores on the GRE, MCAT and LSAT exams. Astin summarized these findings in the Spring, 1993 issue of this newsletter. [Editor's Note: See Article 7 in this text.]

Reason 6. Preparing students for the world of work. At times, higher education has engaged in a debate pitting the goals of liberal education against more narrowly-focused attempts to train students for relatively well-defined jobs. Cooperative learning is a process variable in education in which both sides of this essentially curricular debate may agree. When surveyed by the American Association of Training and Development and the Department of Labor in 1988, employers listed group effectiveness characterized by interpersonal skills, negotiation skills and teamwork as among the highest-rated skills that they look for in an employee. As the workplace becomes more knowledge-based and interdependent, the ability to work in groups will only become more important. So cooperative learning may be one thing that the Classics professor and the MBA professor can agree on in shaping a course of study for the twenty-first century. Cooperative learning can be one tool to prepare students to become oft-lauded but hard to produce life-long learners, able to function in a diverse and interdependent world.

Reason 7. Building a sense of community. When we examine the world around us, it is difficult to feel encouraged about the social fabric of the country and the world. Wherever one looks there appears to be a balkanization of interest groups and a sense of us against them. Ethnic cleansing, militia groups and apparently mindless terrorist activities are some of the symptoms. What is the answer? Well, cooperative learning is not the solution to all that ails this country and the world. But it is something that an administrator or faculty member can do that can have an effect on a significant number of students preparing to take their places in society. These students are the public school teachers, the nurses, the accountants, the politicians, the CEOs (and perhaps most importantly) the parents of the future. Researchers at the University of Minnesota and Concordia University have published research syntheses which document the efficacy of cooperative learning in increasing such outcomes as social support, coping with stress and psychological health. If we can begin the process of developing a shared concern for others, we may begin to turn back the mindless, egocentric world view that seems to be dividing campuses, communities, and countries as we near the end of the twentieth century.

Reason 8. Revitalizing faculty/faculty development. Most faculty value teaching and strive to do the best job they can in the classroom. But few of us were trained in pedagogy. My friend Jack Michael used to say that college teaching was a form of revenge. We do to our students what was done to us. He meant the remark humorously (I think). Reports of teaching practices by NIE, AAC and other groups indicate that the overwhelming percent of class time is spent with students passively engaged with course content. The lecture is still the predominant technique used by a large majority of instructors. When faculty not trained in pedagogy first begin teaching and meet with student resistance for whatever reason it is my experience that dissatisfaction with students and with teaching in general sets in early in many academic careers. On the other hand, if faculty learn skills like cooperative learning and see the impact of well-formed cooperative learning structures on students, the effect on faculty is often dramatic. A colleague of mine at Dominguez Hills reported that he was so burned out on teaching that he was about to take early retirement in the late 1980s. Once he learned and successfully implemented cooperative learning his world changed. Now, in his 60s he is leading workshops on cooperative learning in his discipline and contributes substantially to professional organizations. Once we identify students as willing junior colleagues in a joint exploration, not as the enemy seeking the highest grade for the lowest expenditure of effort, the effect on our attitudes toward the profession are often dramatic. And the impact of this change often influences colleagues, as it did with the instructor just described.

Reason 9. Responding to learning styles. The assessment of learning and cognitive styles and the empirical base for their efficacy is a subject of some debate among researchers. Nonetheless, many students and faculty do express strong preferences for different modes of presentation, styles of processing information and for differing motivational systems. Women and some minority groups express preferences for more collaborative and less competitive systems of instruction. In a recent meta-analysis concerning the relative success of cooperative versus competitive motivational systems in improving problem solving, researchers found that cooperative motivational systems were clearly superior (Qun, Johnson, & Johnson, 1994). Similar results have been found for a number of other student outcomes (although the research is not totally consistent on the relative effects of cooperation versus competition). At the very least it can be argued that cooperative learning presents a change from an overreliance on more passive modes of instruction which have been criticized by national commissions, accrediting agencies and discipline groups for the last twenty years.

Reason 10. Using cooperative learning in university governance. Total Quality Management and its academic counterpart Continuous Quality Improvement have been at the forefront of discussions of academic governance in recent years. These approaches use small-group processes as fundamental elements of governance. Alexander Astin wrote an insightful article (*Change* magazine, 1987) in which he asserted that, although higher education laid claim to such notions as collegiality and community, in fact most levels of academia model competition and striving for status. It is difficult to argue for a commitment to public service and altruism with our students when many members of the academic community are locked in bitter struggles between departments for limited resources, between faculty for career-making tenure decisions and between institutions for the Top Ten listing in *U.S. News and World Report's* yearly ratings of colleges and universities. Robert Slavin of Johns Hopkins University and David and Roger Johnson at the University of Minnesota have begun changing the governance structure of K-12 schools using cooperative learning principles with promising results.

Obviously there is nothing magic about this listing of exactly ten reasons to institutionalize cooperative learning in higher education. There are many other issues which could be addressed, such as assessment, accreditation, writing across the disciplines and math/science reform. All are areas in which cooperative learning principles have been successfully implemented or have the potential for successful use.

When resources are hard to come by and interventions often have little or no impact on institutions, cooperative learning holds great promise for effecting a wide range of outcomes central to the several missions of our colleges and universities.

Section 3
Informal Small-group Procedures

In this section, relatively informal group procedures are presented. In general, they do not require the planning and preparation that is required of more formal, semester-long group-learning experiences such as the Johnson and Johnson base group procedure described in their chapter of this book (see Chapter 1 beginning on page 251).

Article 11, beginning on page 99, is by Barbara Millis and Philip Cottell and describes an informal group-learning strategy known as Think-Pair-Share. In this procedure, the instructor stops the lecture every 15-20 minutes and asks students to privately reflect on an issue or problem for a minute or so, and then turn to a partner to discuss the issue. Finally, the instructor asks pairs to share their thinking with the entire class. Authors Barbara Millis and Phillip Cottell describe the procedure, provide a rationale for its use and identify several applications of the technique. They briefly present an adaptation of the Think-Pair-Share procedure, known as Think-Pair-Square. Article 12 (pages 106-111), written by Joy Ollen, explicates the Think-Pair-Square strategy in more detail and describes how it can be used in a test review class meeting.

Another relatively informal procedure that can be used in college classrooms is Guided Peer Questioning (Article 13, pages 112-121). This technique uses Think-Pair-Share but introduces a set of guided critical-thinking questions to demonstrate the kinds of reflection students might engage in during the Think phase. Author Allison King and her colleagues have used this strategy in a wide variety of disciplines and have convincing data supporting the power of the technique to foster critical thinking.

Susan Prescott Johnston and Jim Cooper wrote Articles 14 (pages 122-134) and 15 (pages 135-145). Article 14 is a description of Quick-thinks; brief, active-learning exercises that can be inserted in lectures or other instructional formats and require students to process information individually and/or collaboratively. Article 15 describes a number of cognitive scaffolding strategies. Scaffolds are forms of support provided by the teacher, or student, to help students bridge the gap between their current abilities and the intended instructional goal. These two strategies form the basis for the Interactive Lecture, a technique delineated in Chapter 7, beginning on page 336, by Cooper, Robinson and Ball later in the book.

In Article 16 (pages 146-151), Mel Silberman describes ten basic activities that can be completed in pairs and provides five ways to structure such activities. Readers interested in the use of informal group and active learning strategies will also be interested in Spencer Kagan's chapter on how group procedures are consistent with brain research. This chapter and the Cooper, Robinson and Ball chapter identify a variety of informal active- and group-learning procedures.

11 A Cooperative Learning Structure for Large Classes: Think-Pair-Share

Barbara J. Millis and Philip G. Cottell Jr.

Originally published in the Cooperative Learning and College Teaching newsletter, Winter, 1995.

Think-Pair-Share is probably the best-known and most widely used Cooperative Learning (CL) structure. Many people use it without, in fact, connecting it to CL or realizing that a single man, Frank Lyman (1981), is responsible for its creation and dissemination. Because of its simplicity and versatility, it offers an entry point for instructors new to CL. It is a relatively low-risk activity.

In Think-Pair-Share, a CL learning structure encouraging increased student participation and higher-order thinking skills, students learn a new response cycle to questions, one based on student interaction and, hence, active learning. This easy-to-use technique has wide applications, even in large lecture classes.

To initiate a Think-Pair-Share activity, the instructor poses a question that cannot be answered facilely with a response based on rote memorization: often the question is a probing one without a single definitive answer. Typically, students are given time, usually less than a minute, to *think* of a response. The importance of the "think time" cannot be overemphasized. Instructors new to CL may find that moments of silence in a class seem too long. They must, however, resist the temptation to hurry the process, since these moments cause students to fully develop their higher-order thinking skills.

An instructor may prefer that this "think" period be used to allow students to write their responses, a practice that ensures most students are on task. This practice also helps instructors fulfill calls for writing across the curriculum. These individual responses can be collected at the conclusion of the class, if desired.

Next, students *pair* with other classmates, often members of their structured learning teams, to discuss their responses to the question. This phase of Think-Pair-Share reinforces the principle of simultaneity in the classroom. In the lecture and recitation technique only two people, the instructor and a designated student, interact. Other students may or may not be attentively listening or actively mulling over their own responses. In Think-Pair-Share, all persons are simultaneously involved in paired discussion: 50 percent of a class are vocal.

In the third phase, the instructor invites students to *share* their responses. If the sharing is done with the class as a whole, instructors will find that students whose ideas have been reinforced, refined, or challenged through discussion with a peer will be eager to volunteer. Instructors will no longer face a paucity of student participants but will have the "problem" of which of many respondents to recognize. Furthermore, the level of responses is intellectually far richer than typical responses from a situation where an instructor merely tosses off a question and waits for the hand of the most assertive students to shoot skyward. As a general rule, it is wise to limit a whole-class follow-up to four to six responses in order to avoid repetition, particularly if the question encouraged complex answers.

Responses during the share period do not necessarily need to involve the whole class however, particularly if instructors have formed students into ongoing structured learning teams. Because much of the benefit from this activity comes from the reflection and subsequent discussion, instructors can simply ask that students share their paired discussions within the small but safe framework of their ongoing structured learning team.

Although a Think-Pair-Share activity can be initiated quickly and easily—sometimes spontaneously during a lecture with random pairs when an instructor senses a need for students to process or reflect on the material—instructors who are committed to the formation of structured learning teams might consider pairing stronger and weaker students to dyads within four-person teams.

Other sharing alternatives for Think-Pair-Share enhance its flexibility. One obvious option is to eliminate the final share phase, because the most important elements of the activity are often accomplished by having students reflect and then verbalize their responses. Too often instructors assume that students expect every contribution to be acknowledged and validated publicly. These whole-class sharings are often unnecessary and time-consuming. Thus, the Think-Pair-Share activity can be initiated without structured learning teams in virtually any setting where people are seated together. In fact, many public speakers have used its power to generate active audience engagement.

Even in its simplest form, Think-Pair-Share offers benefits to students and instructors alike. At a minimum, students have valuable wait time to think through questions before any discussion begins. Moreover, students have an opportunity to rehearse responses mentally and orally with a peer before being asked to share publicly. This process enhances oral communication skills and confidence. All students have an opportunity to share their thinking with at least one other person, thereby increasing their sense of involvement.

Instructors also benefit, since students spend more time actively learning. Students who might have "tuned out" during a traditional lecture and recitation period actively listen to each other during Think-Pair-Share activities. After rehearsing in pairs, they are more capable of volunteering well-thought-out responses. Instructors also have more in-class time to think themselves. They can concentrate on asking higher-order questions, observing reactions, and listening to responses. Think-Pair-Share is easy to learn, easy to use, and easily creates a more relaxed atmosphere than calling on individual, often ill-prepared students.

The Think-Pair-Share structure, a powerful learning tool, can also be used for complex, extended student exchanges. It can be used, for example, to reach consensus by asking students to agree upon a single solution for a problem or issue. With different issues, students can be asked to play devil's advocate with their partners and draw out deeper informed responses by asking carefully phrased, probing questions that might be expected from an opposing viewpoint. The Think-Pair-Share structure is particularly powerful when used for reciprocal teaching, an approach receiving increased attention in higher education. McKeachie, Pintrich, Lin, and Smith (1986), for instance, conclude: "The best answer to the question 'What is the most effective method of teaching?' is that it depends on the goal, the student, the content, and the teacher. But the next best answer is 'Students teaching other students' " (p. 63).

On a basic level, reciprocal teaching can be used efficiently when a vast body of information, such as accounting, biology or other technical concepts and terminology, needs to be committed to long-term memory. Students study the body of material independently, but to ensure mastery, some in-class time is permitted for paired coaching. Students prepare flashcards for pre-test coaching with the word to be defined on the front of the card and the answer on the back. Working in pairs or dyads, one student assumes the role of tutor, holding up the cards with the definitions in rapid succession. If the tutee gives an accurate definition, he or she receives the card. If the answer is incorrect or partially correct, the tutor shows the flip side of the card and allows time for study and reflection. The two might discuss ways to master the elusive definition, such as through a mnemonic device. The card is then placed at the back of the deck for a subsequent response. When the tutee has earned all of the cards through correct responses, the roles are reversed until both partners have mastered the material.

Reciprocal teaching is also useful for material requiring higher-order thinking skills. For example paired essays is an efficient technique used to "front-load" course material, so that class time can be used effectively for processing what students have already learned during independent study.

Think-Pair-Share can also build skills through paired problem solving. A problem-solving period can be extended by asking students to solve exercises using a variation of this structure. Accounting, algebra, or statistics exercises developed in Think-Pair-Share sessions replace the more traditional, but less effective, practice of placing a numerical example on the chalkboard or on an overhead for students to mechanically duplicate in their notes. Because in Think-Pair-Share students actively derive solutions and their underlying concepts, rather than copying them, they feel ownership and are more likely to retain the knowledge.

An Accounting Concept Example

An objective suggested in Ingram's accounting textbook reads as follows: "Explain why risk and return are important to investors." During a lecture, the instructor may explain that investors invest their funds because they want a return. The instructor may also explain why risk occurs in financial markets. Then the instructor poses a question to the class in this manner: "Take 30 seconds to consider what relationship one might expect between risk and return."

After a timed 30 seconds of silence, the instructor says, "Now share your response with your partner." He gives the students one minute to share their responses in dyads than calls the class back into the lecture mode. As the final segment of Think-Pair-Share, the instructor calls for volunteer responses until an exemplary one is given, usually from the first student, due to the reflection and rehearsal time.

Another Think-Pair Share exercise may immediately follow with the question, "What role does accounting play in helping investors assess risk and return?" If the instructor desires, a whole-class discussion or some reinforcing comments may follow these two Think-Pair-Share activities.

Using Cooperative Learning Structures For Group Formation

Once the stage is set, careful team formation can ensure the success of small groups. As discussed earlier, CL advocates agree that heterogeneity enhances the effectiveness of structured group work. To the greatest extent possible, groups should be composed of high, low, and middle achievers of both genders and various ethnic and cultural backgrounds and ages. Three CL structures—Value Line, Corners, and Three-Step Interview—can help instructors create heterogeneous teams rapidly and meaningfully.

These teams may or may not become the semi-permanent structured learning teams that form the heart of the cooperative classroom. For the sake of variety and the opportunity for students to meet other classmates, instructors may create temporary teams for brief in-class assignments and interactions.

Think-Pair-Square

A modification of Think-Pair-Share, Think-Pair-Square (Lyman, 1981) provides instructors with a useful structure when they desire group interaction but not a full class discussion. Instructors will find Think-Pair-Square particularly useful for simple problems where the answers are either right or wrong. It can be used successfully, however, with more complex problems as well.

In Think-Pair-Square students still have time to consider a response and share it with a partner. The difference occurs in the last phase where students share each other's responses in their learning teams instead of in front of the whole class, a less time-consuming, often more focused activity. This within-team sharing is important to be certain that the pairs have solved the problem(s) correctly. Think-Pair-Square is a more advanced structure than Think-Pair-Share because of its reliance on structured learning teams. A Think-Pair-Share activity can be conducted spontaneously with partners who have not previously been acquainted and then brought to closure through whole-class sharing. Think-Pair-Square focuses on learning within a team.

An Example

Instructors may wish to use Think-Pair-Square in conjunction with abbreviated definitions of accounting concepts–accrued revenue, accrued expense, deferred revenue, and deferred expense, each without numerical examples. After hearing the first definition, the students pair with their partners and work a mathematical application of the problem. At the quiet signal, they verify their solutions within the structured learning team. The faculty member actively monitors the groups' conversations to be certain that all students are on target. At another signal, the instructor states the second definition and the students repeat the process with a second problem. Two additional iterations follow. To conclude the class the instructor may plan a brief whole-class discussion to clear up any cloudy areas and bring closure.

12 Think-Pair-Square Applied to a Review Session

Joy Ollen

Originally published in the Cooperative Learning and College Teaching newsletter, Winter, 1996.

Introduction

A review session before an exam can raise questions for an instructor who wants it to be a valuable experience for as many students in the class as possible. How does one choose which topics should be discussed and which left out? If one is reteaching material that students' assignments showed to be misunderstood, how does one really know that they will be able to understand it correctly in time for the exam? What if a small percentage of the class needs a basic concept retaught? Is there any way to prevent high-ability students from being bored by hearing material repeated they have already mastered? A teacher-centered review may not provide answers to these questions that are favorable to all the students.

The Think-Pair-Square cooperative format for exam review was developed in the Fall of 1994 to deal with the various levels of student knowledge that are exhibited in the beginning of the music theory program at the University of British Columbia. Students within the same first-year theory classes may range from having a limited exposure to rudimentary topics to having a relatively sophisticated background in tonal theory. I designed this exam review format as part of the material for my thesis, *Cooperative Learning Strategies for Teaching Undergraduate Tonal Theory*, and had the opportunity to use it in two classes. While this lesson was intended to be used with music students, the format is independent enough from the content that it should be easily transferable to many different disciplines.

The Structure

Think-Pair-Square is a variation of the Think-Pair-Share structure and offers students an additional step in which to interact with peers (Kagan, 1992). In a Think-Pair-Square, the instructor directs students to think alone about a question or problem, then to form pairs for comparison of responses, and finally to form foursomes with another pair for further sharing and discussion. Depending upon the nature of questions posed to students, this structure may only require eight to ten minutes of class time. In the application described here however, the Think-Pair-Square activity filled most of a fifty-minute class period.

The Lesson

I began the class by introducing the review format as an opportunity for the students to ensure that the topics and issues most problematic to them would be addressed. The steps of the Think-Pair-Square structure were outlined briefly and printed on the board. Since it was the students' first cooperative lesson in music theory, I gave these four guidelines for behavior:
1. Keep discussions focused and on-task.
2. Do not talk while I give instructions for each task, otherwise time will be wasted.
3. It is your responsibility to ensure you understand what your group members are saying. I should be able to ask any group member to paraphrase what his/her group is discussing at anytime.
4. Make certain to practice verbalizing your knowledge about the material whenever possible. Even answering someone else's question that you consider simple helps you to gain a better understanding of it and retain the information.

After receiving a handout listing topics and terms on which they were to be examined and a blank index card, individuals spent three minutes on the Think task. Students used the handout as a guide to complete the following two sentences on their index cards:

"One topic I do not understand and need explained is..."

"One topic I do understand and can explain well is..."

Up until now, students had been sitting with the chairs arranged in a circle. At this point, I asked them to pair up with the person seated directly across the circle from them, moving their chairs together into an area of the room in which they could work comfortably. The pairs were given six minutes to work together. Their primary tasks were to compare responses on the index cards, to try to offer explanations for the topics their partners did not understand, and to agree on one topic or question on which they would both like further explanation. If any time remained, partners could practice explaining the topics that they understood well.

During the pair work, I moved around the room, monitoring the topics being discussed. When the time came for students to move into "squares," I attempted to join together as many pairs who might be able to answer each others' questions as possible. Failing that, I directed pairs to link up with each other based on physical proximity.

For the Square task, the sets of pairs had twelve to fifteen minutes in which to present their questions to each other and offer suitable explanations. In this step, students were strongly encouraged to use their texts or class notes to support their explanations and to search as a team for more information. By the end of the time, each foursome had to select one item they would like me to clarify and write it on the board. If this was accomplished before the allotted time was complete, group members were to take turns quizzing each other on any of the material to be tested.

I spent the last fifteen minutes of the period addressing these concerns and offering to listen to any unsettled issues that remained from the students' explanations to their peers. Whenever possible, I would first ask other foursomes for their responses to the questions on the board before answering them myself. I found however, that this method required more time than was available and that students' questions were finely tuned to the point where other students expressed their own confusion with the same issue. In fact, some of the questions were duplicated by other groups or were slight variations on the same topic. After responding to each concern, I checked back with the contributors to ensure they were satisfied.

Comments and Reflections

As this lesson was the first cooperative one the classes received and the first time I was guest-instructing in both classes, it was impossible to predict whether or not the students would be resistant to working in groups. Accordingly, I included several strategies to limit off-task behavior. Asking students to form pairs with people sitting across from them in the circle increased the likelihood that students would not be working with friends. The handout helped to focus students' attention, as did written instructions on the board for each task. I enforced the time limits for each task strictly, giving students notice shortly before each task was about to end. Lastly, I circulated among the groups, observing their discussions and checking on their progress.

During the classes, the students worked diligently at the tasks and were not hesitant to share their knowledge and experience with each other. Often, when students working together discovered that they were all unclear or in disagreement, they requested that I give them the answer or identify whose answer was right. While it would have been simpler to comply, much of the value of the format would have been lost if students received quick, oral solutions from me to their dilemmas. Instead, I reminded the students to follow the task instructions by checking their textbooks for more explanation and by comparing their class notes and assignments. I also directed them to find questions in the textbook and workbook and answer those questions. If students could not find answers in those two sources they were instructed to formulate their own questions. When a group seemed to have exhausted their resources in dealing with a problem, they were encouraged to save the question for the final question period and move on to another topic. Once students were prompted to explore these other methods to find answers, they were able to help themselves successfully in many instances.

While no formal method was used to poll students' opinions of the class, several voiced their reactions after class. Some students said that they found the review format useful because they were able to focus on issues that were problematic for them, and because they were able to receive some personal attention and guidance from me while working in groups. Others were not comfortable with the amount of responsibility they were given to find explanations and assess one anothers' answers. It did not appear that there was a correlation between students' ability level and their appreciation for the class. Most students who had complaints did not think that the group activities should be abandoned completely, but that they be used in addition to a more traditional instructor-led review class.

This lesson plan could be changed slightly to allow more time for the final question period. If students were given the handout one or two classes in advance, informed about how the review class was to proceed, and assigned the Think task as a preparatory assignment, the final question period could be extended for seven to ten minutes. Time could also be saved by randomly assigning students to a partner as they enter the class. This variation may be necessary with classes of more than twenty-four students where the number of questions to discuss is significantly higher. If students tend to be chronically unprepared for classes, one may insist that students present their written sentences before entering the room. Although this tactic may sound extreme, it ensures that all students are ready to begin the Pair task immediately.

The nature of this structure carries with it two dangers when applied to a review format. Because there is a lot of peer tutoring occurring, it is possible that a student may give another an incorrect explanation. The instructor can attempt to minimize this by monitoring the group discussions, but ultimately, the responsibility rests with the students to check the validity of one anothers' answers. Another danger is that students may have questions beyond the scope of the exam or may be concerned about details that are irrelevant. Presumably, an instructor does not want students to use a review class as an opportunity to play a guessing game about exam content. One of the ways to prevent students from missing the important subject matter is to clearly differentiate between the essential and nonessential points of one's lessons. Consistent use of instructional objectives and clear outlines of exam content are two effective methods by which one can communicate this information to students.

Conclusion

As I consider this application of the Think-Pair-Square structure to an exam review session, the main advantage it offers is that problems relevant to the students themselves get addressed. It is the students, not the instructor, who are responsible for generating the review material. Additionally, students who might be too shy or afraid to ask for clarification in front of the entire class are given an opportunity to do so in a smaller and therefore presumably less threatening group. In fact, the Think task *requires* all students to find at least one item with which they are not completely comfortable. The risk of appearing "dumb" in front of a peer is reduced because students know that the person or persons with whom they will form groups during the Pair and Square tasks will also be taking a similar risk in sharing their own item(s). Once students have shared their questions with each other, the emphasis should be placed on group members working together to find answers, rather than testing their ability to provide answers based on their own knowledge. Because of the disparity in students' knowledge, many questions on simpler issues can be answered sufficiently by more experienced peers, and eliminated before reaching the final question period. Since oral rehearsal reinforces and solidifies one's knowledge, the peer coaching not only helps the questioner, but the respondent as well. A question that cannot be answered by four group members will probably interest other class members when it is addressed by the instructor. Finally, such a session can provide valuable feedback to the instructor about his/her own teaching effectiveness.

13 Guided Peer Questioning: A Cooperative Learning Approach to Critical Thinking

Alison King

Originally published in the Cooperative Learning and College Teaching newsletter, Winter, 1995.

Teaching our students to think critically is probably the single most important thing that we as university professors can do. Although most of our students have been raised on fact learning and quick responses, these are not the skills or forms of knowledge that will serve them well in the 21st Century. In the approaching millennium success will not be based on the ability to memorize information and repeat it back; computers and other information technology can perform those skills more quickly and more accurately. Rather, success will depend on the ability to think critically. Both in school and in the work place, individuals will be expected to think about what they have heard or read by analyzing ideas, comparing alternative views, establishing relationships among ideas and principles, integrating ideas across topics, synthesizing concepts into something new, and creating possible solutions to problems. That is, they will be expected to engage in the *production of knowledge* rather than simply the *reproduction of information*.

Critical Thinking and Student Empowerment

The ability to think critically is important on a personal level too. Teaching our students how to think can promote their sense of personal empowerment and autonomy. In a culture so dominated by the media, it will be increasingly difficult for individuals to think for themselves, to critically analyze and evaluate the social and political messages that pervade their lives, and to know that they are making their own decisions rather than being persuaded to follow the agendas of others. Those who are able to critically analyze issues that affect their personal, social, and political decision-making will feel more in control of their lives. In this respect, teaching our students to think critically will help them become empowered autonomous individuals, which presumably will help them lead more successful and fulfilling lives.

Questioning and Thinking

In any college classroom the level of thinking that occurs is influenced by the level of questions asked. We use particular questions to induce in students whatever specific thinking processes we wish. For example, in a beginning anatomy class when we ask a factual question (e.g., "What is a ligament?"), our students are likely to recall and restate only facts (in this case a memorized definition). However, when we ask a critical thinking question (e.g., "How do ligaments differ from tendons?" or "Explain how understanding the function of ligaments would help a paramedic figure out what to do in the following sports injury scenario."), then our students are more likely to engage in critical thinking. Critical thinking questions are ones that require students to not only know the facts, but to go beyond those facts to think about them in a way that is different from what is presented explicitly in class or the text. Essentially, these questions are thought-*provoking*—they induce high-level thinking processes such as analysis, comparison and contrast, inference, application, prediction, and evaluation.

Student Questioning

But, why not have students ask their own questions? After all, they are the ones who know what they don't know and what they are unclear or confused about. When they ask their *own* questions students are not mindlessly searching for "correct" answers to their professors' questions (which may or may not be relevant to their individual learning needs); rather, they are posing and answering questions that are more personally meaningful to them, ones that address their own lack of understanding, their specific gaps in knowledge, and their particular misconceptions.

Unfortunately, students do not ask critical thinking questions without guidance. Research has shown that when students are asked to generate questions on their own they usually pose factual ones rather than ones that are thought-provoking; therefore, if we want them to ask thoughtful questions, we need to teach them how to do so. My research has shown that one way we can train students to generate their own critical thinking questions is by providing them with the structure and guidance of exemplary questions. Figure 1 contains examples of such questions in the form of general thought-provoking question stems; the thinking processes each question is expected to induce are also shown. Guided Peer Questioning is one of a number of different ways in which these and similar questions can be used to promote critical thinking and problem solving (other approaches have been described elsewhere: e.g., King, 1991, 1993, & in press).

Guided Peer Questioning

Guided Peer Questioning can be used in any discipline to facilitate student learning of course content. I and colleagues of mine throughout California have used Guided Peer Questioning in our classrooms in such diverse subject areas as: anthropology, psychology, research methods, business accounting, biology, history, mathematics, and teacher education.

How does this questioning strategy work? After listening to a class lecture, students make up questions on the material covered. Then, in pairs or small groups, they pose their questions to each other and answer each others' questions, thus using their own questions to structure their discussion. In the first step of this strategy students work individually. They use the *generic* questions in Figure 1 as prompts to guide them in generating *specific* questions on the lecture material. Then they engage in *peer* questioning, taking turns posing their questions to their partner or group and answering questions in a reciprocal manner. In this way student discussion and processing of the new material is heavily guided by the nature of the questions they themselves generate. If students follow the form of the generic questions, their specific questions will be thought-provoking; therefore, their discussion is almost guaranteed to be thoughtful.

A Classroom Example

For example, in my beginning cognitive psychology class, one of the topics we study is representation of knowledge in long-term memory. During one of our class sessions I present material on network models of memory. Then, using the overhead projector, I display a list of generic question stems similar to those shown in Figure 1. I ask my students to select question stems they feel are appropriate and write two or three thoughtful questions on the topic of network models using their selected question stems as a guide. To do so they simply adapt the generic question stems for use by "filling in the blanks" with specific content relative to the topic of network models. I encourage them to generate questions that they themselves do not already know answers to. After about three minutes I signal them to turn to their neighbors, form their usual discussion groups, and begin the questioning-answering discussion process with which they have become familiar. Following is a brief excerpt from the interaction of one group of students.

> Fred (reading from his list): "My first question is: How a cognitive network get built up?"
> Sally: "Well, first of all, cognitive networks are made up of nodes and links. The nodes are ideas or concepts—actually, I guess they just represent ideas. And the links are the things that connect the nodes. They show how the ideas—the nodes—relate to each other."
> Sam: "Like one thing causes something else?—Or one node is an example of something represented by another node?"
> Sally: "Yes. That's it! That's a causal relationship and an example

type of relationship; but there are lots of other kinds of relationships between concepts too."
Sam: "Like what, for example?"
Fred: "Like nodes could be related because one is a part of the other or because they are both the same color or used for the same purpose."

Figure 1

GUIDING CRITICAL THINKING

Generic Questions	Specific Thinking Processes Induced
Explain why ___. (Explain how ___.)	analysis
What would happen if ___?	prediction / hypothesizing
What is the nature of ___?	analysis
What are the strengths and weaknesses of ___?	analysis / inferencing
What is the difference between ___ and ___?	comparison-contrast
Why is ___ happening?	analysis / inferencing
What is a new example of ___?	application
How could ___ be used to ___?	application
What are the implications of ___?	analysis / inferencing
What is ___ analogous to?	identification / creation of analogies and metaphors
How does ___ effect ___?	analysis of relationship (cause-effect)
How does ___ tie in with what we learned before?	activation of prior knowledge
Why is ___ important?	analysis of significance
How are ___ and ___ similar?	comparison-contrast
How does ___ apply to everyday life?	application to the real world
What is a counter-argument for ___?	rebuttal to argument
What is the best ___, and why?	evaluation and provision of evidence
What is a solution to the problem of ___?	synthesis of ideas
Compare ___ and ___ with regard to ___.	comparison-contrast & evaluation based on criteria
What do you think causes ___? Why?	analysis of relationship (cause-effect)
Do you agree or disagree with this statement: ___? What evidence is there to support your answer?	evaluation and provision of evidence
What is another way to look at ___?	taking other perspectives
What does ___ mean?	comprehension
Describe ___ in your own words.	comprehension
Summarize ___ in your own words.	comprehension

Section 3. Informal Small-group Procedures

Sally: "So, as I was saying, our memory is organized into this kind of network—so that there is an inter-connectedness among concepts—so that when we think about one idea, the connected nodes are activated too. That way, when we think about one thing we think about things related to it."

Sam: "Sounds a lot like the hierarchical model described in the text—which leads me to two of the questions I wrote: How do network models of memory differ from hierarchical models?, and, How are they similar?"

Fred: "Actually, hierarchical models can be seen as one form of network models—a specialized form—where there is one superordinate node, like birds, and all the other nodes are related to it—underneath it—like they are sub-categories of it—or maybe examples of it, like land birds, water birds, birds that can't fly—that sort of thing. Then robin and bluebird could be nodes underneath the node representing land birds."

Sam: "Okay. So hierarchical and network models of memory are similar, but do they differ in any way?"

Sally: "I guess the difference between them is that one is only organized in a hierarchy of nodes and the other is not strictly hierarchical but it also shows other types of relations among the nodes."

Fred: "But we still have not answered my original question."

Sam: "Could you repeat the question?"

Fred: "Explain how a cognitive network gets built up."

Sally: "Well, of course that happens through our experiences in the world. But let's get specific. I have a question that might help us get specific."

Fred: "Okay, let's hear it."

Sally: "What are the implications of the idea of network models for everyday learning—say for example, learning how a car engine works?"

The students continue discussing network models by asking and answering each others' questions until I signal them to stop. Then, as a whole class, we share some of the questions and ideas that have arisen in the small groups and discuss them further. This final step is important because it provides students with an opportunity to clarify any misconceptions and share new insights they may have gained.

Effectiveness of Guided Peer Questioning

In my program of research we have found that when students are provided with that set of generic question stems as a guide, they learn to generate critical thinking questions very quickly. And, when they use this questioning-answering strategy to study course material, their ability to think critically about the material is markedly enhanced, resulting in improved comprehension and retention (e.g., King, 1989, 1990, 1992, 1993, 1994; King & Rosenshine, 1993).

Why is Guided Peer Questioning so effective in enhancing critical thinking? To begin with, the question stems are designed to promote critical thinking because they act as cognitive prompts to induce analysis, inference, application, evaluation, comparison and contrast, and other critical thinking processes (as shown in Figure 1). Simply formulating the thought-provoking questions, regardless of whether or not they are answered, requires students to think critically about the material. To illustrate from the dialogue above, in order to formulate her question ("What are the implications of the idea of network models for everyday learning—say for example, learning how a car engine works?"), Sally used two critical thinking processes: inferencing and application. First she had to make the inference that network models do have something to say about everyday learning and then she had to think about how the material on networks could be applied to a new situation—learning how a car engine works.

Answering these particular questions further engages students in critical thinking because they must explain concepts to each other, defend their ideas, give examples, and in other ways demonstrate thoughtfulness. Explaining something to someone else often requires the explainer to think about and present the material in new ways such as relating it to the questioner's prior knowledge or experience, translating it into terms familiar to the questioner, or generating new examples. Such cognitive activities force the explainer to clarify concepts, elaborate on them, or in some manner reconceptualize the material. For example, in the dialogue above, as Sally begins to explain what cognitive networks are, she appears to be clarifying her own concept of a network when she says that the nodes may not actually *be* the ideas themselves, rather, "they just represent ideas." Thus, explaining plays an important role in clarifying thinking for the individual doing the explaining.

Asking and answering thought-provoking questions in a group context promotes critical thinking because during thoughtful discussion, differences in opinions and understandings about the topic are exposed, and must be confronted and resolved. When students discover that their own perceptions of a topic, underlying assumptions about an issue, and even their basic factual information about the material differ to a greater or lesser extent from those of others, they experience cognitive dissonance. To reconcile any discrepancies they must engage in critical thinking; they must clearly articulate their own positions, explain their ideas, defend their views, identify their assumptions, verbalize their confusions, acknowledge their gaps in knowledge, recognize any misconceptions, and generally present their thoughts in a reasoned manner. Guided Peer Questioning promotes the process of exposing and reconciling such cognitive discrepancies because the questions are designed to elicit ideas, opinions, analyses, inferences, etc. from others in the group, and the reciprocal nature of the strategy requires that students respond to each other by providing information that addresses their needs. For example, during the questioning and answering excerpt above, it became clear that Sam and Fred held different perceptions of the relationship of hierarchical models to networks. When Sam asked "How do network models of memory differ from hierarchical models?" he tapped in to Fred's differing view on the matter. Sam saw them as two separate models, while Fred saw hierarchical models as a specialized form of networks—a subset. Once the discrepancy in their views was exposed, Fred had to explain and (with Sally's help), justify his view. Apparently Fred's view was accepted by Sam, and their conceptual difference was reconciled.

Using Probing Questions

I have found that students need to be reminded not to simply ask and answer their questions in a rote manner without full discussion of an issue before going on to another question. In some cases within one 10-minute discussion session only one question gets discussed because the discussion that ensues from that question is so extensive. An effective way to get students to extend discussion of a particular point is to teach them to ask probing or follow-up questions such as: "Can you expand on that?", "I don't understand. What do you mean by that?", "Can you give an example of what you mean?", or "Tell me more about that." To illustrate from Sally, Sam and Fred's discussion, when Sally was explaining nodes and links and listed various kinds of relationships among nodes, Sam probed for more examples by asking "Like what, for example?"

Question Sequencing

I've also found it beneficial to teach students how to sequence their questioning to enhance thinking. I emphasize two kinds of sequencing: asking questions that review basic concepts covered in the lecture before going on to more complex critical thinking questions, and asking related critical thinking questions so that their questions build on each other. Sequencing from review-type questions or "memory" questions to critical thinking questions can be accomplished quite easily. Figure 1 includes several generic questions that are simply "comprehension" oriented such as "What does _____ mean?" and "Describe _____ in your own words." Posing a few of these questions at the beginning of their discussion session might help students to define central concepts and recall the main ideas explicitly stated in the lecture—essentially to review the basics—before going on to critically analyze, evaluate, compare and contrast, those ideas. Following is a typical sequence of questions that might have been posed within a discussion group of students in a contemporary art history class after a lecture on post modernism.

Define post modernism in your own words. (comprehension)

Explain how post modernism differs from modernism. (critical thinking)

What is the meaning of the term "appropriation" in post modernist art and architecture? (comprehension)

How do you think the role of "appropriation" in post modernist art and architecture differs from plagiarism? (critical thinking)

Explain why post modernism is said to be a reflection of the wider culture? (critical thinking)

Note that in this sequence, when a shift occurred in the direction of the discussion, a comprehension question was included to review the term to be discussed.

In my classes I have found that teaching students to ask questions and to discuss their own and others' questions thoughtfully through the use of Guided Peer Questioning enhances their ability to think critically. It also promotes self-regulated learning because it empowers them to take charge of their own learning.

14 Quick-thinks: Active-thinking Tasks in Lecture Classes and Televised Instruction

Susan Johnston and Jim Cooper

Originally published in the Cooperative Learning and College Teaching newsletter, Fall, 1997.

Many instructors feel pressured to cover a great deal of information in their courses. For the class sessions that are especially content dense and seem to call for a traditional-lecture format, there is an active-learning strategy that provides a viable alternative to more time-consuming group tasks. We have named the strategy Quick-thinks and they are designed to be easily inserted into lectures so that students are given an opportunity to think about important content as the lesson unfolds. When students are asked to participate instead of passively receive information, they stay more focused, they can check their own understanding, and they are cued to content that has been selected for emphasis.

The research support for incorporating active-thinking opportunities into classroom or televised lectures is impressive and spans many years. In his classic text, *Democracy and Education*, John Dewey noted that learning is "something an individual does when he studies. It is an active, personally conducted affair." Since Dewey's work in the early part of the twentieth century, there has been a large body of theoretical and empirical work to support his assertion.

Theoretical Arguments for Active Learning. The influential cognitive psychologist Jean Piaget stressed the importance of assimilation and accommodation, two processes that he asserted all people use in order to develop beyond primitive stages of cognitive development. These interactive processes of introducing new information into existing cognitive structures and changing those structures to adapt to new information, underscore Piaget's view of people as active, intellectually-engaged learners who are striving to bring meaning to the world. Other theorists concerned with both precollegiate and adult learners, such as Vygotsky, Perry and Belenkey, support Piaget's general approach, suggesting that for cognitive development to occur, students must be engaged in a series of intellectually-meaningful tasks of appropriate difficulty. All of these theorists decry a view of the learner as an essentially empty vessel to be filled with "received knowledge" presented by the lecture method or other techniques which foster little involvement of the learner.

Empirical Arguments for Active Learning. The research documenting the power of active learning in fostering students' cognitive and affective (attitudinal) growth is substantial. Research on undergraduate and medical students exposed to lectures indicates that they were attentive and readily assimilated lecture material during the first 10-20 minutes, but that attention and note-taking dropped dramatically thereafter. A study by Ruhl, Hughes and Schloss (1987) compared lectures presented without pauses with lectures where, every 12-18 minutes teachers paused for two minutes and students discussed and reworked their notes (without interaction with the teacher). Students in the latter group performed better on free-recall quizzes and on a comprehension test. In fact, the differences were so large that they would have raised the performance of the experimental students one-two letter grades (depending on grading scales used).

In large classes, research indicates that "teacher-talk" about academic content (essentially lecturing) accounts for 88% of class time, silence accounts for 6% and student talk for 5% (Lewis and Woodward, 1984). Small wonder that students retain only 45% of lecture material three-four days after lectures and 24% eight weeks after lectures (Menges, 1988). Dissatisfaction with the lecture method caused six professors at Oregon State University to develop a "feedback lecture." This procedure involved having two, twenty-minute lectures per class meeting with an instructor-posed discussion question after each twenty-minute lecture. An evaluation of the system revealed that 99% of the students surveyed said that they found the discussion question useful or extremely useful. Eighty-eight percent said that they would prefer the feedback-lecture approach to straight lecture if they had the choice of formats.

In a discussion of large-class instruction, Bonwell and Eison (1991) suggest that it is the "method of instruction used, not the size of the class" that seems to be the best predictor of learning. They cite the 1987 work by Frederick who suggested that effective large-class instruction implies use of: 1) variation in instructional strategies, 2) visual reinforcements to focus students' attention and reinforce their learning, and 3) opportunities for students to provide personal insights and interpretations.

Research on Televised Instruction. The research on televised instruction on student outcomes has been conducted for several decades. The most common finding when televised courses are compared with the same course or content presented "live" is a no-difference finding. Recently Thomas Russell, Director of the Office of Instructional Telecommunication at North Carolina State University, summarized the findings of 100+ studies conducted over 40 years. He reported that, on standardized and teacher-constructed tests, and on attitudinal measures, there were generally no statistically-significant differences in comparisons of media-based instructional formats (such as television) with more traditional lecture and lecture-discussion using "live" teacher presentations.

For example, Chute, Hulick, Messmer and Hancock (1986) reported in a publication from the University of Wisconsin-Madison "there were no significant differences between the amount of information students learned in classes that were teletrained and the amount they learned in face-to-face instruction." Creswell (1986) reported in the *Journal of Educational Television* that students in live classes performed at the same level as those in the televised classes in both course performance and attitudes. Schlosser and Anderson (1994) reported that "students learning equally well from lessons delivered with any medium, face-to-face or at a distance" and "hundreds of media comparison studies indicated, unequivocally, that there is no inherent significant difference in the educational effectiveness of media." They posit that "The specific medium does not matter." They concur with Moore and Kearsky (1996) who report that "what makes a course good or poor is a consequence of how well it is designed, delivered, and conducted." These authors echo Whittington's (1989) conclusion that "Effective instructional design and techniques are the crucial elements in student achievement whether instruction is delivered by television or by traditional means." V. Bergin (personal communication, June 5, 1986) put it best in suggesting that the question is not about which medium works best, but about effective instruction.

What is effective instruction? Only in the last thirty years has a cumulative base of knowledge emerged which reliably predicts such student outcomes as academic achievement, higher-order thinking skills, reduced attrition and positive attitudes toward subject matter among college populations. Space limitations do not permit an exhaustive description of research-based good practices. However, we would like to highlight some issues which have a bearing on the active-learning Quick-think strategies described later in this document.

In 1984, Herbert Walberg, one of the preeminent researchers working in the area of syntheses of educational research used meta-analysis to examine which educational interventions had the greatest impact on a number of student outcomes. He found that the most powerful predictor of positive student outcomes was feedback to students on their performances. Another strong predictor was instructors offering visual and other cues to students regarding course content and giving feedback to the students when they responded to those cues. In 1987, the American Association for Higher Education published its landmark report, *Seven Principles for Effective Practice in Undergraduate Education*. Unlike Walberg's work, which was focused largely on precollegiate populations, the AAHE group investigated the empirical and theoretical support for teaching techniques used with college populations. They listed "active learning" and "prompt feedback" as two of the seven research-based principles having significant efficacy. They also identified time on task, a procedure fostered by the active-learning strategies described in this article, as one of the seven principles, along with "student-faculty contact" and "cooperation among students."

The research on both class size and televised instruction indicates that it is the method of instructional presentation, not the class size or medium of instruction, that is most predictive of positive student learning and attitudinal outcomes. Over thirty years of qualitative and quantitative research point to active learning as among the most powerful methods for influencing higher-order thinking skills, general academic achievement, student attrition, liking for the subject matter and a host of other outcomes. We believe that use of the set active-learning strategies described below is a relatively low-risk instructional intervention that has the power to transform the classroom from a passive to an engaging learning environment.

Active-learning Strategies

The following "Quick-thinks" were designed for application to a wide range of content areas:
1. SELECT THE BEST RESPONSE
2. CORRECT THE ERROR
3. COMPLETE A SENTENCE STARTER
4. COMPARE OR CONTRAST
5. SUPPORT A STATEMENT
6. REORDER THE STEPS
7. REACH A CONCLUSION
8. PARAPHRASE THE IDEA

One approach to piloting some of these techniques might be to select one course on which to focus. Review the main topic and list the most essential content to be learned at each class session—those concepts, skills, principles, or facts that have the highest priority.

Then match each of these content focal points with a Quick-think task that seems to best fit. For example, if you are going to teach a procedural skill, REORDER THE STEPS might be a good choice so that students can gain familiarity with that procedure. If you are going to teach an abstract concept that has a complex definition, you might want to choose # 8 (PARAPHRASE THE IDEA) so that students can translate technical language into their own words and test their own understanding.

Using the lecture notes or outline that you have on file for each lesson, use arrows to mark the places where you could insert a brief Quick-think task. Referring to the corresponding examples described below, create the tasks you need using the specific content from your target lesson. Then transfer each task to a blank overhead transparency with a fine point overhead transparency pen or a computer printer.

At the first class meeting in which you plan to use Quick-thinks, you will need to explain to your students how you will be using this strategy and how it will positively effect their learning. There is no set formula for how often to stop and ask students to think about the content being explained. Our experience and some quantitative evidence suggests that every fifteen minutes or so results in increased attention, interest, and learning. Participation options vary: students can record their responses individually and then explain their answers to a neighbor, they can verbally generate an answer with a neighbor, or they can be asked to silently think about a possible response. The instructor then needs to provide feedback so that students can hear or share correct or possible answers. Following are specific descriptions of eight Quick-thinks.

1. Select the Best Response

Explanation

This task is most similar to the traditional multiple-choice test item. Students are presented with a question or scenario and then asked to consider which one of three responses best answers it. This task can simply require the recall of information just covered in the lecture or the application of that information.

Format

The original question or scenario can be:
- an incomplete sentence that is completed by the selection of one response.
- an incomplete sentence containing an internal blank line meant to be filled in by the correct answer.
- a complete sentence followed by three possible answers.

Example

Course: Psychology
Content to be learned: Defense mechanism
Format selected: Incomplete Sentence

While Professor Woods was going through a painful divorce, he tended to create unnecessarily difficult tests and gave his students unusually low grades. A psychoanalyst would be most likely to view the professor's treatment of his students as an example of:
    a. repression
    b. projection
    c. displacement
(Correct answer: c. displacement)

2. Correct the Error

Explanation

For this task, the instructor creates an intentional error based on important content just discussed. Students are then asked to correct that mistake. This active-thinking task requires a basic level of comprehension and some immediate processing of content just heard or observed.

Format

The intentional error can contain:
- inaccurate statements, descriptions or procedures.
- illogical conclusions, predictions, or implications.
- weak arguments.
- unlikely quotations.

Example

Course: Teaching Methods
Content to be learned: Learning outcomes
Format selected: Inaccurate Statement
  "A learning outcome in a lesson plan describes how the teacher will present the new content."
(Correct answer: A learning outcome is a description of what *the students* will do to demonstrate their understanding.)

3. Complete a Sentence Starter

Explanation

For this task, instructors create a sentence stem that needs completion to reflect an accurate statement. In order to complete the statement accurately, students need to understand the information that was just explained or discussed. The content described can be presented in a way that requires only a rote level of understanding where students simply recall information just described by the instructor. In order to elicit a deeper level of understanding, the sentence starter would require reflection that goes beyond recall to levels of application, analysis or evaluation.

Format

The sentence starter can focus on:
- a definition.
- a cause/effect relationship.
- an implication.
- a rationale.
- a controversy.

Example

Course: Criminal Justice
Content to be learned: California's "three-strikes" sentencing policy
Format selected: Cause/effect relationship
  "The 'three strikes' mandatory sentencing laws might result in _____."

(Correct answer might include: prison overcrowding, increased pressure on judges to make exceptions, increased employment opportunities in prisons, new prisons built, and/or reduced crime rates.)

4. Compare or Contrast

Explanation

For this task, instructors identify two important parallel elements from the lesson. As students are asked to focus on similarities or differences, they must think about the content at a deep level. This strategy is most effective if the instructor has not already provided a comparison, but has simply presented the two elements separately in some depth.

Format

The items being compared or contrasted can be:
- theories, methods, or models.
- examples of writing, music, art.
- problems or solutions.
- aspects of historical or current events.
- authentic or mythical scenarios.

Example

Course: Art History
Content to be learned: Twentieth-century painting
Format selected: Examples of art

"*After viewing the 1933 Joan Miro painting entitled* **Composition** *and the 1950 Jackson Pollock painting entitled* **One**, *record one similarity between the two paintings.*"

(Correct answer might include: fluidity of design, non-realistic content, or impression of movement.)

5. Support a Statement

Explanation

For this task, instructors create a statement for which students must locate support from their immediate lecture notes or from the homework reading, or they can be asked to generate their own reasons or data to support the statement. Rather than passively accept information given by the instructor, students are asked to think about why a statement might be justified.

Format

The statements requiring support can be:
- conclusions.
- inferences.
- theories.
- opinions.
- descriptions.

Example

Course: Geography
Content to be learned: Negative impact of political decisions on ecology
Format selected: Conclusion

"Warfare has historically had a devastating impact on the earth's resources. Give three pieces of evidence to support this statement."

(Correct answer might include: the systematic scorching of the earth by retreating armies, tank exercises that destroyed animal and vegetative life in the southern California desert, hydrogen bomb testing that rendered some Pacific islands uninhabitable.)

6. Re-order the Steps

Explanation

For this task, instructors present a series of steps in a mixed order and students are asked to re-order the items into the correct sequence. This task can be used either as a motivational technique where students are asked to anticipate the order and make a logical guess before learning the information or as a method to allow students to review the content that they have just learned.

Format

Steps needing to be re-ordered can belong to a:
- sequence.
- method.
- plan.
- strategy.
- technique.

Example

Course: English
Content to be learned: Using the American Psychological Association (APA) format to write in-text citations when paraphrasing someone else's work in a written essay or research paper
Format selected: Procedure

These steps need re-ordering:
1 - write your paragraph or sentence
2 - place an ending period
3 - write the author's full name and the year of publication
4 - enclose with parentheses

(Correct answer: step 1, 3, 4, 2)

7. Reach a Conclusion

Explanation

This task requires students to make a logical inference about the implications of facts, concepts, or principles they just learned. A conclusion can be drawn from: data, opinions, events, or solutions. The statements provided to students may result in multiple responses that can all be logically derived from the content provided.

Format

The conclusion can focus on:
- necessary actions.
- probable results.
- probable causes.
- negative and/or positive outcomes.

Example

Course: Earth Science
Content to be learned: Testing for hardness using common objects equivalent to minerals on Moh's Hardness Scale
Format selected: Probable results

"If you can scratch the smooth surface of a mineral with a tempered-steel file but not with a piece of glass, you could conclude that . . ."

(Correct answer might include: The mineral cannot be quartz, topaz, corundum, or diamond. The mineral has a hardness between 6 and 10 on Moh's scale.)

8. Paraphrase the Idea

Explanation

This task requires students to rephrase an idea using their own words. When students engage in this kind of translation process, they are forced to check their own understanding of what they think they just heard. It is often helpful to have students target their paraphrase toward a specific audience, such as: a novice, a younger sibling, an evaluator, or a client.

Format

The content to be paraphrased can be:
- a definition.
- a theory.
- a statement.
- a procedure.
- a description.

Example

Course: Health
Content to be learned: The body's adaptation to stress
Format selected: A statement

Paraphrase this statement so that a member of your family would understand what is specifically happening to his body during a stressful event.

"When an individual perceives a stressor, the body automatically responds with a three-stage process known as the General Adaptation Syndrome."

These eight tasks are only a sample of generic formats that can be used by instructors in a wide variety of courses and disciplines. The criteria for successful tasks are: that they correlate with the most important content in the lecture, that they require some intellectual effort, and that the specific question or problem is very clearly written. Students resist tasks that appear to be vague or pointless; for example, tasks that ask students to simply "discuss a topic" or to "think about an event" are to be rigorously avoided.

Reported advantages to the instructors who use these tasks are that: teaching becomes more fun and interesting, lectures become more focused on essential content, all students participate, and valuable diagnostic information is gained.

15 Supporting Student Success Through Scaffolding

Susan Johnston and Jim Cooper

Originally published in the Cooperative Learning and College Teaching newsletter, Spring, 1999.

Many college faculty are unfamiliar with how to design their instruction in order to ensure student success. They make the erroneous assumption that lectures and homework assignments are sufficient for students to master new and abstract content. Because of this approach, many students who lack the confidence to learn on their own have experienced unnecessary failure. In order to be effective, all college instructors need to acquire the ability to actively help students bridge the gap between their current knowledge and intended academic outcomes. Powerful instructional techniques known as "scaffolds" are available to college faculty in all disciplines (Rosenshine & Meister, 1995; King, 1995). These are forms of support temporarily provided by instructors when introducing new content and making assignments. Novice learners, like construction workers, need structures of temporary support during their efforts to build something new; once the initial phase of construction is in place, the scaffolds can be withdrawn.

Although we have identified eight such scaffolds, in this article we describe five. They are:

1. ANTICIPATE STUDENT ERRORS
2. PARTIAL SOLUTIONS
3. COMPREHENSION CHECKS
4. THINK-ALOUDS
5. PROCEDURAL GUIDELINES

1. Anticipate Student Errors

DEFINITION: Anticipating and discussing potential student errors is a way of regulating the difficulty in students' understanding of new cognitive strategies. Expert teachers can use prior experience in teaching their courses to pinpoint mistakes that frequently occur and to address these mistakes as course content is being presented (rather than waiting for students to make these common mistakes on tests or papers).

DESCRIPTION: As experts in their fields, teachers tend to forget the mistakes they made when they were novices. They often present content in a way suggesting that all of the material is of equal difficulty rather than pinpointing areas of special difficulty to students and addressing these difficulties at the precise points when the content is being presented. A few minutes spent addressing areas of special difficulty during lectures can improve the quality of assignments, making the grading experience more pleasant for faculty and students as the number of quality assignments increases.

Example #1

COURSE: Secondary Teaching Methods (Susan's course)
SPECIFIC CONTENT: Bloom's taxonomy of the cognitive domain (levels of thinking)

After I read a fairy tale out loud to my students I tell them, "You and your work partner will create questions based on the story at each of the six levels of thinking in the taxonomy (from recall to evaluation). Try hard to avoid the most common mistakes made by my previous students: 1) writing questions with wording that is unclear, making the questions difficult for young students to understand, and 2) using questions that do not reflect what you were really trying to ask because they are too general. For example, telling students to: 'Discuss how you can use the story's moral in your own life' is vague and will not be as successful as the following prompt: 'Describe an event you saw on the playground when someone used force to get her own way and tell what she could have done instead.'"

Section 3. Informal Small-group Procedures

Example #2

COURSE: Research Methods in Education (Jim's course)
SPECIFIC CONTENT: Correctly labeling a correlation scatterplot
After drawing several examples of correlation scatterplots on the board, I ask students to draw one in their notes. Since they are inclined to put the actual numbers of the scores used to present the problem, I caution them to label the X and Y axis using equal-sized intervals, and to NOT put the actual face values of the data on the X and Y axes.

Data Provided to Students:

X	Y
Self Esteem	Stanford 9 Reading %ile
91	43
82	34
70	22
62	14
51	05

Incorrect:

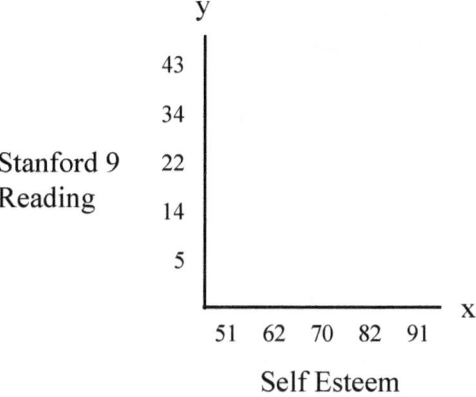

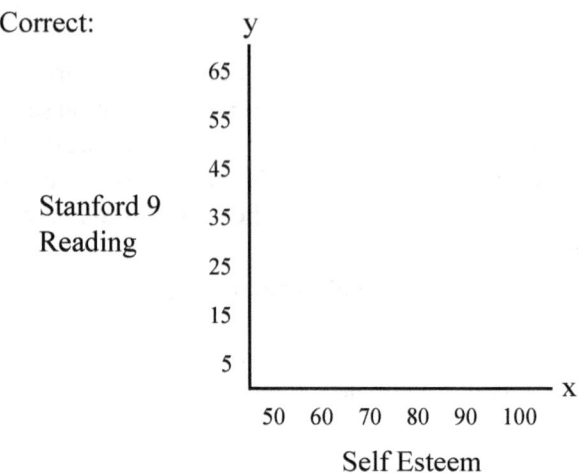

2. Partial Solutions

DEFINITION: Partial Solutions involve presentation of a complex task that is already partially completed by the instructor so that students can more successfully complete the task by focusing on only a few elements while trying to assimilate new information. Partial Solutions also allow instructors to regulate the level of difficulty when students first attempt the application of new ideas or skills. This form of guided practice temporarily reduces the complexity for novice learners while still requiring some application of the content just covered.

DESCRIPTION: Novice learners benefit greatly when not required to independently complete an entirely new and complex learning task. Too often, students are only given brief explanations of new content followed by assignments that will be graded. Typical assignments often include lab reports, critiques of research articles, persuasive essays, sets of word problems, or case-study solutions. Assigning is not teaching, and students need much more specific instructional support than is typically provided. Each of these types of assignments can be broken down to isolate parts that students can practice. For example, using Partial Solutions with persuasive essays, instructors provide the main arguments and supporting points, and students are require in practice sessions, to submit rational evidence for each supporting point made. The next step requires students to give both the supporting points as well as the evidence, and so on.

Giving students the opportunity to practice complex tasks under the guidance of their instructors is an important scaffolding tool that allows them to experience some success at each step of the learning process. Some instructors will often avoid using this strategy because it requires some extra preparation, or it seems to provide students with "unnecessary" assistance. Either argument is an unfortunate abdication of instructors' responsibilities. Students at all levels of schooling have reported that many of their teachers failed to provide opportunities for guided and gradual practice with new complex skills, and then these instructors expected immediate understanding. Such expectations often resulted in additional time spent by students in remedial work after poorly-done tasks or papers were submitted and returned.

Example #1:

COURSE: Secondary Teaching Methods (Susan's course)
SPECIFIC CONTENT: Guided discovery as a teaching strategy

This topic involves teaching my future teachers how to inductively lead their students to understanding important concepts, rules, or sets of factual characteristics by asking guiding questions instead of delivering abstract didactic lectures in which students discover nothing for themselves and are presented with prepackaged conclusions, definitions, descriptions, or rules. After I have demonstrated how guided discovery works with several examples, I present them with a three-column planning chart that requires: 1) a precise identification of the content to be discovered, 2) a description of the stimulus that will function as the focal point of the questions, and 3) the sequence of the main leading questions. When we first practice this in class, I present them with a chart that already has columns one and two filled in and all that remains is to create a set of leading questions in column three. My Partial Solution makes the task much less overwhelming and increases students' motivation to attempt a difficult task.

Example #2: (Jim's course)

COURSE: Research Methods in Education
SPECIFIC CONTENT: Correctly labeling a correlation scatterplot

After drawing several examples of correlation scatterplots of varying sizes on the board, I ask students to draw one in their notes. I often label the X and Y axis the first time I have the students make the drawing and simply have them draw in the data points or dots on the graph. Then, the next time they do the drawing, they draw and label the scatterplot. I also use this technique when teaching my students about frequency polygons. After presenting both scatterplots and polygons I note how they are the same and how the drawings are different, a form of Anticipating Student Errors.

3. Comprehension Checks

DEFINITION: A series of brief thinking tasks inserted into lectures to guarantee that both students and instructors have opportunities to check on the comprehension of the material as it is explained. Students can write their answers quietly in their own notes and/or they can be asked to discuss possible answers with work partners.

DESCRIPTION: Many instructors feel pressured to cover a great deal of information in their courses. For the class sessions that are content dense and seem to call for a traditional lecture format, there are active-learning strategies that are designed to be easily inserted into lectures so that students are given opportunities to think about important content as the lesson unfolds. Comprehension Checks support student learning because when students are asked to actually participate instead of passively receiving information, they can stay more attentive, can check their own understanding, and are provided with valuable diagnostic information during the instructional sequence. Brief tasks for pairs to tackle together ensure participation from everyone. Options include having students solve problems, label examples, select the best responses from multiple-choice questions, correct intentional errors, complete sentence starters, compare or contrast two items, support statements with evidence, reorder steps given out of sequence, reach conclusions, and paraphrase ideas. Research on student achievement and critical thinking (Mazur, 1997) presents a convincing argument for inserting Comprehension Checks throughout the teaming sequence.

Example #1:

COURSE: Secondary Teaching Methods (Susan's course)
SPECIFIC CONTENT: Graphic organizers as an alternative note-taking format

I show and explain each model of several visual graphic organizers (e.g., spider map, chart matrix, network tree) that can be used as note-taking formats for adolescents whose learning style requires an alternative to the traditional linear-outline format. As each model is covered, I ask my students to match each model to a lecture topic from their own teaching subject by completing this sentence starter: The graphic organizer entitled _____ _____ could be used when I teach _____. Then I call on students to share their choices so I can check their understanding of the uses of each model.

Example #2:

COURSE: Research Methods in Education (Jim's course)
SPECIFIC CONTENT: Identification of sampling procedures

This content deals with identifying sampling procedures when presented with real educationally-related descriptions that might appear in journal articles. After I explain the sampling procedures, I have students identify *key words* in the descriptions which discriminate one procedure from another. I usually teach six sampling techniques during the lecture which, are often perceived as technical and somewhat confusing to students. Therefore, after presenting just three of the techniques (random, stratified and systematic) I have students silently read three examples of sampling procedures in the course workbook. After they identify which procedure is described in each example, they underline the key words that "tipped them off." Then, working in pairs, they share this information. I then solicit the identification and keyword information from pairs and briefly elaborate on their responses with the total class.

4. Think-Alouds

DEFINITION: After some direct instruction on a topic, the teacher presents new applications of the content and verbally models how an advanced practitioner would attempt to address the issue.

DESCRIPTION: College teachers are inclined to present students with the *results* of their thinking in class rather than identifying the *process* that they follow to come to those results. Thus, students lack a model of an expert coming to terms with complex issues. Little wonder then, that students are often incapable of creatively solving problems or addressing issues on tests or papers, preferring instead to provide memorized answers or rote solutions. Think-alouds are designed to make teachers explicitly address the steps that they use in thinking about content. For most professors, these steps are so automatic that they assume the steps are self-evident to students.

Example #1:

COURSE: Secondary Teaching Methods (Susan's course)
SPECIFIC CONTENT: Selecting the appropriate content type (fact, concept, or skill) for a lesson

After I finish the explanation of the different content-type options that can be used to focus lessons, I tell my students: "Tonight in class you will have to decide if the lesson plan you will be turning in should focus on factual information, a concept, or a skill. Let me walk you through how I might approach that problem by thinking out loud so you can hear my reasoning process. Let's assume that my eighth-grade English class is beginning a two-week series of lessons on writing business letters. A skill lesson that emphasizes how to organize the parts of the letter would probably not be appropriate for their first lesson since they don't even have a concept of what a business letter is, what purpose it serves, or how it differs from other types of letters. Therefore, I think that several concept lessons should precede any skill lessons. I could ask students to list questions they have about people they admire, future professions, or interesting current issues. Then I could teach a lesson focused on the concept of business letters that are requests for information. I could follow this lesson with several more concept lessons on other types of business letters, such as letters of complaint, opinion, or recommendation. Once these basic concepts are in place, then I can design letter-writing skill lessons that focus on procedures and usage rules. This two-week unit on business letters doesn't seem to require fact-based lessons. If individual students want to research factual information on the persons or companies of their choice, they can do that outside of class using the Internet research guidelines taught at the start of the year."

Example #2:

COURSE: Research Methods in Education (Jim's course)
SPECIFIC CONTENT: Distinguishing stratified from purposive sampling

After lecturing on stratified and purposive sampling, and before providing students scenarios or examples to complete without my assistance, I give students a sampling example, such as: "A researcher wanted to assess how the Success for All reading program affected reading performance of at-risk third graders, so she identified 100 third graders who scored below the fifteenth percentile on the Stanford Nine reading subscale." I would then verbalize my thought process in distinguishing whether this was stratified or purposive sampling. I might say that "it appears not to be stratified since with stratified one is typically interested in ensuring that students from all levels of reading achievement in the population are represented in the sample (e.g. students scoring above, at, and below reading level for their grades). In purposive we are often interested in identifying a specific group of people to be in the sample. In the example presented, it appears that the researcher is specifically interested in just the at-risk kids, based on prior test performance (the kids scoring below the fifteenth percentile). So, it seems that this is a purposive sample."

5. Procedural Guidelines

DEFINITION: Procedural guidelines function as concrete references students can rely on for support as they attempt to complete new and complex assignments. This scaffolding strategy is often used when assignments involve a particular series of steps, procedures, or questions. The sequence or checklist is presented during instruction and is used later as a guide by students as they work independently on the assignment.

DESCRIPTION: Too often novice learners are given only brief explanations of assignments and then expected to somehow replicate the steps on their own. Even if examples of desired end products are provided by instructors, the steps taken to achieve those end products often remain a mystery to students. While it is true that those learners with the most confidence or persistence might make appointments with their instructors in order to make clear the necessary procedures, these extraordinary measures should not be prerequisite for successful performance on required assignments. Providing students with a set of procedural guidelines to follow when working independently from teachers is what effective instructors do on a regular basis. These teachers force themselves to become consciously aware of the steps that they (as experts) intuitively follow when critiquing plays, creating personal fitness schedules, writing persuasive essays, recording lab results, selecting math formulas, or designing marketing plans. They then record the sequence of steps that they took and share it with their students. When assignments or problems are complex in nature, students' intellectual energies can be best spent engaged in the struggle of the application of the new content rather than in inefficient and frustrating attempts to divine how the experts arrived at the solutions.

Example # 1:

COURSE: Secondary Teaching Methods (Susan's course)
SPECIFIC CONTENT: How to write a lesson plan

Here is a summary of the procedural guidelines I give to my students to follow when writing lesson plans:

1. Identify the essential content to be learned.
2. Create a learning outcome to match.
3. Design the initial concrete experience to engage learners and provide a context.
4. Write the detailed instructional sequence using inductive and deductive strategies.
5. Design the reflection or practice activity to show evidence of meeting the learning outcome.

Example #2:

COURSE: Research Methods in Education (Jim's course)
SPECIFIC CONTENT: Steps in writing a proposal for a qualitative research study

After describing the features of qualitative research and giving a number of examples of qualitative research studies conducted nationally and with my own students at CSUDH, I have my students develop possible qualitative study proposals using the following steps:

1. Identify the general goal of the study (called a Foreshadowed Problem in qualitative research).
2. Construct several Research Question–more specific questions or issues to be answered in addressing the goal.
3. Develop methodology to answer each Research Question, including: a) sample to be studied (students, teachers, parents, others), b) specific procedures to be followed (classroom observation, interviews, videotaping, etc.), and c) time line to complete the study.

These are just five of many scaffolds that teachers can use with their students. Many scaffolds have significant amounts of research documenting their efficacy in promoting academic achievement and fostering critical thinking. For additional material on scaffolding we recommend Angela O'Donnell's article (CL&CT Vol. 4 No. 2), the Alison King article (Article 13, pages 112-121), and the Rosenshine and Meister chapter (Scaffolds for Teaching Higher-order Cognitive Strategies. In A. C. Ornstein (Ed.), *Teaching: Theory into Practice* (pp. 134-153). Boston: Allyn & Bacon.

16 The Use of Pairs in Cooperative Learning

Mel Silberman

Originally published in the Cooperative Learning and College Teaching newsletter, Fall, 1996.

Let's face it, when you place students in cooperative-learning groups, lots of things can go wrong. Among the possibilities are:
- *Confusion*: Students don't know what to do because they didn't follow the directions.
- *Off-task*: Students don't stick to the topic or worse yet, they talk about the weather.
- *Unequal Participation*: Some people dominate, some remain quiet.
- *One-way Communication*: Students don't listen and respond to each other.
- *No Division of Labor*: Some people don't pull their own weight or let the group down.
- *Perfunctory Examination of the Issues*: Students are done before you know it, breezing through the assignment in the fastest way possible.

Experienced practitioners of cooperative learning know how to minimize these problems but their occurrence is still too frequent. In groups, it takes time to work out the several issues that delay the onset of learning and productivity. As many know, these issues are often referred to as forming, storming, and norming, and time and patience are required to let them happen.

Pairs are not immune to these problems and issues, but their ability to work through them is usually more rapid and less painful. It's hard to *hide* in a pair. It's also hard to get *left out* in one.

The communication network is simpler and there are more chances to work out conflicts.

There is a practical side to the use of pairs, as well. Pair activity tends to be less time-consuming and requires less movement of furniture. (Even a lecture hall can easily accommodate pair-learning activities.) In addition, pairs can more easily negotiate times to meet outside of the classroom.

The major disadvantage of pairs is the lack of several perspectives that exist in larger groupings. Therefore, one of the important goals in designing cooperative learning in pairs is to heighten an active exchange of viewpoints, information, and skills.

Ten Basic Activities in Pairs

I have developed a handy list of ten basic things you can ask students to do in pairs that begin the process of active learning:

1. **Discuss** a short written document together.
2. **Interview** each other concerning partners' reactions to an assigned reading, a lecture, a video, or any other educational activity.
3. **Critique** or edit one another's written work.
4. **Question** a partner about an assigned reading.
5. **Recap** a lecture or class session together.
6. **Develop** questions together to ask the instructor.
7. **Analyze** a case problem, experiment, or exercise together.
8. **Test** each other.
9. **Respond** to a question posed by the instructor.
10. **Compare** notes taken in class.

Of course, more complex assignments are also possible.

Five Structured Activities in Pairs

There are many ways to structure pair activity. Here are some of my favorites:

Active Knowledge Sharing

Overview: This a great way to draw students immediately into the subject matter of your course. You can also use it to assess the knowledge level of students, while at the same time, do some team building. It would work with any class and with any subject matter.

Procedure:
1. Provide a list of questions pertaining to the subject matter you would be teaching. You could include some or all of the following categories:
- words to define (e.g., "What does ambivalent mean?")
- multiple choice questions concerning facts or concepts (e.g., "A psychological test is valid if it: a) measures an attribute consistently over time; b) measures what it purports to measure.")
- people to identify (e.g., "Who is George Washington Carver?")
- questions concerning actions one could take in certain situations (e.g., "How do you register to vote?")
- incomplete sentences (e.g., "A _____ identifies the basic categories of tasks you can perform with a computer program.")

2. Create pairs and ask them to answer the questions as well as they can.

3. Then, invite them to mill around the room, finding other pairs who can answer questions they cannot. Encourage students to help each other.

4. Reconvene the full class and review the answers. Fill in answers unknown to any of the students. Use the information as a way to introduce topics of importance in the class.

Learning Starts With a Question

Overview: The process of learning something new is more effective if the learner is in an active, searching mode rather than a passive, receptive one. One way to create this mode of active learning is to stimulate students to delve into or inquire into subject matter on their own without prior explanation from the teacher. This simple strategy stimulates question asking, one key to learning.

Procedure:

1. Distribute an instructional handout of your own choosing. [You may use a page in a textbook instead of a handout.] Key to your choice of material is the need to stimulate questions on the part of the readers. A handout that provides broad information but lacks details or explanatory backup is ideal. An interesting chart or diagram that illustrates some knowledge is a good choice. A text that's open to interpretation is another good choice. The goal is to evoke curiosity.

2. Ask students to study the handout with partners. Request that pairs make as much sense of the handout as possible and identify what they do not understand by marking up the document with questions next to information they do not understand. Encourage students to insert as many question marks as they wish. If time permits, form pairs into quartets and allow time for pairs to help other pairs.

A physics teacher, for example, might distribute a diagram illustrating how potential energy converts to kinetic energy by showing a circus diver leaping from a 50-foot pole. Students work with partners to review the illustration and determine questions (i.e., "When exactly does the potential energy become kinetic energy?" "What is the basic difference between kinetic and potential energy?").

3. Reconvene the class and field questions that students have. In essence, you are teaching through your answers to student questions rather than through a preset lesson. Or, if you wish, listen to the questions all together and then teach a preset lesson, making special efforts to respond to the questions students posed.

The Power of Two

Overview: This activity is used to promote cooperative learning and reinforce the importance and benefits of synergy, that is, that two heads are indeed better than one.

Procedure:

1. Give students one or more questions that require reflection and thinking.

Here are some examples:
- How do our bodies digest food?
- What is knowledge?
- What is "due process?"
- How is the human brain like a computer?
- Why do bad things sometimes happen to good people?

2. Ask students to answer the questions individually.

3. After all students have completed their answers, arrange them into pairs to share their answers.

4. Ask the pairs to create a new answer to each question, improving on individual responses.

5. When all pairs have written new answers, compare the answers of each pair to the others in the class.

Jigsaw Learning In Pairs

Overview: Jigsaw learning is a widely-practiced technique in which each student learns something which, when combined with the material learned by others, forms a coherent body of knowledge or skill. While Jigsaw learning can be utilized with different-size groups, pairs are an ideal choice.

Procedure:

1. Choose learning material that can be broken into parts. A segment can be as short as one sentence or as long as several pages. (If the material is lengthy, ask students to read their assignments before class.)

Examples include:
- A multi-point handout
- Parts of a science experiment
- A text that has different sections or sub-headings
- A list of definitions
- A group of magazine-length articles or other kinds of short reading material

2. Divide the learning material into two segments. Assign each

member of the pair one of the two segments and ask him or her to read and learn the material assigned.

3. After the study period, reconvene the pair.

4. Ask the partners to teach each other what they have learned. Or give the pair a set of questions or a task to do that requires the separate knowledge of each partner.

5. Reconvene the full class for review to ensure accurate understanding.

Pair Review

Overview: This strategy gently challenges students to recall in pairs what was learned in each of the topics or units of the class. It is an excellent way to help students revisit the content you have covered.

Procedure:

1. At the end of a class, present students with a list of the topics you have covered. Explain that you want to find out what they remember about the topics and what they have forgotten. Keep the atmosphere informal so that they do not feel threatened by the activity.

2. Form pairs and ask partners to recall what each topic was about and as many things as they can remember about it. Ask questions such as:
- What does this topic refer to?
- Why is it important?
- Who can give me an example of what we learned about this topic?
- What value does this topic have for you?
- What were some of the learning activities we experienced with each topic?

If little is recalled, handle their forgetting humorously or place the blame on yourself for not making the topic "unforgettable."

3. Continue in chronological order until you have touched upon all the course material (or as much of it as you have time and student interest).

4. As you proceed through the content, make any final remarks you wish.

Section 4
Formal Cooperative-learning Strategies

In this section of the book, more complex cooperative team strategies are presented. In the first two articles (Articles 17 and 18, pages 155-165) Susan Prescott Johnston describes issues that should be addressed as faculty begin to plan more formal teamwork. In her articles, Susan treats such issues as optimal team size, team formation and grading. She also describes how to manage teams, including developing team folders.

In Article 19, beginning on page 166, Nancy Stetson describes cooperative base groups, groups that work together for a semester or term to address complex issues, and which require more time than the informal procedures described in Section 3. Nancy describes the phases that groups often go through as members learn to work together. In Article 20 (pages 171-178), Susan Gruber and Darlene Habanek build on Nancy's work and offer suggestions regarding how to ensure that base groups function successfully.

Specific techniques for using base groups are described in Articles 21 and 22. In Article 21 (pages 179-182), David and Roger Johnson and Karl Smith report on a technique that they call Structured Controversy (also known as Constructive Controversy). In this technique, pairs of students within four-person base groups research and present two sides of an issue, then switch sides within the base groups in order to adduce as much information as possible (as opposed to defeating another team as in many forms of debate). In Article 22, beginning on page 183, Shlomo Sharan describes Group Investigation, a technique he developed for his students to use to research complex issues using base groups. In Group Investigation, students test hypotheses in the same way that mature researchers conduct empirical research. This approach requires significant amounts of teacher planning and organization.

17 More Tips for Getting Started in Cooperative Learning (CL)

Susan Prescott-Johnston

Originally published in the Cooperative Learning and College Teaching newsletter, Spring, 1992.

Following are some answers to frequently asked questions. These guidelines are not meant to be prescriptive, but can be adapted to fit the unique needs and styles of individual professors and students.

Q. How do I let my students know we will be trying a new strategy and that it is important to make it work well?

A. You can put a statement in your course syllabus to emphasize its importance. An example from my syllabus follows:

> During class we will be practicing important concepts and skills in small work groups of 3 to 5 students. This strategy is known as cooperative learning and is designed to increase your mastery of the course content. You will be expected to actively participate in an effort to ensure your own and your teammates' understanding of the ideas presented in class. We need your commitment to demonstrate a willingness to contribute ideas, to listen to others, and to be a constructive force in the learning process.

You can also explain the advantages of CL to the students and how they will benefit in terms of increased learning, enjoyment, peer contact, and access to the instructor. If you feel it is appropriate, you might hand out an article describing the research base for CL.

It is also helpful to make the connection between participating in learning teams now and students' future or current experience in the workplace. Most careers require people to plan and work together productively. Employers report that their biggest problems center on the inability of people to interact productively. Students need to hear that class groupwork is valuable preparation for future problem solving in team settings in the work place as well as an opportunity to more effectively learn the course curriculum.

Q. When do I actually start using learning teams in class?
A. That can vary. At my university some colleagues start on the second class meeting; information cards filled out during the first class session provide the data (GPA, language proficiency, sex, ethnicity, age, etc.) needed to form heterogeneous groups. Others prefer to wait several weeks in order to diagnose students' abilities, and to learn as much as possible about individual students. In very large classes, such careful grouping is not as practical. My teacher education classes usually have 30-35 students, and we meet once a week. For the first three to four weeks I make sure students sit in pairs; these can change each week. During instruction I ask students to turn to their partners and think of examples of principles we have just discussed, and I also design short practice activities for them to do together. By about the fourth week of class they are used to interacting in pairs and I have had an opportunity to learn more about individual personalities, so we are ready to move into larger permanent work groups.

Q. How many students should be on a team?
A. Teams of four seem to be ideal because that size allows each member to be heard and allows partners within a team to work together and then share their results with their other pair. Larger teams can be risky because a shy or unmotivated student can more easily choose to not participate or can be overlooked by teammates intent on completing a task. Some of my colleagues report that they have great success with teams of three and five when that is necessary. We do not recommend teams larger than five since the opportunity for equal participation is greatly decreased.

Section 4. Formal Cooperative-learning Strategies 157

Q. How do the students find out who is on their team?
A. This can also vary. In my class I have written their names in clusters on an overhead transparency. When they come in, the directions on the overhead ask them to find each other and arrange their seats so they are in a foursome facing each other and also able to see me. During the previous class meeting I explained this procedure so they know what to expect. I review the advantages of CL and emphasize that these are to be work groups not friendship groups. Respect for each other is expected, even though many would not have chosen to work with each other. I tell them that, if friendships result that is wonderful, but it is not a prerequisite for productive group work (just as in the workplace).

One of my colleagues simply reads off students' names by teams and then asks them to find their new seats. Another gives cards with names to each team leader and that person is responsible for finding his own teammates. On that initial day there is always momentary chaos that is usually of short duration. Most of us always have students sit in their teams when they enter the classroom. This eliminates wasted movement time later and allows teams to brainstorm answers together when the instructor poses questions during the lecture or discussion.

Q. What can I do to establish some team spirit when students first form their groups?
A. An effective strategy is to have some brief teambuilding activities that are designed to help teammates learn more about each other. These can be simple interview questions. Some examples include: place of birth, career goals, special talents, scariest moment, or favorite pastimes, sports, vacation, foods, etc. Students can also give themselves a team name; freshmen through graduate students enjoy this activity. It is risky to omit teambuilding activities; because learning is an emotional as well as cognitive process, students need to feel some sense of connection in order to work together productively.

Q. Do I keep the same teams all semester?
A. It takes a while for students to learn how to work with the people in their group; most instructors are hesitant to disrupt the

process. If classes meet frequently throughout the week and engage in CL each time, students might be ready for some variety. When in doubt, privately ask some students in the class for their reaction to changing the composition of the teams.

Q. Do I need to have students assume roles within the team?

A. Again, the answer varies. Some faculty use a less-structured format called Collaborative Learning that does not require roles or stable teams. Most of my colleagues feel that permanent teams with roles help students stay on task, feel more organized, and increase the involvement of all members. Role titles can be traditional or creative. The only requirement is that the responsibilities are made clear to the students. (See the following article for a specific description of team roles and how a team folder can be used to assign roles and keep a record of student attendance and performance.)

Q. What kind of activities can I design for learning teams to do together?

A. Activities can range from the simple to complex. Here are some helpful guidelines to use when planning the task that students will complete in class.

The task needs to be very clearly structured in terms of what the students are expected to produce and how each member is expected to contribute. When the activity is vague (i.e. "Discuss this topic...") students are usually frustrated and waste valuable learning time trying to figure out the instructor's intent. Both young and older adult learners appreciate clarity; a tightly structured task often frees them to think critically and creatively. Often, a visual structure like a chart, sentence starter, sequential diagram, or specific question with space for an answer can provide a format that helps students organize their thinking and writing.

Some instructors refer to unit exams in order to select priority content that serves as the basis for planning tasks that might require teams to answer questions, solve problems, generate mythical scenarios, critique viewpoints, analyze pros and cons, locate evidence, correct intentional errors, or create persuasive arguments. Tasks that reflect important course concepts and skills vs. trivial information result in greater student enthusiasm and participation. Students need to feel that their group work directly relates to their understanding and mastery of the more complex subject matter for which they will later be held accountable through tests, quizzes, or projects.

Q. Do I need to grade these practice activities?
A. We advise instructors not to grade group practice tasks. Grades need to be based on individually completed quizzes, tests, or projects. These activities can sometimes be turned in via the team folder; so that several points can be awarded to give credit for effort and completion. If the instructor explains to students the rationale for group practice tasks and students experience the connection between helpful team interaction and increased individual understanding and performance, then the need for having each activity evaluated is greatly reduced.

Q. How long should the practice activities take and how often should we actually meet in cooperative groups?
A. Practice activities following a presentation by the instructor can range from twenty minutes to an hour. The length of the task will be determined by the complexity of the content to be grasped and the total length of the class session. Groups often appreciate and need an opportunity to also share their answers or products with the whole class. This is a valuable use of learning time and serves to increase mastery of content and clear up misunderstandings that still exist. In classes of only one hour duration, teamwork can still occur at brief intervals within a lecture or discussion.

There is no set formula for how often groups should meet. Ideally, students should be given some opportunity for interaction at each meeting. The more frequently they work together, the more effective they become in offering and asking for meaningful explanations from each other, engaging in critical thinking, and becoming actively engaged with important ideas. It is always a challenge for instructors to strike a productive balance between direct instruction and necessary practice.

We encourage instructors to experiment with all the facets of implementing Cooperative Learning and to seek opportunities for dialogue with colleagues who are trying to increase learning and motivation through the use of this strategy.

18 Getting Started with Cooperative Learning

Susan Prescott-Johnston

Originally published in the Cooperative Learning and College Teaching newsletter, Winter, 1992.

The successful application of Cooperative Learning (CL) in the classroom requires careful attention to details of implementation that can be easily overlooked. In this article I will describe how a team folder can work to help both the instructor and student feel more organized and productive. Folders also seem to provide a greater feeling of team identity for students.

Once teams are formed, I give each group a file folder with their names on the outside. The three classes I teach meet once a week for three hours and are color-coded. Monday's folders are red; Wednesday's, blue; and Thursday's, yellow. In this way I can immediately identify which stack of folders to take to class or which folders I need in order to insert the papers I want to return to students. The folders function as an important channel of communication. All homework, notes, projects and tests can be turned in and returned using the folders. I tape each team's Polaroid photo on the folder cover; it's fun, the students love it, and the team monitor can locate his team's folders quickly. An alternative might be to have the students bring in personal photos or put a team insignia on the cover.

Stapled to the inside of the front and back covers are two important data sheets. The first is a chart describing the team roles and responsibilities (see Figure 1); the second is a record-keeping chart on which information about students' attendance, homework, tests, and points for team practice activities is recorded (see Figure 2).

Some faculty use a less-structured format called Collaborative Learning that does not incorporate any roles. However, most of my colleagues feel that roles help students stay on task, feel more organized, and increase the involvement of all members. Role

Figure 1

TEAM ROLES AND RESPONSIBILITIES			
ROLES	NAMES		
	round #1	round #2	round #3
LEADER 1. MAKES SURE EVERYONE UNDERSTANDS THE NEW LEARNING AND ASSIGNMENT PROCEDURE 2. ENSURES THAT ALL MEMBERS PARTICIPATE AND WORK PRODUCTIVELY 3. FACILITATES RESOLUTION OF ANY CONFLICTS AMONG TEAM MEMBERS 4. APPOINTS OR SERVES AS SUBSTITUTE FOR ANY ABSENT TEAMMEMBER (ON TEAMS OF FOUR)			
RECORDER 1. RECORDS TEAM RESPONSES FOR PRESENTATION TO CLASS 2. ENSURES THAT PRACTICE ACTIVITY IS COMPLETE IF ASSIGNMENT IS TO BE GIVEN TO INSTRUCTOR 3. RECORDS ALL ABSENCES AND TEAM POINTS			
MONITOR 1. PICKS UP AND RETURNS TEAM FOLDER 2. ENSURES THAT ALL PAPERS IN FOLDER ARE DISTRIBUTED TO TEAMMATES 3. MAKES A COPY OF CLASS NOTES FOR ABSENT MEMBER(S) AND CALLS BEFORE NEXT CLASS 4. WRITES ABSENT MEMBERS' NAMES ON ALL HANDOUTS AND KEEPS THEM IN TEAM FOLDER			
SPOKESPERSON 1. MAKES SURE THAT EVERYONE UNDERSTANDS ANSWERS/IDEAS TO BE SHARED 2. REPORTS TEAM IDEAS TO CLASS (USES RECORDER'S NOTES WHEN NEEDED)			
SUBSTITUTE 1. ASSUMES RESPONSIBILITIES FOR ANY ABSENT TEAM MEMBER			

titles can be traditional or creative. The only requirement is that the responsibilities for each role are made clear to the students.

Some faculty let students choose who will take each role. I prefer to assign all the roles the first time; students find out their roles when I hand out the team folders with names already filled in. A colleague of mine assigns the leader role based on highest GPA and lets the team self-select the remaining roles. He assigns each student a preplanned number on the day teams are formed and then tells them that all the number ones are the team leaders. None of these strategies seem to meet with resistance; once students know the rationale and see the benefits they are usually grateful and enthusiastic. The frequency of class meetings during the week may determine if or how often roles are rotated throughout the semester. My classes meet once a week for three hours, so I give each team the option of keeping or changing their team roles.

Some faculty members are concerned about the issue of record keeping and wonder how much is necessary and if it will be time-consuming. There seems to be a minimal amount of record keeping required, and the students can manage it themselves. Teachers only need to provide them with their folders and an explanation of how the charts are to be used. Team recorders are responsible for entering all the data for test grades, and bonus points for each practice activity that meets the criteria. Because my students are asked to sit with their teams upon entering the classroom, information gathering happens quickly and quietly at the start of class.

This record sheet (Figure 2) is only an example and can be changed in any way to suit the maturity level of the students and the policies of the instructor. The days that the class meets are circled and attendance is taken each day. A new sheet will need to be stapled in at the start of the sixth week of CL. The recorder can also record a plus or minus in the homework category; this section of the chart can be eliminated if not appropriate, but some students report that it makes them feel more accountable. If during any week the teams complete a practice activity that is worth a small amount of bonus points (much easier to award points than grades), then the recorder looks at the paper returned by the instructor in the team folder to see the number of points earned. These are then recorded in the box at the bottom of the chart. If a student is absent during any week in which a team activity was completed for points, that student's total semester score does not include those particular points when the instructor adds bonus points to each student's individual point total at the end of the semester.

Not all team tasks need to be turned in for bonus points. However, the amount of points needs to be small (three to five) so that if ten team tasks are worked on in class during the semester, the resulting thirty or fifty points won't significantly alter any student's overall point total that is used to compute the grade for the course. The principle of individual accountability is important and should not be violated by giving group grades.

Figure 2

			TEAM RECORD		
NAMES	week #1 MTWTF	week #2 MTWTF	week #3 MTWTF	week #4 MTWTF	week #5 MTWTF
	ATTENDANCE				
1.					
2.					
3.					
4.					
5.					
	HOMEWORK				
1.					
2.					
3.					
4.					
5.					
	INDIVIDUAL ASSIGNMENTS Š PROJECTS				
1.					
2.					
3.					
4.					
5.					
	TEAM PRACTICE ACTIVITIES				

The team folder is not a prerequisite to successfully implementing CL in the college classroom. However, it can be viewed as an optional strategy that can serve as a valuable motivational hook for students as well as a helpful management tool for instructors.

19 Using Small-Group Development to Facilitate Cooperative Learning Base Groups

Nancy E. Stetson

> Originally published in the *Cooperative Learning and College Teaching* newsletter, Winter, 1996.

Cooperative learning base groups are long-term groups with stable membership that usually stay together for at least a term. Base groups are appropriate when you have large numbers of students in your classes and the subject matter is complex.

When you facilitate base groups, it will help you to understand small-group development. Regardless of size or type, small groups typically go through predictable stages over time. Small-group development experts such as Kent Curtis, M. A. C. Jensen, R. B. Lacoursiere, George Manning, Steve McMillen, and B. W. Tuckman have named and described these stages. According to these experts, small groups move through four developmental stages: forming, storming, norming, and performing. Obviously, it is in the best interest of base groups to move through the first three stages as quickly as possible in order to develop high performance teams. If you, as facilitator, understand the stages of small-group development, you likely will be better able to facilitate base groups moving more quickly toward the fourth, high-performing stage.

Stage I, Forming. According to the experts, when groups first come together and form, they need to deal with the issue of trust. New groups are unclear on their purpose and members don't know what to expect. They are facing a new social situation, with some discomfort and apprehension. Consequently, they likely will be cautious. They'll be trying to figure out what is going to happen, who's who in the group, where they fit in, and how they will be treated by other group members. They'll also be trying to figure out what is OK behavior, what is the nature of their group's tasks, and how they will deal with each other to accomplish the task. Interactions likely will be light and superficial and mostly directed toward you, the formal leader. At this stage, groups will not have developed any skill and knowledge as teams. When you first form your base groups you can expect them to be cautious, excited, anxious, and to perform at a low level. You also can expect individual members to be anxious, searching for structure, silent, and cautious with you and group members.

Stage II, Storming. Once the base groups have formed, they usually move into a period of storming, when they need to deal with the issue of conflict. In this stage, individual members will react to what has to be done, question your authority, and feel increasingly comfortable being themselves. The groups likely will exhibit conflict and resistance to the task and structure, even as they increase their productivity through increased skills and knowledge. Members may express their concerns and frustrations more openly, and feel freer to exchange ideas. At this stage, they are learning to deal with differences in order to work together to meet their goals. Typically, members will exhibit power struggles for influence. Groups that don't get through the storming stage successfully will exhibit divisiveness and low creativity. After your base groups have formed you can expect them to exhibit conflict over the task and the structure. On some occasions you may have individual members who: confront you, the cooperative learning facilitator; polarize among the team members; test group tolerance; and behave in a fight or flight manner.

Stage III, Norming. This is the stage in which explicit or implicit norms of behavior are developed that are considered essential for the groups to accomplish their task. Order forms, as does group cohesiveness. Members begin to identify with their groups and develop acceptable ways to complete assignments, resolve differences, make decisions, and solve problems. They enjoy meetings and exchange information among themselves freely. Group (or team) productivity increases as skills and knowledge continue to develop. After your base groups have successfully stormed, you can expect them to reach agreement on roles and tasks, and norms of behavior, including team member and leadership behavior; and to increase their cohesiveness, morale, and productivity. You also can expect individual members to shift from power struggles to affiliation; from confusion to clarity; from personal advantage to group success; and from detachment to involvement.

Stage IV, Performing. The fourth stage, the payoff stage, is performing. If your base groups have successfully moved through issues of membership, purpose, structure, and roles, they will now be able to focus their energies on group performance: completing tasks and solving problems together. They will take initiative and achieve results. As they achieve progress, morale will go up and they will have positive feelings about each other and their accomplishments as a team. Base groups will now be teams that business and industry call "self-directed work teams." They will no longer be dependent upon you for direction and support; instead, members can take on leadership roles as necessary. You can expect your performing base groups to exhibit good communication and teamwork, individual commitment, high morale and group pride, and high team performance. You can also expect base groups to use a wide range of task and process behaviors: monitor and take pride in group accomplishments; focus on goals as well as interpersonal needs; and maintain the values and norms of the group. Individual members will exhibit interpersonal trust and mutual respect, actively resolve conflict, actively participate, and be personally committed to the success of the group.

Your Role as Small-Group Development Facilitator. As cooperative learning facilitator, you can help base groups move through the first three stages of small-group development as quickly as possible so they can reach the high performance stage. According to Manning et al. your small-group development facilitator role in each of the four stages is slightly different.

In the forming stage, you can **reduce uncertainty** by: (1) explaining the purpose of the groups and their goals, (2) providing time for questions, (3) allowing time for members to get to know each other, and (4) modeling expected behaviors.

In the storming stage, you can **reduce conflict** by: (1) hearing all points of view; (2) acknowledging conflict as an opportunity for improvement; (3) adhering to core values, such as truth, trust, and respect; and (4) maintaining democratic and humanistic ideals.

In the norming stage, you can **encourage norm development** by: (1) modeling listening skills, (2) fostering an atmosphere of trust, (3) teaching and facilitating consensus, and (4) providing team-centered learning.

In the performing stage, you can **help groups succeed** by: (1) being prepared for temporary setbacks, (2) focusing on task accomplishments and interpersonal support, (3) providing feedback on the work of the groups, and (4) promoting and representing the groups.

Manning et al. believe it is helpful to view each of the stages in the life of groups from two points of view. "The first is *interpersonal relationships*. The group moves through predictable stages of testing and dependency (forming), tension and conflict (storming), building cohesion (norming), and finally, establishing functional role relationships (performing)."

"At the same time, the group is struggling with *accomplishing tasks*. The initial stage focuses on task definition and the exchange of information (forming). This is followed by discussion and conflict over the task (storming). Next comes a period of sharing interpretations and perspectives (norming). Finally, a stage of effective group performance is reached (performing)."

If you and your base groups have done your jobs exceedingly well, you will have groups that exhibit the "dazzling dozen" characteristics of effective teams described by Manning, et al.:

1. Clear mission
2. Informal atmosphere
3. Lots of discussion
4. Active listening
5. Trust and openness
6. Disagreement is OK
7. Criticism is issue oriented, never personal
8. Consensus is the norm

9. Effective leadership
10. Clarity of assignments
11. Shared values and norms of behavior
12. Commitment

Stage V, Adjourning. If you're an experienced cooperative learning base-group facilitator, you undoubtedly know the fifth stage in small-group development, one most of the experts don't address: adjourning. As your base groups near the end of the term, they typically will begin to think about how they will feel when the groups are no longer groups. They usually will experience some sadness or regret at the idea of separation.

In the adjourning stage, you can **encourage closure** by: (1) acknowledging and honoring the feelings about relationships that have developed; and (2) allowing farewell rituals. If you have super high-performing groups, they may not even need your encouragement. They may perform the task of closure—their final task together—all by themselves.

20 College Classrooms' Lost Gold Mine: The Cooperative Base Group

Susan E. Gruber and Darlene Vanselow Habanek

Originally published in the *Cooperative Learning and College Teaching* newsletter, Fall, 1996.

Included in the list of challenges for contemporary college classrooms is empowering students to become not only successful, but also caring adults who are committed to the academic success of their peers. The popular press enumerates the need for modern-day citizens to have well-developed communication and collaboration skills. Unfortunately, these skills are not generally reinforced in traditional classrooms, which maintain one-way communication flowing from the instructor to the students and the lecture-practice-test sequence for learning. Cooperative-learning structures used in college classrooms provide organized and systematic choices for varied learning experiences which foster the development of social skills needed for collaboration and communication around academic tasks.

One valuable cooperative structure is base groups. In our college courses we begin each class session with a base-group meeting. Base groups are heterogeneous, long-term cooperative-learning groups with stable membership which meet regularly. The purpose of these meetings is to provide each member with support, encouragement, and assistance needed to complete assignments and make good academic progress. Members hold each other accountable for striving to make academic progress.

For faculty members to use base groups, they must understand how to set them up, as well as what activities to use initially, in the middle and at the close of the term. There is a solid research foundation supporting the use of base groups; they are also generally enjoyed by both students and instructors.

Setting Up

Group Size

In setting up base groups, the first decision that must be made is the size of the groups. We have found that it is easier for a group of four students to get together outside of class to work on projects or to build academic support for study and review together. This size also allows for absenteeism or for students who drop the course before the end of the term.

Assigning Students to Groups

The next decision to be made is the assignment of students to groups. There are several methods that can be used to assign students to groups: team-of-instructors' assignment, random assignment, student self-assignment, or individual-instructor assignment. There are two types of classes which influence the group assignments: cohort and regular classes. With a cohort of students who are taking most of their courses together, a team of instructors would meet to assign students to groups based on jointly-determined criteria. These criteria might be based on: a) where students live, b) transportation issues, or c) academic interests. These base groups would then remain constant for all courses for the duration of the program (as long as four years in some cases).

For regular-class base groups, students might be assigned randomly. Students would count off and join students with the same number. For example, in a class of 32, students would count off from 1-8, forming eight teams of four. Another group-formation procedure would be to have students self-assign according to criteria such as living in the same area, people you don't know, different gender and age, and full- and part-time students. After students find each other, a data sheet can be produced as an initial assignment where group members report information based on criteria specified for forming groups. This sheet would be turned in to the instructor for review to assure heterogeneity, and then placed in the base-group folder for future reference by students and instructor.

Section 4. Formal Cooperative-learning Strategies

If the class is small, the instructor might employ other methods to determine group membership, such as a sociogram and/or information gained from informal observations. A sociogram, often used by sociologists, is a method of gaining information about group dynamics and/or interaction patterns among people. When using a sociogram, the instructor asks students to list two or three peers in class with whom they would like to go to a movie or have a cup of coffee (social events) and to list two or three different peers with whom they would like to work on a project or paper (academic tasks). The instructor would then form groups of three or four people around isolated students, always reserving the right to adjust the final group assignment based on academic ability, social skills and other criteria important to the course. To use informal observations for assigning students to groups an instructor would gather data early in the course by observing student interactions during group work and whole-class discussions. For example, the instructor would note which students talk a great deal or seem to pull away from the group, and which students appear to have a solid knowledge base versus those who struggle with the course content. This information is then used to form effective heterogeneous cooperative base groups.

After deciding on group size and composition, decisions must be made as to what the members will do in their base groups. Below are activities that can be used at the beginning, during or at the end of a session.

Activities

Base groups meet at the beginning of each class session. Members pick up their base groups' folders, arrange their desks or sit two-by-two if in a lecture hall (or a room without moveable chairs) and carry out basic activities.

***Folders.** Groups give themselves names which they write on the tabs of their folders along with their group numbers. Group members also write their names on the outside of the folders. Some groups may choose to decorate their folders with things they have in common or symbols that represent their groups. This might be an ongoing task for the groups. In a class of 100 with 25 or more base groups, we take pictures of the groups on the day they are assigned to their base groups. During the next session students tape these pictures to the inside of their folders, writing their names across their pictures. This practice helps us learn students' names faster so we can refer to them by name, in and outside of class and when they send E-mail during and after the course.

Routine Tasks. Attendance can be taken in the group. The Membership Grid (see Trust/Self Disclosure Tasks) can be used as the attendance record by having students write absent on it if a person is missing rather than allowing it to be filled in the next time the person attends class. Other records can be kept by the base group as well if this is important in the course (i.e., hours spent in lab or internship or fieldwork since the last session, or interviews completed).

Homework Check. Students check one anothers' homework to see if it is complete, if there were any problems with the assignment or with understanding the material. Arrangements can be made for a time outside of class when the base group can meet to provide academic or cognitive support to group members. Checklists of skills, concepts, processes and procedures can be completed within groups to determine the kind of support members need in order to understand the information in the course.

Other interesting activities to complete at the beginning of class meetings include:

Trust/Self Disclosure Tasks. With this task students share something personal about themselves. This is entered on a Membership Grid which gives the history of the group. Questions can be posed, such as favorite teacher and why, favorite relative and why, farthest place from this room traveled, most dangerous experience, hobby, qualities of a best friend, famous person you would like to learn from, person who had the most impact on your life, where and with whom you learned to resolve conflict, favorite movie, best thing that happened to you since last session, and so forth. These questions provoke self disclosure which facilitates the personal support that group members need to become a connected productive group. (For more information on using and understanding small groups see the previous article.)

Section 4. Formal Cooperative-learning Strategies 175

*Review of Relevant Learning. Periodically, we check what the students have read, thought about, or done that is relevant to the course since the last session. Each member gives a succinct summary of this to his/her base group. Sometimes students are asked to do a One Minute Paper individually before they share with their groups. This can be turned in via the group folder for the instructor to review. Students might bring resources they have found or copies of articles and other work they wish to share with their group members.

*Peer Editing of Required Papers. Before papers are handed in to the instructor, base group members can peer edit them. They might check grammar, organization, style and other aspects of the writing process. We find that papers are of much higher quality when students are given some class time for peer editing.

*Group Processing. To assist groups to function better, students are periodically asked to reflect on and give feedback to each other and the instructor about working together. Students might answer questions on what they like about each other, what they like about themselves, how they would rate themselves and the other group members on their involvement in their groups. Students might be asked to write about what is going well in their groups, what needs to be improved and how they will do this. Team members sign these papers, put them in the folders for the instructor to review and use for group processing activities. Reflection on how the groups are working helps to improve the functioning of the groups. Without this reflection, dysfunctional groups tend to remain that way throughout the term and students become angry and bitter about group work. To have honest processing, however, the trust level must be high in the groups. Trust activities are an important aspect of building effective group functioning.

During class sessions, base groups can be used for both informal and formal cooperative-group work.

*Informal Group Interactions. When lecturing or making a longer presentation, instructors break "teacher talk" into shorter periods of time (for adults about 10-15 minute time blocks). At the end of that "talk" time, students are asked to turn to their base groups or to one member of their base group and answer a ques-

tion that the instructor has posed based on the information just presented. This process transforms the students into active rather than passive learners. Students are randomly selected from different groups to present a response based on the interaction with their partners. Sometimes they give written responses which are then placed in the folders. During an hour session, this may be done three or four times.

Formal Group Work. Students complete a formally-structured group project in their base groups on an area of concern or issue in the field. We use base groups when heterogeneity is important or changing groups is not critical to the project. At other times we use other team configurations based on grade level or subject area when base groups would not be as effective. The decision to use base groups or to form different groups for a project is dependent on the outcome desired. For example, a case study analysis can be done by forming groups using one person from three different base groups. Or, a Jigsaw of course material could be structured with the base group being the teaching/learning group with individuals studying and planning how to teach their section with members of other base groups who have responsibility for the same section of the materials.

At the end of class sessions, base groups can be used for closure. Some of these tasks might be similar to those used at the beginning or during the class session.

Closing Tasks. At the end of the session, base-group members should check to see that each member understands the assignment(s) and if anyone will need support. This checking might take the form of a meeting or just talking with each other on the telephone between sessions. Group members might set goals about what they will read or have completed before the next session. In addition, members might discuss what they learned during the session. They might even check their notes to be sure they have all of the important information. Further, members might discuss how they can apply what they learned during the session in a real-life situation. Group members might rate themselves as to how well they worked together during the day. And, of course, there should be a celebration of the hard work and learning which took place. Someone in each group is responsible for being sure all papers are in the base-group folder and that the folder is returned to the instructor prior to leaving class.

Research Support

The research support for using cooperative base groups is extensive.

Social Support. Social psychology tells us that "receiving social support and being held accountable for appropriate behavior by peers who care about you and have a long-term commitment to your success and well-being is an important aspect of progressing through college" (Johnson & Johnson, 1989).

Achievement and Productivity. Cooperative efforts result in high achievement and greater productivity than competitive or individualistic efforts (Johnson & Johnson, 1997).

Concern for Self and Others. Conger (1988) found that without a balance between concern for self and concern for others, concern for self led to a banality of life and, even worse, to self-destructiveness, rootlessness, loneliness, and alienation. Individuals are empowered, are given hope and purpose, and experience meaning when they contribute to the well-being of others within an interdependent effort.

Sense of Belonging. When students feel they are supported and known by other students, they tend to feel less alienated and more positive about remaining in college. This kind of support has been shown to combat dropping out of school (Johnson & Johnson, 1989).

Conclusion

Cooperative-learning base groups are at the heart of all our courses. We have collected data and comments from students concerning their feelings about being in base groups. Not only do students benefit through both personal and academic support, we as instructors benefit.

Student Comments: Some students have reported that:

"Base groups helped me to develop a connection with other students. It forced me to expand my friendships,"

"As a new student to college, it was a reassuring way to get adjusted to classes,"

"I had people to count on when I missed class,"

"The tasks we did at the beginning of each class as a base group got us on task and kept me on schedule for readings and assignments,"

"Having feedback from other students and forming answers made the material clearer," and

"I felt more prepared for large group discussions."

Authors' Experiences. After using base groups over several years in teaching both undergraduate and graduate courses, we have found that:

*We can both view and be part of the social interaction,

*We hear and can address student concerns quickly and housekeeping chores can be taken care of expeditiously,

*Absent students can get remedial assistance from their base-group members,

*Ready-made groups are set up for activities, and

*Base groups provide constant, appropriate modeling of collaborative efforts in the classroom.

As more careers use teamwork to meet goals, institutions of higher education have an obligation to change the paradigm of how we conduct courses. When students interact with each other, we see that they not only achieve at higher levels, they also care more about each other. Even though structuring and organizing base groups requires time and thought initially, the benefits more than pay back the time and effort for both instructors and students. Base groups have been a gold mine in our courses.

21 Structured Controversy/ Constructive Controversy

David W. Johnson, Roger T. Johnson and Karl A. Smith

Originally published in the *Cooperative Learning and College Teaching* newsletter, Spring, 1993.

Using academic conflicts for instructional purposes is one of the most dynamic and involving, yet least-used teaching strategies. Although creating a conflict is an accepted writer's tool for capturing an audience, teachers often suppress students' academic disagreements and consequently miss out on valuable opportunities to capture their own audiences and enhance learning.

Controversy exists when one student's ideas, information, conclusions, theories, and opinions are incompatible with those of another. Structured academic controversies are most often contrasted with concurrence seeking, debate, and individualistic learning. For instance, students can inhibit discussion to avoid any disagreement and compromise quickly to reach a consensus while they discuss the issue (concurrence-seeking). Or students can appoint a judge and then debate the different positions with the expectation that the judge will determine who presented the better position (debate). Finally, students can work independently with their own set of materials at their own pace (individualistic learning).

Structured Controversy in Environmental Education

Topics on which we have developed curriculum units include the following and many others: "What caused the dinosaurs extinction? Should the wolf be a protected species? Should coal be used as an energy source? Should nuclear energy be used as an energy source? Should the regulation of hazardous wastes be increased? Should the Boundary Waters Canoe Area be a national park? How should acid precipitation be controlled?" An example of Structured Controversy using the topic of hazardous wastes regulation follows. The teacher assigns students to groups of four and asks them to prepare a report entitled, "The role of regulations in the management of hazardous waste." There is to be one report from the group representing the members' best analysis of the issue. The groups are divided into two-person advocacy teams with one team being given the position that "more regulations are needed" and the other team being given the "fewer regulations are needed" position. Teams are often composed of one low-achieving and one high-achieving student. Both advocacy teams are given articles and technical materials supporting their assigned positions. They are then given time to read and discuss the material with their partners and to plan how best to advocate their assigned positions.

Five Steps in Structured Controversy

First, students research the issue, organize their information, and prepare their positions. Learning begins with students gathering information. They then categorize and organize their present information and experiences so that a conclusion is derived. Second, the two advocacy teams actively present and advocate their positions. Each pair presents its position and reasoning to the opposition, thereby engaging in considerable cognitive rehearsal and elaboration of their position and its rationale. When the other team presents, students' reasoning and conclusions are challenged by the opposing view and they experience conceptual conflict and uncertainty. Third, students engage in general discussion in which they advocate their positions, rebut attacks on their positions, refute the opposing positions, and seek to learn both positions. The group discusses the issue, critically evaluates the opposing position and its rationale, defends its position, and compares the strengths and weaknesses of the two positions. When students are challenged by conclusions and information that are incompatible with their reasoning and conclusions, conceptual conflict, uncertainty, and disequilibrium result. As a result of their uncertainty, students experience epistemic curiosity and, therefore, actively: (a) search for more information and experiences to support their positions, and (b) seek to understand the opposing positions, and its supporting rationale. During this time students' uncertainty and information search are encouraged and promoted by the teacher. Fourth, students reverse perspectives and present the opposing position. Each advocacy pair presents the best case possible for the opposing position. Fifth, the group of four reaches a consensus and prepares a group report. The emphasis during this instructional period is on students reconceptualizing their positions and synthesizing the best information and reasoning from both sides. Group reports should reflect their best reasoned judgment. Each group member then individually takes an examination on the factual information contained in the reading materials.

Instructional Materials For Structured Controversy

Prepare the instructional materials so that group members know what position they have been assigned and where they can find supporting information. The following materials are needed for each position:
1. A clear description of the group's task.
2. A description of the phases of the controversy procedure and the interpersonal and small group skills to be used during each phase.
3. A definition of the position to be advocated with a summary of the key arguments supporting the position.
4. Resource materials (including a bibliography) to provide evidence for the elaboration of the arguments supporting the position to be advocated.

Implementation Tips For Structured Controversy

No matter how carefully teachers structure controversies, if students do not have the interpersonal and small-group skills to manage conflicts constructively, the controversy does not produce its potential effects. Students should be taught the following skills.

1. Emphasize the mutuality of the situation and avoid win-lose dynamics. Focus on coming to the best decision possible, not on winning.
2. Confirm others' competence while disagreeing with their positions and challenging their reasoning. Be critical of ideas, not people. Challenge and refute the ideas of the opposing pair, not them personally.
3. Separate your personal worth from criticism of your ideas.
4. Listen to everyone's ideas, even if you do not agree with them.
5. First bring out all the ideas and facts supporting both sides and then try to put them together in a way that makes sense. Be able to differentiate the differences between positions before attempting to integrate ideas.
6. Be able to take the opposing perspective in order to understand the opposing position. Try to understand both sides of the issue.
7. Change your mind when the evidence clearly indicates that you should.
8. Paraphrase what someone has said if it is not clear.
9. Emphasize rationality in seeking the best possible answer, given the available data.
10. Follow the golden rule of conflict: act towards your opponents as you would have them act toward you. If you want people to listen to you, then listen to them. If you want others to include your ideas in their thinking, then include their ideas in your thinking. If you want others to take your perspective, then take their perspective.

22 Group Investigation in the University Classroom

Shlomo Sharan

> Originally published in the *Cooperative Learning and College Teaching* newsletter, Winter, 1994.

The Group Investigation approach seeks to stimulate learning as an "inside to outside" process rather than an "outside to inside" process, as is commonly practiced even in most Cooperative Learning methods. That is to say, Group Investigation organizes students to *seek* and solve problems in given areas of study, and to understand, and try to solve these problems. Group Investigation also can be used to produce knowledge, through use and synthesis of a wide variety of informational sources and experiences. This approach stands in contrast with those methods where students are expected to learn (often used synonymously with memorize) or consume quantities of knowledge predetermined by the teacher. In this sense, Group Investigation was designed to follow the steps typical of mature research: to test hypotheses formulated in advance by those who seek to acquire the information necessary to determine whether the hypotheses support the theory from which they were derived. Group Investigation is thus an exercise in *the pursuit of knowledge*, and not in the consumption of given knowledge. However, this pursuit of knowledge is conducted with a small number of peers who interact with one another in many ways during their collective effort to study and solve a problem.

Group Investigation and the Four I's

Group Investigation works effectively because it incorporates four features which are consistent with good practice in teaching and learning: Investigation, Interaction, Interpretation and Intrinsic Motivation.

Investigation. This is Group Investigation's distinguishing characteristic, and the entire class must be directed toward this form of learning in order to create the social environment that sustains this approach. Small groups of students, rarely numbering more than five per group and usually only four, engage in planning precisely what the group wishes to investigate as part of the class' broad topic. The group also plans how and where it will seek information or experiences relevant to the topic they choose. It is suggested that the topic be formulated as a problem that requires solution. (Why do human beings walk on two feet? What cultural influence did China receive from India? What are the basic features of prophecy in ancient Israel versus philosophy in ancient Greece? What kinds of effects does demographic change in Africa, India and China have on ecological problems in those countries? What are the major moral, philosophical and practical implications of Galileo's discovery that the earth revolves around the sun?).

One way of generating a series of problems that relate to a central class-wide topic is to have the class proceed through a series of steps whereby it proposes and lists problems. These problems can then be organized into categories and selected by the different groups in the class as their topics for investigation. For example, pairs of students can be asked to write down all the problems they consider a necessary part of understanding a broad topic introduced by the instructor. Pairs sitting close to one another are then combined into fours, and two "fours" can be combined later into groups of eight. Each stage lasts only a few minutes, although the last stage of octets requires more time. At each stage, the component groups (of two, four or eight members) generate lists of suggestions for subtopics needing study, compare their lists, eliminate duplication and continue to suggest new problems or sub-topics that need study to achieve a broad understanding of the major topic at hand. At the level of the octets, students in each group are asked to categorize all of the suggestions listed thus far into a small number of categories. All of these categories from each octet in the class are posted on a placard or on a blackboard, duplications eliminated, and a series of topics are identified as appropriate for investigation. This latter step is carried out with the entire class as a whole.

Students are counseled about locating sources of information needed for various investigations, such as printed materials in libraries, sites to be visited, people to be interviewed, experiments to be conducted, and observations to be made. The variety and richness of the materials depend, of course, upon local conditions and upon the initiative of the instructor and the students.

Interaction. During the process of carrying out these stages, the students, working in small groups, will interact with one another in many different ways including exchanging ideas, feelings, and points of view, mutual assisting, and assuming responsibility for different aspects of the work to be done. Of course, investigations can always be performed by individuals, and in some of the humanities (history, literature, etc.) the tradition of individual research is still very strong. However, given the complexity of the information needed, research in many fields by persons working entirely alone is becoming less common, particularly in the natural and social sciences. The point is not so much that investigation CAN be done by individuals, but that it can also be accomplished in a very rewarding and motivating way by small groups of individuals working together. This small-group setting for investigation provides many positive features that cannot be experienced by individuals working alone, namely, the entire dimension of constant communication with others about a topic of common concern.

Interpretation. Information is made meaningful when it is placed in a broader context by connecting to existing ideas and relating to past experiences. Knowledge emerges when information is made meaningful; it is not inherent in the information itself. The small group setting is an ideal forum for having students attribute meaning to the information they uncover about the problem at hand, and hence to have that information gradually become knowledge for those students. Such knowledge is all the more important to students because they interpreted its meaning rather than had the meaning presented by the instructor as interpreted by him/herself or other scholars. Interpretation is thus an essential feature in the pursuit of knowledge and can be greatly enhanced by the communication occurring between members of small groups.

Intrinsic Motivation. Research and theory in teaching and learning suggest that the combined functioning of the three I's just described will activate and sustain students' genuine interest in the subject they study. Thus, students will devote themselves to their investigation not only because they want good grades but also because the topics engage their interest. The study of academic subject matter out of interest rather than for external reward is an essential element in all quality education. Failure to engage students' genuine interest in the pursuit of knowledge is a widespread and deeply regrettable feature of today's education at all levels. Granted, not all learning experiences can or need be intrinsically motivated, it is still of significant importance that some critical mass of students' educational experiences be so motivated if they are to cultivate any interest in learning that will survive their years in formal educational settings. Group Investigation invites students to take active roles in determining the content and method of study they pursue within an interactive social context. Expanding students' control over their learning behavior, together with the motivating aspects of a relatively free form of peer interaction devoted to a common goal appear to promote and heighten students' intrinsic interest in the work of investigating a topic. Hence, intrinsic motivation is one anticipated result of implementing the first three of the four I's.

When all four I's operate as anticipated, Group Investigation typically leads to many other beneficial results including increases in academic achievement, and improved relations between students of different social classes and ethnic groups (Sharan & Sharan, 1992).

The Six Stages of Group Investigation

The four I's are embodied in the procedures to be carried out by students when conducting a study according to the Group Investigation method. These procedures can be divided into six consecutive stages.

Stage 1: Class Determines Subtopics and Organizes Into Research Groups.

Students scan sources, propose questions, and sort them into categories. The categories become subtopics. Students join groups studying the subtopic of their choice. As a prelude to this stage, instructors may wish to show slides, a videotape or film, invite a visiting lecturer, visit a site, have students examine documents or scan books. The main questions to be asked at this stage are: What do we know about the problem or issue? What do we want to know?

Stage 2: Groups Plan Their Investigations

When the sub-topics have been identified, students sign up to be members of groups on the basis of their interest in a particular sub-topic. Instructors may have to negotiate with some students to ensure that groups do not become over or undersized, that cliques do not dominate particular groups, and that groups are otherwise heterogeneous.

Group members plan their investigations cooperatively: They decide what they will investigate, how they will go about it, and how they will divide the work among themselves. The procedural and organizational questions to be posed at this stage are: How will we find information about what we want to know? How will we divide the investigation into parts, and who will assume responsibility for which parts? What resources will we need to investigate this topic? Where will we find these resources?

Selection of particular questions to be investigated by students allows for the expression of individual preferences and talents. Not everyone has to do everything! All members have the responsibility to become thoroughly acquainted with all aspects of the groups' work, but no one individual needs to carry out the study of each and every problem dealt with by the entire group.

The instructor can, of course, identify some particular source or portion of a task that must be mastered by all of the students in the class. The entire class can always be assigned some task as required study for everyone apart from the topics investigated by the different groups. Such assignments are more likely to be accepted willingly by students within the context of their investigations than outside such a context, particularly if the instructor highlights the relevance of the assigned work for students' understanding of the topics they are investigating.

Instructors must perform the role of resource person in guiding students to appropriate resources. A wide variety of sources probably will have to be examined to fully investigate any genuine problem. Groups must be encouraged to identify for themselves sources of information regarding the topic at hand. On occasion, the group may discover gradually that its initial plan for the investigation was unrealistic or impractical, for whatever reason, and new planning must take place.

Stage 3: Groups Carry Out Their Investigations

This is typically the longest stage and may span any number of class sessions or may require a great deal of time to be spent outside of class. The question of time and group cooperation to implement its plan must be discussed in detail in each group.

Group members gather, organize, and analyze information from several sources. It may be advisable to have different students assume particular roles to make group organization efficient, such as: coordinator, recorder, secretary, etc., as the situation dictates.

Students pool their findings, interpret them as a group and form conclusions. Group members discuss their work in progress in order to exchange ideas and information, and to expand, clarify and integrate them. The more experience students have with Group Investigation, the more skilled they become in integrating all of the group members' contributions into the final group product.

Stage 4: Groups Plan Their Presentations

Group members determine the main ideas developed during their investigation. In this stage the groups plan how to present their findings by answering the following questions: Which of their findings does the group wish to present to the class? How will these findings be presented so the class will find them interesting?

Group representatives meet as a steering committee to coordinate plans for the final presentation to the class and consult with the instructor. Ideas for the presentation probably have been developing during the course of the investigation. Again, diverse talents can be given creative expression in the group presentation.

Stage 5: Groups Make Their Presentations

A schedule of presentations can be posted or copied and distributed to everyone. Presentations are made to the class in a variety of forms that emphasize class participation and minimize lectures by the presenting group. A few possibilities include setting up an exhibition, performing a skit or role play, conducting an experiment, building a model, constructing a chart, or preparing a slide presentation.

Stage 6: Teacher and Students Evaluate Their Projects

The audience evaluates the clarity and appeal of each presentation, in addition to evaluating its intellectual and informational value for those who participated in the investigation and for the class as a whole. Students share feedback about their investigations and about their affective experiences. Teachers and students collaborate to evaluate individual, group, and classwide learning. Evaluation can include a test, if the instructor feels it is necessary. Often students can be asked to contribute questions that will make up the test. However, the groups' presentations may well suffice as a solid basis for evaluating student learning.

Teaching the Group Investigation Method

One way of teaching students the Group Investigation method is to pose several major problems about the method itself and to have students propose specific questions for investigation. Students can then form study groups that focus their investigations on different features of the Group Investigation method.

Suggestions for problems that could be investigated are: 1.

What are the theoretical foundations of Group Investigation? Students are asked to study, discuss and present the implications of the four main components of Group Investigation: Investigation, Interaction, Interpretation and Intrinsic Motivation. How do these differ from prevailing pedagogical principles? 2. What is the teacher's role or the students' roles in each stage of Group Investigation? What changes occur in these roles in contrast with expectations regarding those roles in traditional instruction? 3. How should the learning task be designed? 4. What are the effects of the learning task on group functioning? (Why will certain task designs fail to engage the group while others succeed?) 5. What is the role of students' cooperative planning in all stages of the Group Investigation method? What is the contribution of students' planning to achieving the goals of Group Investigation?

Findings from the investigation of Group Investigation are discussed by a panel consisting of representatives from each of the study groups. This panel discussion can serve as the final presentation of the groups' work, or other presentations can be planned, depending on time, conditions and other constraints. Having students study the Group Investigation method is recommended when the goal is to have students become aware of the method by which they conduct their work. That is often an important goal not only for students of education, but for anyone who wishes to become acquainted with team research as practiced in many professional environments.

Section 5
Implementing Interactive Group Instruction: Practical Advice

In this section advice on good practice for college teaching is offered. The emphasis is on active and cooperative strategies, although the recommendations are generally applicable to all pedagogies. This section is dominated by the work of Susan Prescott Johnston, who served as Contributing Editor to the newsletter from its inception. Susan's skill in application was matched by Contributing Editor Joe Cuseo's work that focused on research and theory in college teaching. Between the two of them, the newsletter attempted to maintain a firm grounding in research and theory, while focusing on the practical issues that faculty must address in their teaching.

In Article 23 (pages 193-200) Ted Panitz identifies resistances to the use of group work among faculty and students. He also describes how these concerns can be addressed. The editors of the current volume believe that getting a firm foundation in the research, theory and practice of small-group instruction is the best way to combat resistances which prevent many faculty from taking the risks associated with interactive teaching. We hope that the articles and chapters included in this text offer support to novices considering interactive teaching, and for those currently using some of the strategies discussed and want to extend the range of active- and group-learning techniques they are using.

Toward that end, Marcy Hamby Towns offers advice in Article 24 (pages 201-206) for planning and implementing small-group strategies. Jim Cooper, in Article 25 (pages 207-210) summarizes the advice that he received concerning how to form groups, a concern that many instructors have in considering the use of team learning. Six national leaders in group learning offered their recommendations on this issue, including advice relating to group size and formation, and reasons why some groups fail.

Supplementing these two articles is one that Susan Prescott Johnston wrote (Article 26, pages 211-215) which attempts to answer the "what if " questions that instructors commonly ask in thinking about adopting group learning (e.g. "What if students complain about a teammate?" "What if a student tells me he/she wants to work alone?"). Article 27 (pages 216-221) is another article by Susan, addressing practical implementation strategies in group learning. In this article, Susan describes *when* to include group work in the instructional sequence. In Article 28 (pages 222-230) Susan offer examples of specific tasks that could be used in the cooperative classroom and ties these tasks to a variety of content areas including the humanities, science and technology, and professional programs such as nursing and education.

In Article 29 (pages 231-235), Susan addresses the issue of Peer Revision, providing a four-step sequence that teachers may use to implement this powerful pedagogy. Finally, in Article 30 (pages 236-246) Susan addresses seven deadly assumptions that instructors often have which can have a lethal effect on students. She responds to each of these, offering advice based on her three decades in higher education as an award-winning teacher and influential workshop presenter and author.

23 Faculty and Student Resistance to Cooperative Learning

Ted Panitz

Originally published in the Cooperative Learning and College Teaching newsletter, Winter, 1997.

Considering the significant benefits created by the use of cooperative-learning methods, it is surprising more instructors don't use it. It is my view that the current educational system often supports practices which are inconsistent with cooperative learning and include an emphasis on content memorization and individual student competition.

Although cooperative learning has been around for well over 25 years at the K-12 level, and a decade or more at the college level, relatively few professors or students have had significant exposure to cooperative-learning techniques. Most college instructors are not taught cooperative methods during their graduate training. If instructors are taught by the lecture method during their undergraduate and graduate training, then it is hardly surprising that this will be the method of choice when their turn arrives to take over the classroom.

Reasons Why Teachers Resist Cooperative Learning

Loss of Control in the Classroom

Perhaps the biggest impediment to cooperative learning lies in the fact that many teachers feel they give up control of the class if they give more responsibility to the students for their learning. Cooperative-learning techniques often encourage students to formulate their own ways of understanding the material. The constructivist ideology is foreign to many teachers who have been trained in more teacher-centered pedagogies such as the lecture method.

Lack of Self Confidence by Teachers

It takes a great deal of confidence in one's self and one's students to transfer the responsibility of learning to the students or even to share some of the responsibility. In my view, many teachers lack the self confidence needed to try methods which may expose them to potentially difficult situations. These situations may occur when students ask unanticipated questions or act in socially unacceptable ways. Cooperative learning changes the roles of teachers from experts to facilitators. The focus on students reduces the opportunities teachers have to demonstrate their expertise and might call into question their teaching ability.

Fear of the Loss of Content Coverage

Some teachers fear a loss in content coverage when they use cooperative-learning methods because group interactions often take longer to cover the same content than simple lectures. Students in groups often need time to accumulate enough information in order to be able to use it within their groups. They need time to work together to reach a consensus and/or formulate opinions for presentation to the whole class. A major function of cooperative learning involves teaching students how to work together effectively. Also, teachers superimpose onto cooperative learning their experiences using the lecture method. For example, many students do not understand the material despite excellent lecture presentations by their teachers and therefore perform poorly on content-based tests. Teachers therefore conclude that the situation would be even worse if students work with other students who may be having similar problems. The reality is that when students become involved in their learning their performance improves, often quite dramatically.

Initially, groups do work slowly as they learn how to function cooperatively, analyze what works and what doesn't work for them and receive training in conflict resolution. But as students get used to the process, their content mastery and critical thinking increases to the point where they can move through the curriculum faster.

Lack of Prepared Materials for Use in Class

Cooperative-learning techniques may require teachers to build a set of handouts which create interdependence among students and provide a basis for them to work together. Current textbooks generally offer a set of questions at the end of each chapter which may be individually answered by students. A few publishers are beginning to tailor their texts to offer one or two questions which can be answered by groups, but supporting materials are not generally included. In addition, few suggestions are provided in teachers' manuals about how to institute group activities. This is a major impediment for teachers who are new to cooperative learning. Since a significant expenditure of effort and time is required to revamp curricular materials, teachers generally adhere to the methods and materials with which they are most familiar.

Lack of Familiarity with Alternate Assessment Techniques

Assessment is a major concern frequently expressed by teachers who are unfamiliar with cooperative learning. They presume that individual accountability will be lost or that one student will dominate the group or do all the work for the group. They are unfamiliar with how to assess group efforts and individual contributions to group efforts. Often they assume that only one process is appropriate for assessing students' performances.

Techniques available for assessing groups include: teacher observations during group work; group grading for projects; students grading each other or evaluating the level of contribution made by each member to a team project; extra credit given when groups exceed their previous average or when individuals within a group exceed their previous performance by a specified amount; use of a mastery approach whereby students may retake tests after receiving extra help from their groups or the teacher; and the use of quizzes, exams or assignments graded to ensure individual accountability.

Students' Resistances to Cooperative-learning Techniques

A cause for concern by teachers starting cooperative learning is the students' initial reactions. Most students have not been trained to cooperate in an academic environment. The approach in our colleges and universities is all too often one of competition for grades and recognition. Teachers need to sell the concept of cooperative learning to the students by making clear what the objectives are and what the benefits will be. Until the students become comfortable with this new method, they may express concerns about cooperative, small-group techniques.

Students may feel that the lecture method is "easier" because they are passive during the class while apparently receiving the necessary information. In contrast, interactive classes are very intense. The responsibility for learning is shifted to the students, often involving activities requiring critical thinking. This situation can be both mentally and physically tiring. When students respond by complaining and lobbying for a return to the good old lecture days it can be very disconcerting for a new cooperative-learning practitioner. Such resistance will decrease as the teachers become more experienced using cooperative learning. In well-structured cooperative-learning tasks these complaints are rare once students have experienced the benefits of small-group work.

Also, students may perceive their teachers as not doing their jobs. Cooperative classrooms are student-centered whereas in typical classes the focus is on the teachers' performances. In order to address this concern, teachers need to make clear to the students why they use particular cooperative techniques and what the outcomes will be from the procedures.

Another way for teachers to overcome this perception is to spend time with the groups or with individuals during the class. Teachers may walk around during class to observe groups interacting, make suggestions, or ask leading questions in order to help facilitate the groups.

Lack of Familiarity with Cooperative-learning Techniques and Class Management

Teachers are often concerned about the potential dominance by one or two students during small-group discussions or by inequitable work loads carried by individuals within teams. These issues can be addressed by: a) assigning roles to students and rotating the roles, b) allowing students to assign performance grades to each other anonymously and specifying what percent of the total assignment was completed by each member, and c) observing groups and making suggestions for more equal participation. Group processing concerning how the groups are functioning throughout the semester also helps address these issues.

Not every activity works exactly as planned and constant modification is needed. Some activities work better with some groups than with others and classes react differently to each situation. In some institutions cooperative learning is seen as cheating because the educational pedagogy recognizes and rewards individual effort and competition, and discourages cooperation among students.

If the program, department or institution has a content-coverage perspective instead of a content-mastery approach then the teachers will be less concerned about what students are learning and more concerned about including as much material as they can in a class period. Thinking about learning primarily as a social interaction is a foreign idea for many instructors, students and administrators, who expect to see the teacher controlling the class through lectures and/or teacher-directed class discussion.

Lack of Pedagogical Training in Cooperative Procedures in Graduate School

There is a great deal of comfort in propagating the familiar. At the university level the preferred pedagogy, judging by frequency of use, is the lecture; thus there are few role models for future professors who might be interested in using cooperative-learning methods. Many professors are more concerned with doing research than with teaching. This situation is reflected in the fact that many institutions and faculty use the terms teaching "loads" compared to research "opportunities." Except within some education departments, very little research goes on in support of good teaching practices. Within some institutions there are very few role models to provide mentoring for teachers. In fact, professors are often criticized by their peers when they do try to institute cooperative learning. Critical comments by teachers about room noise and "touchy-feely" teaching in the classroom are often used to discourage people from using cooperative-learning techniques.

Because most teachers receive little training in cooperative learning they are unaccustomed to what takes place in the cooperative-learning class. One consequence is that they find it hard to believe that students can be learning the content while they are socializing in their groups. Social learning creates an enjoyable as well as interesting environment. This is not very surprising; human beings are social animals, so many situations which encourage and enhance this basic need are frequently satisfying and enjoyable. Additionally, students' self esteem builds in cooperative groups as they gain confidence in themselves and their peers, leading to additional enjoyment of the learning process. In real-life situations people often work, learn and socialize at the same time. If we are to help our students move into employment situations, particularly the more interesting and responsible ones, then we need to provide a model for them to follow, which includes cooperation and team efforts, as well as individual efforts.

Another consequence of teachers' lack of familiarity with cooperative-learning classes is the feeling of guilt which can arise. Some teachers do not feel they are teaching if they are not dispensing information. They may appear to be inactive, since in cooperative learning it is necessary to allow time for the groups to interact without teacher intervention. Even if teachers move around the classroom observing the students or talking to individuals or groups, in their minds they still do not fit the picture of a productive teacher. Students may comment on the fact that they do not see the teacher "teaching."

Large Class Sizes and Inappropriate Classroom Setup

There is a growing trend in colleges to attempt to economize by increasing class size. This runs contrary to the nature of cooperative learning where smaller, student-centered groups have access to the professor, who in turn serves as a facilitator, not an information giver. Fixed-seating arrangements in large amphitheaters may make it difficult for students to interact comfortably.

Reasons Why Students Resist Cooperative Learning

Students' Lack of Familiarity with Cooperative Techniques

A major problem in implementing cooperative learning arises because students lack an understanding of the underlying rationale for the technique. Our current system encourages competition and individual responsibility and discourages student interaction and group responsibility. Some resentment may arise when students are asked to share information and study techniques, or to help their peers. The superior students have figured out how to get good grades in a competitive situation and to share that information may be uncomfortable for them. Cooperative learning redefines the role of students and teachers and their interrelationships by creating a nurturing cooperative environment versus a competitive one.

Fear of Loss of Content Mastery and Ability to Achieve High Grades

Initially, students in groups may not know if the work they are doing is correct. Student-centered discovery and construction of knowledge are new to many students. It is exactly these processes that help students develop critical-thinking skills, but they may initially resent the fact that group work shifts the burden of learning to themselves. They may feel much more comfortable hearing their teachers present the important facts instead of having to sort out what is important. A common fear among students is that all the group members will be wrong, leading to failure.

The cooperative-learning process often calls for constant review and summary through whole-class discussions and presentation of material by individuals and groups. In addition, teachers should continuously observe the groups and make suggestions about how to proceed or where to go to find necessary information. Over time students become more comfortable with the process as they understand that their questions will be addressed and that teachers are active participants in the process, taking on the role of facilitators or coaches instead of expert information presenters.

24 Building Community One Brick at a Time

Marcy Hamby Towns

Originally published in the Cooperative Learning and College Teaching newsletter, Winter, 1997.

Implementing Cooperative Learning

Some teachers discover cooperative learning through workshops or reading journals, and become very excited about integrating a new technique into their classrooms. They put their students into groups, turn them loose, and wait to see the positive outcomes associated with cooperative learning blossom. Unfortunately, these new cooperative-learning enthusiasts may become disenchanted and disappointed when those outcomes do not always occur.

The implementation of cooperative learning requires preparation. Simply placing students into groups and telling them to work together invokes two fallacies. One, that students actually know how to work together, and two, that students who do know how to work together will actually do so. Thus the question before you implement cooperative learning is, how do you get your students to work together?

Novice practitioners of cooperative learning can find answers in two texts which are especially helpful for those who are trying to understand the principles and applications of cooperative learning. Roger and David Johnson have written many texts and articles on cooperative learning; however one text (Johnson, Johnson & Smith, 1991) focuses exclusively on cooperative learning in the college classroom. This book: 1) contrasts the perspective of students as passive recipients of knowledge with the perspective of knowledge as constructed in the mind of the learner, 2) reviews cooperative-learning research, and 3) outlines in depth the essential elements of cooperative learning. It also provides many applications of different types of cooperative-learning activities. As a chemistry instructor, I found Nurrenbern's (1995) book on cooperative learning especially helpful. In it Nurrenburn discusses what cooperative learning is and why it should be employed, the role of the teacher within a cooperative classroom, how to design tasks, how to manage groups, and it also addresses the common concerns facing many practitioners of cooperative learning. There are a plethora of field-tested examples contributed by chemistry instructors.

Reading these two texts helped me generate the materials and the approach I now use in my chemistry classroom.

How Do I Get My Students To Work Together?

At my first class meeting I talk to my students about the cooperative-learning activities they will be doing during the semester. I discuss with them why I think it is important to learn to work with other people, and I emphasize the benefits of explaining concepts and problems to other students. From experience, I have found that it is helpful to use activities at the beginning of the semester which let group members get to know each other and set operating rules. The handouts and activities described below represent the present incarnation of my course.

Getting to Know You

The first day of class my students fill out a getting-to-know-you questionnaire which identifies their intended career paths, previous group-work experience, and attitudes toward group work. I collect the questionnaires and form the students into heterogeneous groups based on their responses, academic ability, and gender. It is very important that the instructor form heterogeneous groups. The workplace of the twenty-first century will be composed of more women and minorities than ever before. In order for students to flourish and succeed in this type of workplace, they must learn to value and respect diversity (i.e., they need to

Individual and Group Responsibilities

The first homework assignment asks the students to respond to four items prior to their first cooperative-learning activity: 1) list your responsibilities to the group, 2) list the responsibilities the group has to each member, 3) describe the advantages of working in a group or as a team, and 4) describe the disadvantages of working in a group or as a team (Nurrenbern, 1995). I want the students to think about what they expect from the group and what they expect to contribute to the group. During their first cooperative-learning activity the students assemble in their assigned groups and compare their responses to each question. This allows the groups to draft "Group Covenants" which describe the group members' responsibilities to their groups, and the groups' responsibilities to each member (Nurrenbern, 1995). In essence, this sets up the operating rules for each group. It helps to define acceptable behavior and how group members will interact in order to accomplish tasks. Each group member keeps a copy of the Group Covenants, and one copy, signed by each group member, is delivered to me.

Looks Like, Sounds Like

After the groups have had the opportunity to write their covenants, we compare what each group has written as individual responsibilities and group responsibilities. During this class discussion students are asked "What does each one of these responsibilities look like and sound like?" (Johnson, Johnson, & Smith, 1991). This is not a trivial question. Students need to know that verbal and non-verbal behavior play a role in how people perceive them. For example, groups often include listening to each other as a responsibility of each member to the group. But when asked, what does listening "look like" the students are usually stumped. They ask, "What do you mean, look like?" Listening to a person involves actually looking at him/her, making eye contact, and holding a facial expression that communicates that you are listening. Students need to realize that behaviors such as not looking at a person when they are speaking, rolling their eyes, or continuing to doodle delivers a message to the speaker. It "says" louder than words that what the speaker is saying is not important. Asking students what these responsibilities look like and sound like forces the students to think about how they are going to operationalize their Group Covenants.

Salaries and the Real World

At the beginning of the semester I emphasize that the interpersonal and communication skills the students develop during cooperative-learning activities will have a profound effect on their future success in the workplace. Since I teach a chemistry course, I discuss the starting salaries for BS, MS, and Ph. D. chemists (Chemical and Engineering News, 1996). I emphasize that many of the most interesting and highest-paying jobs in the workplace involve getting people to cooperate, leading others, and understanding and coping with complex power issues (Johnson & Johnson, 1989). Thus, learning how to effectively function in a group will contribute to their employability, productivity, and subsequent earning power.

Let's Get Started

The first cooperative-learning activities in any course can be fairly easy. I like to begin with an activity that is creative, non-threatening, and somewhat silly. The students are asked to estimate the number of ping-pong balls it would take to fill our classroom (Nurrenbern, 1995). They must describe their procedure in 150 words, not counting equations. I generally see the students splitting up the tasks such as trying to remember the equation of a sphere and pacing the length and width of the room, then pooling their efforts to calculate a reasonable answer. Laughter rings out as the groups try to evaluate whether or not our classroom could hold

10 million ping-pong balls! Its a great activity to get cooperative learning started on a positive note.

How Are We Doing?

Groups need to regularly reflect on how well they are functioning. Group processing is critical to improving performance and is analogous to evaluation and team-building efforts that occur in industrial settings (Johnson, Johnson, & Smith, 1991; Manning, Curtis, & McMillen, 1996). Processing can be facilitated by using a simple evaluation form where each team member is evaluated on the criteria outlined in their Group Covenants, and by responding to the following statements: 1) "to operate as an effective team we need to continue to do the following," 2) "things we should start doing are," and 3) "we should monitor our progress towards these goals by." Completing these three statements encourages students to think about what their groups are doing well and what they need to do to function more effectively as a group. It also reminds group members that building an effective group is not a static endeavor, it is a dynamic process which requires effort.

Building Classroom Community

Cooperative learning helps students build a coherent classroom community based on trust. The friendships students build as they share insights and ideas nurture that trust. For students to disclose their own reasoning and to share information they must trust their teammates to listen with respect and to critically evaluate their input. This enables students to form a classroom community based on positive relationships. When students experience this feeling of community they become willing to take on tough tasks because they expect to succeed, their attitudes toward courses become more positive, their potential for achievement becomes enormous, and absenteeism drops.

Building this community requires that the students know and trust each other. Working through the activities described in this article will help students get to know each other, decide operating rules for their groups, and evaluate and improve how their groups function. Groups which function effectively and thus build a sense of community unlock their potential to achieve and perform at a high level.

25 Group Formation in Cooperative Learning: What the Experts Say

Jim Cooper

Originally published in the Cooperative Learning and College Teaching newsletter, Fall, 1996.

In the Winter, 1996 issue of the newsletter we published the results of an E-mail survey concerning several issues that seem to consistently emerge in workshops, conferences and publications dealing with cooperative learning. A number of distinguished colleagues who have extensive experience in using cooperative learning and who have been studying the topic for many years were nice enough to respond to the questions that we posed. The survey included questions relating to the research base for cooperative learning, advice to both beginning and intermediate practitioners, and thoughts concerning the future of cooperative learning. That article was so well received that we have asked these colleagues to respond to some additional issues that seem to emerge in discussions concerning cooperative learning at the college level. The issues presented in this second survey relate to applied topics, particularly issues associated with group formation.

We want to thank Spencer Kagan, Barbara Millis, Jane Promnitz, Larry Michaelson, Karl Smith and Susan Prescott for their thoughtful responses to the survey.

The first item on the survey asked the respondents to share any general thoughts relating to optimal group size. As with all of the items included on the survey, respondents tended to qualify their answers, indicating that this decision depended on a number of factors. However, most respondents tended to favor groups of 2-4. Spencer Kagan responded that, unless there is an overriding reason to do otherwise, "groups of four are by far the best." One reason for favoring groups of four, according to Spencer, is that there are six possible learning pairs that can be formed within such groups. He reported that groups of three often produce a pair with the third person left out. Barbara Millis shares Spencer's enthusiasm for groups of four, and noted that this size generates appropriate amounts of diversity while ensuring that no one gets left out. Karl Smith prefers groups of 2-4, opting for smaller groups if time is short and the task is simple. He also wrote that smaller groups are more appropriate for auditoriums and other rooms where desks are bolted to the floor. Susan Prescott prefers to start the semester using pairs. She then forms teams of four after observing the pairs for a month or so to determine what would be the best groupings. Larry Michaelson noted that the larger the group is, the greater the resources for intellectual exchange. But, on the negative side, larger groups make it harder to build and maintain cohesiveness. Larry recommended using groups of 6-7 but only if one is careful about group management. He also wrote that temporary groups can be much smaller.

The second item on the survey asked our panel of experts how groups should be formed, whether by the teacher, student self-selection, or random formation. In the case of teacher-formed groups, respondents were asked to describe the criteria they would apply. They were also asked about homogeneous versus heterogeneous team formation. Karl Smith reported that random assignment of students to groups often works well, that it is quick and is perceived as fair by students. He also likes stratified random formation where students of varying levels of skill are placed into heterogeneous groups ensuring high, medium and low skill representatives on each team. Homogeneous formation of teams based on a shared interest often works well for long, complex projects, according to Karl. Susan Prescott likes to have students work in pairs for a month or so, then form heterogeneous teams based on such factors as course achievement, gender and ethnicity. For extremely advanced students, however, Susan ensures that there are very advanced partners on the team to dissipate burnout and morale problems among these high-achieving students. She also reported that when using pairs is the sole cooperative-learning technique used, student self selection of partners may be appropriate.

Barbara also advises forming heterogeneous teams on the basis of such criteria as achievement level, gender, ethnicity and learning style. She indicated that homogeneous teams based on a common interest may occasionally be formed for a specific project. She warns against same gender and same ethnicity teams unless there are compelling reasons to use such groupings. Jane Promnitz reported that early in her implementation of cooperative learning she was a strong believer in teacher-formed, heterogeneous teams. More recently she has observed successful use of student-formed teams, particularly when teams are clear as to the purposes of cooperative learning and the nature of the learning tasks in the class. If groups have to meet outside of class, homogeneity of class schedule or geography may be primary criteria for group formation, according to Jane. As with many of the respondents, Spencer Kagan indicated that this question is highly dependent on the nature of the learning task and other educational goals to be fostered. Larry Michaelson agrees with Karl and others who report good results by using a stratified, random approach so all teams have a mix of skill levels. He pointed to difficulties associated with students' self-selection to teams, such as a lack of diverse viewpoints and a perception by some students as being "leftovers" when they are not asked to join a team.

The third survey item asked respondents how long cooperative-learning teams should stay together. There was a diversity of opinion expressed by our experts. This diversity was typically associated with the educational goals of a given assignment. The value of relatively long-term groups lasting from a half to a whole semester was often recommended, in order to allow students to form emotional bonds with one another. Susan keeps her students together for the entire semester. She has colleagues who successfully form base groups that stay together for a semester, but are supplemented by temporary groups used for specific, short-term assignments. Barbara Millis likes to keep her groups together for at least half the semester so they can work through the forming, storming, norming and performing phases of interacting described in the group dynamics literature. Spencer Kagan reported using base groups who stay together all semester to work on complex multi-media group projects. Karl Smith reported using informal groups that stay together for a class period or less. More formal groups in Karl's classes stay together for longer periods of time, up to a semester. However, he likes the idea of changing groups at least once a semester, so that students in less functional groups have the chance for a better group experience. Larry Michaelson is perhaps the most adamant about leaving groups together for the entire semester. He cited research that he and his colleagues have done, indicating that understanding and trust are best developed only after students have worked together in excess of 20-25 hours. He cautioned against using cooperative learning to reduce racial stereotyping unless groups are together for the entire semester.

The fourth and final item on the survey asked for the respondents to identify reasons for failure when groups did not work well. Many of the responses focused on issues relating to clarity, organization and structure of the tasks. In addition to these issues, Larry Michaelson noted that out-of-class group-learning experiences where the instructor is not able to monitor the groups' work is problematic. He also suggested that assigning an extended written document often results in a lack of collaboration because students tend to simply write their own sections of a larger document and not engage in give and take discussions over all elements of the work. Spencer Kagan listed lack of structure, lack of social skills and unclear task definition as among the major reasons for poorly functioning groups, problems that he indicated can be addressed by appropriate choices of learning structures (techniques). Karl Smith pointed to spending too much time doing cooperative learning without proper training of students in organization and management skills for group work. He also criticized faculty who have vaguely-structured learning tasks which are often weak in ensuring positive interdependence and individual accountability. Jane Promnitz noted that groups often fail if there are not clear ground rules for how students are to proceed and if faculty fail to adequately monitor groups, particularly in the beginning of their work. Barbara Millis pointed to the importance of clear assignments and expectations and the importance of appropriate team-building. She also indicated that problems may occur if students are unused to small-group work and are unwilling to devote the time and effort to become productive group members.

26 Trouble-Shooting Cooperative Learning

Susan Prescott Johnston

(Originally published in the Cooperative Learning and College Teaching newsletter, Winter, 1993)

In this article I will focus on questions that reflect instructors' concerns about things that might go wrong as they incorporate CL into their classrooms. While glitches will always occur in any human endeavor, the instructor must feel and project a sense of optimism that a solution for the problem can be found. It is important to remember that the positive outcomes of this strategy far outweigh any malfunctions that will inevitably occur. It is also the instructor's responsibility to minimize the negative conditions that can lead to potential problems in learning teams. Practices to avoid include: giving group grades, assigning team projects that require fluent and extensive meetings outside of class, poorly structured team practice activities with unclear unions, not monitoring and observing students as they work together, and evading necessary interventions with individual students.

Q. What if a student tells me he would rather work alone?

Whenever a student expresses a negative feeling, it is crucial to stay calm and not to take it as a personal attack. Try to respond in a caring manner that sends a message of objective interest. Students' reactions can always be viewed as a source of valuable information about their own needs and fears. If a student makes this statement in front of others, I would tell him that I was most interested in hearing his concerns and ask for a conference at break or after class. I would then ask him to tell me more about why he wished to work alone in an effort to determine: if he had experienced a previous negative group situation in which he had been exploited, if be had some fear of feeling exposed and inadequate in this subject area, if he felt uncomfortable communicating in his nonnative language, if groupwork represented a new and unfamiliar method of learning, or if be simply preferred working alone. Depending on his response, I would provide appropriate reassurance and repeated explanations of my rationale. Occasionally, it is necessary to ask a student to consider a fair compromise and agree to try groupwork for at least three weeks, and if he still feels the same way he will be allowed to work alone. In only one case that I know of did an instructor have a student choose to be alone after several weeks of intensive involvement with a team of peers.

Q. What if some students dominate in their teams and others rarely contribute?

Both young and older adult learners need to be given a clear set of expectations in the course syllabus as well as in a class discussion regarding skills of participation and communication. Students can also brainstorm behaviors that have the potential to help or hinder teamwork. It helps to have the instructor and students demonstrate specific verbal and nonverbal strategies for: making everyone feel included, expressing disagreement constructively, offering encouragement and support, eliciting responses from quiet members, asking for clarification, avoiding negative and critical styles, etc. When this kind of roleplaying is conducted in an informal and humorous setting, a positive feeling tone is set for the semester.

In addition to these preventative methods, instructors can carefully monitor group interaction and make notations of students who are contributing too much or too little. I have pulled students aside during groupwork time and conducted brief very private conferences in which I expressed my concerns. During these friendly and very supportive talks, I tell them that I am obligated to ensure that an equal amount of participation occurs in each team, but my clipboard notes indicate that their team pattern seems to be unbalanced. I acknowledge their equal desire to have things go well and ask for their observations and ideas to improve the situation. If a student's response indicates absolutely no awareness of his own behavior pattern, then I become more explicit in my description of what I have seen and more directive with specific strategies for him/her to try. While I try to be sensitive to the possibility that a student's family or cultural background might reflect a different set of expectations for interactions, we usually reach some agreement on how to proceed.

Q. What if a group activity requires previously completed individual work and some students come to class unprepared?

Again, clear expectations recorded in the course syllabus as well as a lively class discussion focused on both the responsibilities and rewards of team membership can go a long way to prevent these sorts of problems. My students also report that having to record completed homework on the team folder information sheet seems to increase their motivation to come to class prepared. Even the most conscientious of students will occasionally find themselves in this predicament; the important thing is to intervene if it becomes a pattern with a particular student. Depending on a student's maturity level and personality, either a team captain will be asked to help solve the problem or I might need to get involved. One colleague who teaches freshmen and sophomores simply does not allow students to join their teammates if they come unprepared; they are asked to sit as individuals at the back of the room and complete the missing assignment. While this strategy is extreme, it may be scary if an individual consistently chooses not to do the required work. Before consequences are used, I assume that a student with this type of chronic problem would be offered access to support services on campus to help find a solution.

Q. What if I can't tell how students are feeling about working in their teams?

The easiest way is to ask them; several options are available. One strategy is to give them a questionnaire asking them to record what they liked about CL, what they wished was different, and any specific suggestions they have. Another method is to conduct a class discussion asking the same questions. While the responses may not reflect the degree of frankness found in the anonymously completed survey, they will still be helpful. Another colleague identifies several students whose judgment he trusts and targets them as his *barometers* by consulting with them privately and asking them how they feel about the class and if they have any ideas for improvement.

Q. What if students complain about someone on their teams?

This problem rarely occurs. When it does, it is a delicate situation and the solution depends on many factors including the nature of the complaint, the personality of the offending teammate, and your assessment of the ability of the distressed students to handle the situation themselves. The ideal would be to coach them through an independent resolution; if this is not possible, then a direct intervention by the instructor may be required. In the past I have approached a student privately by stating that I have noticed a disturbing pattern emerging and am concerned that the classroom climate for learning [for which I am ultimately responsible] is being adversely affected and I need some help in making changes. More frequently, however, I am the one to first register a complaint because many students would rather tolerate inappropriate behavior than approach the instructor with a negative situation. On one occasion, I met with a student who had some emotional problems and kept distracting his teammates. Very firmly I described the conditions for staying on a team and things improved. I also met with each of his teammates and expressed gratitude for their willingness to work with this person and stated that I would make a change at their request. They all assured me that everything would be fine, they could handle it, and they then set out to prove to me that they were capable of saving the situation. Once, in a colleague's class, a student informed him [after the fact] that he bad switched with a person on a different team and things were much improved. There was not much to be done at that point, but trading places is generally not a helpful strategy and can lead to a breakdown of the team structure.

Q. What if students on a team visit with each other during my instruction or the small group activity?

This is a frustration and it occasionally happens in my classes. Since CL results in students feeling more positively connected, they may forget to set appropriate boundaries when necessary. Usually I will make eye contact with someone on their team who will then motion to them to stop talking. If it persists, I then meet with one or both students and ask if they are aware of the problem. I ask them to consider how their choice to engage in disruptive behavior is affecting their own and their teammates' learning. I mention that since I am ultimately responsible for a classroom climate that is conducive to learning, I would appreciate hearing their plan for solving the problem.. This approach has always worked for me, and students generally respond in a constructive manner.

While it can be productive to anticipate as many problems as possible so that we are ready with both preventive and coping strategies, the odds are great that, some unexpected event will still occur. When it does, our responses can greatly influence our students' attitudes toward the CL process in our classrooms. It is difficult to think of any problem that cannot be brought directly to an individual or whole class for a constructive problem-solving session.

27 Trouble-Shooting Cooperative Learning

Susan Prescott Johnston

Originally published in the Cooperative Learning and College Teaching newsletter, Winter, 1994.

Dear Susan:

I want to create more cooperative activities in my classes, but I'm not always sure when to include them. Sometimes it feels like I'm simply having students work together because it's a good thing to do, and I'm not always clear on my purpose behind the groupwork.

Puzzled in Peoria

Dear Puzzled,

Your concern is an important one. As you plan your instructional program, it might be helpful to think about the needs you have as a teacher and then design cooperative activities in order to meet them. Following is a list to help you decide when to use groupwork and what the content of a task should be. As teachers we have the need to:

1. Motivate students by capturing their attention and interest before introducing a new concept or skill.

— For a variety of reasons ranging from anxiety to apathy, many students need to be helped to focus on the new material being presented. While it may be frustrating to teach students who do not share our enthusiasm for the subject matter, it is in the instructor's best interest to try to increase their desire to learn. Most learners are intrigued when attention is first focused on their personal opinions or experiences or when cognitive dissonance is created. Motivational strategies include asking students to: explain a puzzling scenario, share personal responses related to the topic, experience a visual or auditory stimulus, or guess the answers to questions that will be tried again at the end of the lesson.

2. Provide an initial concrete experience to use as a referent during lecture when explaining an abstract idea or procedure.

— Because instructors have already achieved an in-depth comprehension of the underlying concepts and principles of their discipline, it is easy to assume that explanations alone will be sufficient to transfer this understanding to students. Unfortunately these explanations often lack meaning because of their abstract nature. Students greatly appreciate any effort to first provide some kind of concrete experience that can be used to add meaning to definitions, rules, characteristics, procedures, or laws subsequently presented in lectures. Strategies include: teacher demonstration, video or audio tape, artifacts and primary resources, analyzing data, recording observations of an event, inferring the critical differences between visual examples presented in columns labeled as effective vs. ineffective (or correct vs. incorrect), and manipulating physical objects.

3. Check for understanding and active listening during explanations and demonstrations.

— As teachers we should be on a mission to reduce passive listening on the part of our students. It is our responsibility to incorporate methods that will increase the likelihood that learners are actively processing the information. The first time that students are asked to demonstrate, verbalize, or question their understanding should not be on the homework or on an exam. Active listening strategies can easily be inserted during a presentation and include having students: complete a sentence starter, find an intentional error presented on the board or overhead, think of a question that would test comprehension, generate an example, or search their notes for evidence that supports or contradicts a statement presented to the class.

4. Give students an opportunity to reflect on or practice newly presented information, concepts, or skills.

— Ideally, students should be able to consolidate their learning after important ideas have been discussed or presented. Many learners need to talk about ideas or procedures in order to integrate the new learning. Content that appeared clear during an instructor's fluid explanation can present special challenges as students begin to grapple with it on their own. These practice sessions need not be lengthy to be effective. Sessions can include: creating pro/con arguments, writing summaries, producing dialogues, analyzing data, writing a critique, explaining events, signalling agreement or disagreement with oral or written statements, or solving problems.

5. Review material prior to an exam.

— In an effort to help their students, many instructors conduct review sessions prior to exams. Typically, they will spend time presenting summaries of key ideas and functioning as the primary resource if any questions are asked. An alternative approach is to design review sessions in which students assume a much greater responsibility for their own learning. These strategies can include having students: write questions for tests, become topic experts and quiz each other, design a short review for the class, or make summaries of important information to use during the exam.

6. Cover extensive textual information efficiently.

— Many students become discouraged when asked to read unfamiliar and lengthy material all alone. It is also risky for teachers to assume that simply because students have read a text selection that they have fully comprehended its meaning. Students can be asked to effectively help each other learn from assigned readings. Section experts can present oral summaries of readings which contain answers to questions their teammates will complete.

7. Be sure that students have learned from their performance on their most recent exams or projects.

— Many teachers experience an uneasy feeling after exams or projects are returned with errors and grades noted. There is always the concern that students may never really understand the nature of the weakness in their thinking. Small group test debriefing sessions can be a wonderful solution; teammates help each member to understand more effective alternative responses. So that students demonstrate sensitivity and encouragement, instructors need to set clear expectations regarding how they are to discuss each others' errors.

This list of needs or "task functions" can now be used to provide a rationale for both the content and timing of cooperative tasks. When an instructor identifies the instructional need that has priority for the next lesson, a group activity can be designed that best functions to meet a particular purpose. The planning chart (Figure 1) provides some examples of how a teacher can connect groupwork to curriculum based on the conscious reflection of the requirements of both teacher and students. The benefit of using this chart format for planning is that it forces the correlation of groupwork with both the desired instructional function and the most essential content of the course.

A major topic from the course syllabus is entered in the first column. Topics in a syllabus can be titles of instructional units, broad fundamental concepts/principles/skills, or essential questions that form the framework of inquiry for the course. The number of times the same major topic is entered in column one is dependent on both the number of class meetings it requires and the number of different functions that groupwork can serve within that topic.

The second column focuses on a very specific learning outcome related to the major topic. Here the instructor must identify an important concept, principle, skill, or fact cluster to be explored in a single class meeting. This content decision is an important prerequisite to creating a group task, since it is difficult to plan a clear activity when the learning outcome has been only vaguely described. In column three the instructor must decide which of the instructional functions best suits the lesson in question. Will students need a group practice session to consolidate their new learning, or will some brief comprehension checks during instruction suffice? It is also possible to have several functions and tasks match up with a single column two entry, especially in classes of two to three hours duration.

The fourth column contains a description of the group activity that reflects both its predetermined content emphasis and instructional purpose. The purpose will often determine a task's length and complexity; some will demand critical and creative thinking, while others will require a simpler expression of understanding.

This systematic method is meant to help instructors feel more in control of the process of designing groupwork. Individual charts

Figure 1.

ACTIVITY PLANNING CHART

Major Topic From Syllabus	Specific Content To Be Learned	Instructional Need/Function	Cooperative Activity
mythology	critical features of a hero	motivational hook before lecture	teammates tell each other a current personal hero/heroine
origins of western classical architecture	influence of ancient Egypt on Greek classical style	provide concrete experience prior to explanation of abstract ideas	show slides of Egyptian and Greek temples and ask teams to list similarities using their own descriptive language
statistics	mean, median mode	check for understanding during lecture	show data re: school sports teams S groups compute each type of stat as it is discussed
genetics	predicting traits of offspring	opportunity to practice after lecture	give class three parent scenarios S teams chart all offspring characteristics
writing the research paper	information resources available in the library	review material prior to exam	teams create questions of article to read at home and teach in group next day
the legislative process	effects of political action committees	cover extensive background reading	team assigns sections of article to read at home and teach in group next day
forms of small business ownership	pros/cons of corporate, partnership, sole proprietor	learn from performance on exam or project	when tests are returned teams help each student understand alternative responses

can be created to focus on single syllabus topics and kept in labeled teaching files for easy access as needed. The charts also provide a structured format that facilitates sharing among department or cross-disciplinary teaching colleagues.

28 Trouble-Shooting

Susan Prescott Johnston

Originally published in the Cooperative Learning and College Teaching newsletter, Spring, 1995.

Dear Susan:

I could sure use some more ideas for group activities that can be applied to my own content area. I would like to start building a file of task options that can be tailored to fit specific concepts and skills that I cover throughout the semester.

> Signed,
> Ready in Raleigh

Dear Ready,

I would be happy to share some more ideas for groupwork that can be used to help students master the essential content of your course. An important resource is the handbook for college teachers by Thomas A. Angelo and K. Patricia Cross entitled *Classroom Assessment Techniques*, 2nd edition, Jossey-Bass Publishers San Francisco, CA, 1993. The authors have compiled a collection of fifty specific strategies designed to give instructors feedback about students' understanding, attitudes, and reactions. As teachers gain valuable information through observing their students' performance on these assessment tasks, subsequent instruction can be tailored to better meet students' needs.

Those of us committed to constructivist classrooms know that teachers also need to provide opportunities for students to consolidate understanding and to practice what they have learned through activities that require reflection and conversation about important course content. The techniques intended by Angelo and Cross as assessment tools can be adapted for use as Cooperative Learning (CL) activities that precede or follow instruction.

Section 5. Implementing Interactive Group Instruction

This article will describe four techniques that have potential for use in a wide variety of disciplines. Most of the descriptions will be direct statements from the handbook [with permission from the authors]. These quotations will be shown in italics.

1. Pro and Con Grid

Description: This technique requires students to *focus on a decision, a judgement, a dilemma, or an issue* from multiple perspectives. It provides an opportunity to engage students in a critical thinking task dependent on logical reasoning instead of a single set of obvious right answers. *For some college students, this is a difficult but valuable step in their intellectual development. The Pro and Con Grid can be put to good use in any course where questions of value are an explicit part of the syllabus,* such as . . . *humanities, social science, and public policy courses. It can also be used to focus on potential costs and benefits or alternate technical solutions to the same problem . . . in many science and mathematics courses, as well as in preprofessional and vocational training.*

Procedure:

-Focus on a decision, a judgement, a dilemma, or an issue that has teaching and learning implications in your discipline and for your students.

-Write out a prompt that will elicit thoughtful pros and cons in relation to this issue or dilemma.

-Let students know how many pros and cons you expect and how they are to be expressed. Are parallel lists of words and phrases adequate, or should the pros and cons be expressed in sentences?

Content Examples:

A. Business [Personal Financial Planning] *After reading a short case outlining the financial situation of a two-career couple, list the potential costs and benefits to these two individuals of filing their federal income taxes jointly.*

B. Biology [Issues in Bioethics] *You have read several recent articles on the current debate about patenting human genetic material. From your viewpoint as consumers, what are the principal pros and cons of allowing the patenting of genes?*

C. Political Science [U.S. Electoral Politics] *In the wake of the last federal census, the state legislature has just issued a draft plan for redistricting. Study this plan carefully, as though you were the governor's special assistant for legislative relations. Then write a short list of political costs and benefits that the governor should consider before deciding whether to support this plan.*

Cooperative Adaptation: When student teams produce a pro/con grid, their participation can be structured in a variety of ways. Partner pairs can be assigned either the pro or con category. Upon completion pairs exchange lists for feedback and revision. Final ideas are combined onto a T-chart for use during the whole class discussion. A less structured strategy might have one person record ideas as teammates brainstorm ideas for both sides of the chart. Another option includes having each individual first silently record their own ideas followed by the team working together to consolidate all ideas onto one chart.

2. Invented Dialogues

Description: *By inventing dialogues, students synthesize their knowledge of issues, personalities, and historical periods into the form of a carefully structured, illustrative conversation. There are two levels of "invention" possible with this technique. On the first level, students can create Invented Dialogues by carefully selecting and weaving together actual quotes from primary sources. On a second, more challenging, level they may invent reasonable quotes that fit the character of the speakers and the context. Invented Dialogues . . . capture the essence of people's personalities and styles of expression—as well as . . . theories, controversies, and opinions. Dialogues are particularly useful in humanities and social science courses such as history, literature, political science, philosophy, sociology, and theology. . . . Students can speculate on conversations that might have taken place between contemporar-*

ies . . . *within a given historical context. A U.S. History student might invent a dialogue between an abolitionist and a slaveholder. Or the students can juxtapose times and places, reinventing history to achieve an effect. A student in a course on political leadership might convene Alexander, Caesar, and Napoleon to discuss the difference between the leadership skills required to conquer an empire and those needed to maintain one.*

Procedure:

   -*Select one or more controversial issues, theories, decisions, or personalities that are important topics in your course and lend themselves to the dialogue format.*

   -Provide a model to serve as a guide when this activity is first introduced. *You can write a short dialogue yourself [no more than ten to twenty exchanges], or if transcripts of relevant dialogue exist, collect a few and make them available.*

   -Make an instructive handout to help students get started. *Suggest a few possible topics, give time and length guidelines, and list your criteria for a successful dialogue. Let students know how much they can invent and how much should consist of actual quotations.*

Content Examples:

   A. *Philosophy [Greek Politics]* In order to focus on the *fundamental differences between Socrates' and Aristotle's views of the individual's role in political life*, students were asked to *invent a dialogue by juxtaposing selected quotes on citizenship and political involvement from Aristotle's Politics and from any of the several Socratic dialogues they had studied.*

   B. *Fine Arts [Shakespeare on Film]* In order to focus on the *critical differences between staging Shakespeare's plays in the theater and presenting them on film, this art instructor asked students to come up with a short dialogue in which William Shakespeare and Orson Welles compared notes on their quite different "stagings" of Othello. The class had read Othello, seen a traditional theatrical staging, and seen the restored version of Welles's film.*

Cooperative Adaptation: Invented dialogues are a natural match for CL groups. The most obvious strategy for organizing students' participation is to use partner pairs to create a dialogue to be performed for the opposite pair within the team. The listeners can then be asked to give feedback as to how well each dialogue met the criteria. Standards for excellence often increase when students know in advance that their efforts will be shared with an audience [whether it is their opposite partner pair, another team, or the whole class]. Before splitting off to work in pairs, cooperative groups might need to spend a little time sharpening the main content focus that both dialogues will have in common.

3. Directed Paraphrasing

Description: *In many fields, particularly in the professions and the service sector, success depends on one's ability to translate highly specialized information into language that clients or customers will understand. . . . Students are directed to paraphrase part of a lesson for a specific audience and purpose, using their own words. . . . In fields such as marketing, social work, public health, education, law, and criminal justice, much of a students' eventual success depends on the ability to internalize specialized and often complex information and then to communicate it effectively to the public.*

Procedure:

Select an important theory, concept, or argument that students have studied in some depth. This should be a topic with some implications outside the classroom.

Direct the students to prepare a paraphrase of the chosen topic. Tell them who the intended audience is, what the purpose is, and what the limits are on speaking time or on number of words or sentences.

Content Examples:

A. *Nursing [Gerontology]* *In one or two sentences, paraphrase what you have learned about hospice care to inform a dying, but still lucid, patient of its possible advantages over hospital or home care.*

B. *Computer Systems [Database Systems]* *In plain language and in less than five minutes, paraphrase what you have read about computer viruses--such as the Michelangelo virus--for a vice president of a large insurance firm who is ultimately responsible for database security. Your aim is to convince her to spend time and money "revaccinating" thousands of workstations.*

C. *Education [Science in the Secondary Schools]* *First, in no more than two or three sentences, paraphrase the "punctuated equilibrium" theory of evolution advanced by Niles Eldredge and Stephen Jay Gould. Direct your paraphrase to a veteran science teacher who has taught the "modern synthesis" view for years and has never heard of this more recent theory. Next, write a paraphrase of the same theory but for a very different audience. Paraphrase "punctuated equilibrium" in two or three sentences for a bright seventh grader who knows a lot about dinosaurs but little about evolutionary theory.*

Cooperative Adaptation: Team members might first discuss their understanding of the assigned topic with each person contributing one idea that reflects their best thinking. Then anyone needing clarification asks for assistance from teammates. At this point, each person silently writes his own paraphrase. Once completed, each member reads his personal summary to the team. Individuals can take notes for later reflection. If time permits, the cooperative group can consolidate the four versions into one team effort for the purpose of sharing with the larger class. An alternative strategy relies on the use of partner pairs. Each pair member helps the other clarify his/her thinking until a concise and clear paraphrase is created. The paraphrase version is then presented to the other pair who act as the intended audience. Teammates then give each other feedback as to the clarity and helpfulness of each of the two Directed Paraphrase statements.

4. Applications Cards

Description: *After students have heard or read about an important principle, generalization, theory, or procedure, the instructor hands out an index card and asks them to write down at least one possible, real-world application for what they have just learned. This technique prompts students to think about possible applications and, as a consequence, to connect newly-learned concepts with prior knowledge.*

Procedure:

-Identify an important—and clearly applicable—principle, theory, generalization, or procedure that your students . . . have just studied.
-Figure out exactly how you will word the . . . prompt.
-Hand out small index cards or slips of paper.
-Remind students to come up with their own ideas, *not to repeat applications they have heard in class or read in the text.*

Content Examples:

A. *Economics [Microeconomics] Gresham's law basically states that "good money drives out bad." Give at least one contemporary application of Gresham's law to something other than money.*

B. *Statistics [Statistics for Health Professionals] After the class had studied statistical significance testing, the professor asked her students to provide three possible applications of statistical significance testing to public health issues in the news.*

C. *Psychology [Educational Psychology] Psychologists have long noted the effects of "primacy" and "recency" on recall of information. These effects have some implications for classroom teaching and learning. Suggest one or two applications of these implications for teachers using the lecture method.*

D. *Physics [Foundations of Physics] In his Principia, Sir Isaac Newton set forth . . . his Third Law, the heart of which is "To every action there is always opposed an equal reaction." Give three* *applications of Newton's Third Law to everyday life around the house.*

Cooperative Adaptation: Because it is easy to block when trying to make a connection between course content and life experience, students are more likely to generate multiple applications if allowed to help each other so that one person's association can trigger related ideas from teammates. However, in order to guarantee each student's participation within the cooperative groups, instructors might first require several minutes of quiet thinking time during which each student records any applications that come to mind. Group leaders can then conduct a roundtable sharing session asking each member for an idea followed by open brainstorming. When the recorder reads back the list of ideas, the group can select several that represent their best thinking for sharing to the larger class or for recording into their personal class notes.

Conclusion

1. When I consult with instructors across the country, I encourage them to build a collection of generic cooperative task ideas that can be scanned for a match with specific content to be taught each week. This speeds up the planning process and therefore increases the likelihood that students will have opportunities to experience interactive learning. Faculty who seem to be most efficient have developed a file system for each course. Each file is labeled with a key topic from the syllabus and contains notes, overhead transparencies, and a description of the cooperative task for use again.

2. The primary challenge prior to selecting cooperative tasks is the clear identification of essential content. Until the instructor can specify the learning outcome, a cooperative task and strategy will remain elusive and ambiguous. In workshops, teachers' first attempts at describing content will often sound like these examples: "characters in literature," "business letters," "propaganda." My response to all three is "This is a good first step, but what **about** it; what exactly do you want them to understand?" As worded here, these ideas are not yet sufficiently crystallized to design or select a

cooperative task; we don't yet know what students should do in response to "characters, business letters, or propaganda." The heart of the problem seems to be a lack of clarity about the purpose of teaching a particular topic. Some instructors fall victim to what I call the "textbook trap"--focusing on abstract content labels simply because that is how they are presented in the text or in the table of contents. Once the workshop participants were able to ascertain which aspect of the content was important because it related to the broader goals of the course, we worked to refine the content and emerged with the following:

American Literature: "A character's personality and motivation is revealed by the author through dialogue, inner thoughts, and actions."

Practical Writing: "Business letters need to state their purpose clearly and concisely in the opening paragraph."

European History: "Propaganda often exploits people's fears."

Now that the intended educational outcomes are clearly specified it becomes much easier to design original cooperative tasks or to select from techniques one through four described above.

I have found that the following procedures and CL techniques are particularly useful in the three disciplines just described.

American Literature: Invented Dialogues, Applications Cards

Practical Writing: Rewrite a badly written example of an opening paragraph.

European History: Pro/Con Grid, Applications Cards

The complaint most often mentioned by college students during groupwork is the frustration experienced when content is vague and task directions are confusing. Effective CL classrooms depend on a combination of clear content selection and activity design.

29 Peer Revision: Sharing the Power and the Work

Susan Johnston

Originally published in the Cooperative Learning and College Teaching newsletter, Winter, 1998.

Peer revision is a process by which students are asked to give each other specific and constructive feedback on assigned work. Students are provided with an excellent opportunity to review important content, engage in higher-order thinking, consolidate understanding and receive valuable feedback regarding performance. Students consistently report that they enjoy the experience and feel empowered by being trusted with the important task of providing each other with feedback; they also gain confidence in their mastery of the new content to be learned.

The revision process can be conducted in the context of learning pairs or in cooperative teams. A wide range of student work can be improved using peer revision: papers, critiques, reports, data analyses, creative writing, debate preparation, problem solutions, answers to chapter questions, and persuasive arguments. This type of cooperative activity needs to be planned after students have had sufficient time to get to know and trust each other, since some students may initially feel hesitant about exposing their work to peer review. Although the procedure requires class time that could be spent covering new material, the benefits in terms of increased learning and motivation make it an efficient use of the instructional hours available. In addition, peer revision relieves instructors of the tremendous burden of being the sole reviewer of student work.

The instructor's role in the process includes creating the initial assignment, specifying the criteria for success and preparing the students for the revision process. Steps involved in preparing the students for the revision process will be examined below in more depth using one of my classes as the focus of the discussion.

I teach in the School of Education, and this class is an Introductory Teaching Methods course for future junior and senior high school teachers. Some of the topics of the course are: principles of effective instruction, lesson design, higher-order thinking and cooperative learning. One assignment I use for peer revision is the first draft of a design for a cooperative-learning lesson plan. The actual revision session has been preceded by several class meetings in which the topic as well as the assignment was taught in depth.

Step One: Inform Students of the Benefits of Peer Revision

Because peer revision will be new to some students, the instructor needs to anticipate the natural resistance that occurs with all things unfamiliar and take a proactive stance by informing the class of the positive opportunities the process provides. I tell my students that previous participants have reported that they enjoyed the experience, learned a great deal and greatly appreciated the chance to receive help from and offer help to their teammates. I also tell them that because my work load precludes me from being able to take this assignment home in order to make personalized comments on their first drafts, peer revision will allow them to obtain valuable feedback in order to make necessary changes before turning it in for a final grade.

Step Two: Review the Criteria for Success

We also take time to review the criteria that I gave to them when introducing the assignment and that I will also use when grading it. These same criteria will be the factors that they are to keep in mind as they read each other's papers. Examples of criteria for the cooperative-learning activity include: a logical sequence of steps, a consistent curricular match between the lesson topic and the activity itself, and a clear description of the specific interactive strategies to be demonstrated by the participants.

Once they understand the complete list of criteria, I take the time to briefly present hypothetical violations of each of the crite-

Section 5. Implementing Interactive Group Instruction   233

ria. For example, with the third criterion given above [a clear description of the specific interaction strategies to be used] I would role play a scenario in which I was providing feedback for a cooperative geography activity on reading the distance scale on a map. In response to the written statement [each team works together to compute the daily vacation miles traveled using the scale on the state map] found on "my teammate's" first draft, I would point out that I didn't think that the interaction strategy for that phase of the activity had been described in sufficient detail.

Anticipating potential problems in this manner is an important step because the probability is increased that revision comments will focus on important criteria instead of trivial details. My students appreciate this guidance because it makes them feel more prepared to deal with the kinds of problems that they will be likely to encounter on their colleagues' first drafts. They also seem relieved when I assure them that they do not need to be experts in order to make a useful contribution, and although suggestions by teammates should be given careful consideration, it is not a requirement that they be incorporated into the final draft.

Step Three: Model How to Phrase the Written Comments

Although to the uninitiated this step may appear to be overkill in the "providing structure" department, it most definitely is not. I have learned to think through all aspects of complex cooperative tasks in an effort to limit the stress that results from confusion due to vague or incomplete directions.

My students do not think it is strange that we take time to discuss optional ways to phrase their written comments, so that they are perceived as concise and constructive in nature when returned to the recipient of each first draft. I model how to use a question [Do you think that your students will know what you mean when you tell them to "discuss" their vacation plans?], how to offer an alternative solution, [Perhaps having each student compute the distance for later comparison would provide better participation.] and how to make a comment starting with an "I" statement

[I'm not clear on how these two steps in the activity support the content that you are trying to teach.]. We also discuss the importance of including several compliments, adding their initials to each comment and writing in the margins with clear handwriting.

Step Four: Structure the Interaction

The purpose of this step is to pre-empt the following inevitable questions: Whose paper do we read? How many do we read? Do we get to ask each other questions? I tell the team leaders that they have several options. In order to get started, they can let team members hand their drafts to teammates, distribute them randomly, or ask them to pass their papers to the right. I ask the leaders to keep an eye on the process and make sure that each first draft receives at least two sets of comments and to limit conversations among team members to clarification of confusing language.

Once I have signaled that time is up for writing comments, teams are to move into the next phase of peer revision which involves reading the feedback written on their own first draft and then engaging in conversation with those whose initials appear next to a comment that triggers a need for further dialogue.

Closing Comments

This last phase has proven to be the most interesting; my students would extend it well over the time limit if permitted. Their conversations about each other's feedback comments are very intense and thorough, reflecting the seriousness with which they undertake this task. [One explanation might be that this lesson-plan assignment is an important part of their course grade, and they know that I will not be offering any first-draft feedback.] These post-revision conversations within teams consist of asking for clarification of the brief critiques written in the margins, explaining to the critiquers the original intents of particular entries, and the offering of specific suggestions to improve ideas.

With this assignment I schedule 1 hour and 45 minutes of a three-hour class. The preparation [steps 1- 4 described above] takes approximately 30 minutes. The actual peer revision is 45 minutes in duration. The post-revision conversations are given 30 minutes. The length of the peer-revision process will always be dependent on the nature of the assignment, the maturity of the students and their previous experiences.

The students always report during our short debriefing discussion at the end of the class that they learned a lot from seeing others' work and from experiencing their own work through others' eyes.

30 Supporting Student Success in the Classroom

Susan Johnston

Originally published in the Cooperative Learning and College Teaching newsletter, Spring, 1998.

I teach a course that is required for future secondary teachers. The focus is on "effective teaching methods." College faculty from across the country who attend my workshops tell me that they feel cheated that a similar course was never part of their professional preparation. While these faculty have advanced degrees and a high level of expertise in their own disciplines, they often learn about effective instruction through trial and error in their own classrooms. For some faculty this article about the principles of effective instruction will be an affirmation of their own classroom practices, for others some new ideas will be presented. Those in mentoring or administrative positions will receive a potential framework for helping new faculty effectively support their students' learning.

I think it is important that faculty are able to articulate how they manipulate principles of instruction, so decisions regarding teaching and learning are made beyond the intuitive level and so faculty can enter into a dialogue with colleagues on their campuses about specific strategies that can support their students' success and achievement.

Following are seven assumptions held by many college instructors. I have labeled these assumptions "deadly" because they can sometimes have a lethal effect on students' achievement, motivation, and desire to stay in school.

Seven Deadly Assumptions

1. Students will apply the content on their own after class.
2. Students don't need instruction or tasks to be structured.
3. Students learn best by hearing the expert version first.
4. Students can integrate new information by just listening well.
5. Students should do their own work during class time.
6. Students don't need much guidance from the instructor.
7. Students overcome complexity gaps between classwork and tests.

I was originally going to label these the seven deadly sins of college teaching, but I didn't feel that I had the authority to label these as official "sins." Besides, I wanted to honor the separation of church and state. I did become curious about the origin of the seven deadly sins. After consulting a professor of theology, I learned that St. Thomas Aquinas referred to them as the seven capital vices and took the list from the moral teachings of Pope St. Gregory the First. These moral teachings represent a 35-volume work that was written between 578 and 595 A.D. These particular seven sins [pride, covetousness, lust, anger, gluttony, envy, and sloth] were considered to be "capital" in nature because they so often give rise to other vices. Just as these problems seem to be universal, so are the assumptions that we make about how college students learn.

Assumption #1: Students Will Apply the Content on Their Own After Class

The assumption here is that students will understand the new information from listening in class, have sufficient confidence and motivation to work at home alone with new content, and have the ability to independently design an appropriate task that requires application-level thinking. The reality is that no learners can, or will, do this and it's not necessarily because they are lazy, have bad attitudes, or are immature.

Because of research and experiential evidence, I believe very strongly that we owe our students in-class opportunities to apply their learning to well-designed tasks, questions, or problems. When I look back on my undergraduate education, I have serious questions about the ethics of the methodology used by the majority of my instructors. The emphasis was on the expertise of the faculty instead of where it should have been—on the understanding of the learners.

I cannot recall having an opportunity during class time to consolidate what I thought I had learned. But I do recall feeling great tension and anxiety as mysterious statistical computations covered the blackboard, as philosophers were described in a barrage of metaphysical terms, as examples of subtle imagery were pointed out in a stream of endless poems, and as a myriad of chemical equations were rapidly and magically balanced on the overhead projector screen. My classmates and I would have greatly welcomed the opportunity to take some time in class to solve a few standard deviation problems ourselves, view current problems through the eyes of the philosophers being discussed, try to find examples of imagery in a new poem, or work through the balancing of several chemical equations. My teachers assumed that teaching meant telling us what they knew and then on exams many weeks later letting us tell them what we knew.

Assumption #2: Students Don't Need Instruction or Tasks to be Structured

The assumption here is that instructors of learners at the college level do not need to be overly concerned with issues of clarity. For many professors, the word "structure" has only negative connotations. However, I have yet to meet a group of college students whose motivation was not adversely affected by the following kinds of scenarios that are devoid of the kind of structure so necessary for learning: 1) instructors beginning a lecture without stopping to give a clear statement of the new content to be learned that day and a clear statement of how students would later be asked to demonstrate their understanding of that content, 2) instructors delivering an overwhelming and steady stream of information without breaking it up into meaningful chunks or categories, 3) instructors expecting students to take copious notes without providing them with some kind of visual format to organize their thoughts, 4) instructors asking students to work together on assignments in class without providing clear criteria for the finished products or clear expectations for how each student will participate, and 5) instructors assigning vague homework tasks requiring students to discuss or analyze a reading without specifying what those verbs actually mean.

I believe that students have a right to expect a clearly-structured learning environment when they pay their tuition or sign up for a class. We, of course, also have a right to expect effort from them in return. But, many of our students lack the confidence to ask us for clarification and will often cope as best they can, or drop out, rather than risk a potentially negative or uncomfortable confrontation.

Some faculty fear that providing structure is antithetical to creativity and critical thinking. Actually it is quite the contrary; my students tell me that the structure frees them to think at a high level rather than waste valuable time and energy trying to figure out what they are supposed to be learning or doing in class. Most students resent what I call "fuzzy" teaching, and they are usually powerless to change the situation, even when they like the instructor. I recall a sociology professor who tried to involve us by having us meet in groups to "discuss" the homework reading. Unfortunately those were her only directions, and what could have been a productive use of our time quickly degenerated into chaos because of her inability to clearly structure the task.

Assumption #3: Students Learn Best by Hearing the Expert Version First

This assumption requires students to assume a passive role in the learning process. Little thinking is required as they listen to the instructor present the perfectly-formed definition, conclusion, rule, attribute list, procedure, or inference. What appears on the surface to be an efficient teaching strategy is, in reality, just the opposite.

Many of our students do not learn well this way. Expert explanations are often abstract and devoid of meaning to students unfamiliar with the content. Far more effective is an inductive approach where students are led to new understandings by examining material with helpful questions posed by the teacher to guide the process. For example, when I wanted my students to learn the rule for writing lesson-plan objectives, I asked them to examine examples in our textbook and with their work partners try to infer what the different examples of objectives had in common. From these student-generated lists, they constructed a rule that now held personal and concrete meaning for them. I then gave them the "official" rule so they would have both versions in their notes. I could have first lectured on the topic and given an expert and technical explanation. They would have nodded, written down every word, and not have had a clue how to write an objective. It is important not to assume that the expert version must be the first thing that occurs. It is often most effective when it comes after students have had a chance to examine data, photographs, examples, a series of events, writing samples, or solutions to problems. This is a powerful teaching strategy because it draws in and empowers learners; students report that they feel much more connected to potentially intimidating content and learning seems to be an enjoyable process.

Assumption #4: Students Can Integrate New Information by Just Listening Well

This assumption is a dangerous one because there is often a bias on the part of some instructors that the students who are not learning are simply not good listeners. The reality is that listening is only one way to process information and those of us with different cognitive requirements will not do well when instruction is consistently delivered in only one way. I include myself here because I spent most of my undergraduate years convinced that I did not belong because there was so much that I did not understand during lectures. It was clear that many instructors did not explain abstract and complex content in a manner designed for the novice learner. It was almost as if they were delivering information to an audience who would already have to be well-grounded in their subjects. Perhaps they were unable to see their own content through the eyes of those who had never seen it before. They were too expert, too fluid, and then couldn't understand why we couldn't understand.

Much of my energy was spent desperately trying to make visual connections between the seemingly fragmented pieces of information and trying to digest what was being explained before the next big idea was presented. I think I was listening well. That wasn't the problem; the problem seemed to be that I needed to do more than just listen in order to integrate the knowledge. I needed to have brief time-outs to work with partners, or in my notes, to answer specific questions, summarize understanding, paraphrase ideas in my own words, or give a reason or evidence for a solution or conclusion.

Assumption #5: Students Should Do Their Own Work During Class Time

This assumption is grounded in the belief that collaboration is unfair and may even give the appearance that a form of cheating is being allowed in the classroom. It is important not to confuse practice time with evaluation time. We now have many studies that show increased achievement among students who are given the opportunity to work together in order to practice or reflect on new content just introduced in class. Many students actually need to think out loud and engage in active dialogue to understand and internalize new ideas or skills.

When pairs or small groups of students are assigned questions, problems, or scenarios to work on together, a safety net is automatically created. I have seen students who would never raise their hands and ask questions in a large lecture class, or even in a class of thirty, be assertive and happily ask their partners for clarification.

The important guideline here is that tasks need to be clear and well structured so that students never feel that their time is being wasted or that they are simply being asked to pool their own ignorance. When the content selected for group work is of the highest priority and needs to be mastered for future individual exams or projects, students welcome the chance to work together. Alexander Astin at UCLA completed a longitudinal study of 27,000 students at 309 four-year institutions to test which environmental factors affected students' academic and personal development. Out of 192 environmental factors studied, two were most predictive of positive change: interaction among students and interaction between faculty and students. It is not surprising then, that our social natures should be considered when planning the instructional strategies to use in our teaching.

Assumption #6: Students Don't Need Much Guidance From the Instructor

This assumption is in keeping with one version of a traditional model of the college teacher—as the fount of wisdom with little responsibility for the learning of his students. We now have evidence that a college teacher can have a powerful impact on student learning by using strategies designed to create a support system as students struggle to learn new concepts, skills, and principles. This support system is often referred to as "scaffolding" in the education literature, much in the same way construction workers use a temporary scaffold for support when building a new structure. One type of scaffolding is the use of concrete prompts. One type of prompt is a series of questions provided to serve as a note-taking guide when students listen to lectures or read texts. The series of question prompts can also be used by students when solving complex problems or preparing a piece of writing for a specific audience. These prompts often mimic what the expert does when faced with similar situations; they let the students in on the secret.

I have worked with many faculty who never directly teach how to think through a problem or question. They simply assign difficult tasks and hope that the students will somehow intuitively figure out what to do. So, a second type of scaffold is called the

Section 5. Implementing Interactive Group Instruction   243

"think-aloud." These are internal, private monologues used by an expert when faced with a problem to be solved, and are now made public for the students' benefit. Think-alouds can be used for a wide variety of content: planning a persuasive argument, interpreting data, detecting political bias in an editorial, setting up a mathematical equation to match a business scenario, creating a fitness plan, etc. They should certainly be used to teach students how to answer typical essay questions that contain words like "discuss, compare, describe, or analyze."

A third type of scaffold is to provide models or demonstrations of final products or procedures. One instructor I know was terribly frustrated by her students inability to include evidence to support opinions in their persuasive writing papers. I asked her if she had taken the time to show them models of a persuasive piece that cited evidence effectively and ones that did not. She looked at me blankly; it had never occurred to her. I think that she believed in her heart that college students shouldn't need that kind of guidance. However, since persuasive writing was a topic on her syllabus, a safe assumption could be made that she did not expect her students to enter class already knowing this skill. Therefore she had an obligation to explicitly teach them how to use evidence, not just assign the paper requiring it and then blame her students for not mastering that skill.

Another type of scaffold is "partially completed examples." This method is powerful because students experience success during the initial stages of mastering new content. For example, a bar graph can be given with the x- and y-axis already labeled; students are left with the task of labeling the individual fields and filling in the bars to match the data. For the next practice session, they might be given a blank graph with no scaffolding help provided.

Assumption #7: Students Can Overcome Complexity Gaps Between Classwork and Tests

This assumption minimizes the negative impact of test questions that shock the student because the level of difficulty appears to be so different from the way the content was treated in class. Instructors assume that students should be able to make the leap to complex analysis of content after simply being exposed to that information in class. These same instructors would never claim that their goal is to deliberately trick the students or to use tests as a sorting mechanism; but sometimes it must appear so to the students.

There needs to be congruence between the kind of thinking required during lessons and the level of thinking required during evaluative assessment. The following testing tasks would need parallel prior experiences: critiquing the logic of an argument, formulating data into a visual graph, comparing two short stories, conducting a nutritional analysis, etc. I am not making an argument for teaching to the test; I am making a case for testing what we teach. Using tests with questions that require higher-order thinking is an admirable teaching practice, but so is teaching to higher-order thinking by providing models, think-alouds, and collaborative practice tasks in class.

Closing Thoughts

Developing expertise in the ability to teach effectively is an ongoing and challenging process. Rather than being discouraged by that fact, I think that is precisely what makes the field of education so rewarding, stimulating, and fascinating for us. In keeping with our initial discussion of Saint Gregory's seven deadly sins, I would like to close with a poem from an unknown author who reminds us that we are all works in progress:

"I dreamt of heaven the other night
and the pearly gates swung wide
an angel with halo bright
ushered me inside,
And there to my astonishment
stood folks I'd judged and labeled
as quite unfit, of little worth
and spiritually disabled.
Indignant words rose to my lips

but never were set free
for every face showed stunned surprise
not one expected me!!"

[This article is adapted from a keynote address delivered by Susan Johnston, April 1998 in Monterey at the National Conference on Teaching and Learning Diversity.]

Part II
What the Experts Are Thinking

For this part of the book we asked a number of leading researchers and practitioners in group learning to address issues that they found to be of interest as they examined the area of small group instruction. Their responses were varied, ranging from the Johnson brothers sweeping piece on the future of higher education to very applied works, such as Barbara Millis' chapter on using games as instructional procedures to foster deep learning.

In the first chapter written expressly for this book, David and Roger Johnson focus on higher education in the 21st century. They reflect on their 35 years of experience in education and report that a high quality college experience is based on the *Three Cs*: cooperative community, constructive conflict resolution and civic values. Cooperative community implies building learning communities based on cooperative learning principles, in which learners develop a sense of positive interdependence, a sense that they *are* their brothers' or sisters' keepers. Constructive conflict resolution implies using conflict as an opportunity for growth and transformation, rather than an unpleasant, anxiety producing experience to be avoided. Civic values implies that our colleges need to focus on preparing students to become local and even global citizens, ready to function in a diverse, technology based world.

The Johnsons' interest in civic values is further developed by Jim Mitchell in his chapter on service learning. Service learning, in which university course work is closely linked to students' engagement in the larger community, is at the top of the agenda for many interested in shaping the higher education curriculum for the future. Jim identifies a number of types of service learning and explains how cooperative learning is a natural ally of service learning. The power of reflection in making both cooperative and service learning achieve their greatest impacts on students, is a focal point of his chapter.

The third chapter in this portion of the book is a survey of leading figures in higher education who share an interest in teaching and learning. The editors of this book surveyed these leaders to get their take on where we have been and where we should be going with respect to group learning in higher education. These experts also offer advice to those who are relatively new to group learning and who wish to learn more about this powerful pedagogy.

The fourth chapter in this volume, written by Spencer Kagan, picks up on one issue addressed in the survey described above, the research and theory base for group learning. Spencer describes the recent findings in brain research. He outlines a number of active and group learning procedures that he created and identifies how these procedures are consistent with what we know about how the brain functions. The reader will not only find out about this fascinating research base but will also find out about some of Spencer's recent cooperative learning strategies.

The next three chapters focus on practical group learning procedures. In Chapter 5, Mark Maier identifies how surveys and other student-generated information can be used cooperatively to make group learning more relevant. He describes applications of group learning to a wide range of content areas, from poetry to his own discipline of economics.

In Chapter 6, Barbara Millis describes how cooperative games may be used to engage students for the serious purpose of fostering critical thinking and a number of other cognitive and affective student outcomes. Barbara sets her chapter within the context of the *Seven Principles for Good Practice in Undergraduate Instruction*, a landmark 1987 work by Arthur Chickering and Zelda Gamson.

Chapter 7 is by Jim, Pamela and David and describes the Interactive Lecture. The Interactive Lecture is a lecture in which active and group learning exercises are embedded at frequent intervals in order to foster deeper processing of content. The authors assert that it promises significant impact on student thinking and is a relatively low-risk procedure which may be used by most faculty, including those uncomfortable with more formal group learning procedures. As they note, this chapter is heavily influenced by Susan Prescott Johnston.

It is fitting that the last chapter in this volume be written by Contributing Editor Susan Prescott Johnston. For nine years she contributed many articles to the newsletter and served as a beacon of thoughtful and sensible advice to our readers interested in applications of active and group learning in the college classroom. According to Susan, what is ultimately important if we want to teach our students, no matter the pedagogy, is *clarity*.

We hope that clear thinking about research and practice in college teaching is a characteristic feature of the nine years that Jim and Pamela edited the *Cooperative Learning and College Teaching* newsletter. We hope that some of that clear thinking is demonstrated in this volume.

The 21st Century College: The Three Cs

David W. Johnson and Roger T. Johnson

The Three Cs

For over thirty-five years we have been conducting a program of theory, research, and practice focused on creating a high quality college experience for students. A high quality college experience is built on the *Three Cs*: Cooperative community, constructive conflict resolution, and civic values. The college or university is a cooperative system in which faculty, staff, students, and other stakeholders work together to achieve mutual goals concerning quality education. Doing so creates conflicts over how best to achieve goals and coordinate actions. Such conflicts have to be resolved constructively if the community is to survive. Both cooperative community and constructive conflict resolution are based on civic values that recognize and support the long-term benefits of working together to achieve mutual goals.

The First C: Cooperative Community

A high quality college or university experience begins with establishing a learning community based on cooperation (i.e., working together to achieve mutual goals). A community is a group of people who live in the same locality and share common goals and a common culture. The heart of community is social interdependence, which exists when each individual's outcomes are affected by the actions of others (Deutsch, 1962; Johnson & Johnson, 1989). Social interdependence may be positive (cooperation), negative (competition), or absent (individualistic efforts). The type of interdependence structured among individuals determines how they interact with each other, which in turn largely determines outcomes. Structuring situations cooperatively results in individuals promoting each other's success;, structuring situations competitively results in individuals opposing each other's success; and structuring situations individualistically results in no interaction among individuals. According to Johnson & Johnson (1989), these interaction patterns affect numerous variables, which may be subsumed within the three broad and interrelated outcomes of:

1. Effort exerted to achieve (higher achievement and greater productivity, more frequent use of higher-level reasoning, more frequent generation of new ideas and solutions, greater intrinsic and achievement motivation, greater long-term retention, more on-task behavior, and greater transfer of what is learned from one situation to another).
2. Quality of relationships among participants (greater interpersonal attraction, liking, cohesion and esprit de corps, valuing of heterogeneity, and greater task-oriented and personal support).
3. Psychological adjustment (greater psychological health, greater social competency, higher self-esteem, shared identity, and greater ability to cope with stress and adversity).

These outcomes result only when cooperation is effectively implemented. Effective cooperation requires that five basic elements be carefully structured into the situation (Johnson & Johnson, 1989; Johnson, Johnson, & Smith, 1998). First, there must be a strong sense of positive interdependence, so individuals believe they are linked with others and cannot succeed unless the others do (and vice versa). Positive interdependence may be structured through mutual goals, joint rewards, divided resources, complementary roles, and a shared identity. Second, each collaborator must be individually accountable to do his or her fair share of the work. Third, collaborators must have the opportunity to promote each other's success by helping, assisting, supporting, encouraging, and praising each other's efforts to achieve. Fourth, working together cooperatively requires interpersonal and small group skills, such as leadership, decision-making, trust-building, communication, and conflict-management skills. Finally, cooperative groups must engage in group processing, discussing how well they are: a) achieving their goals, and b) maintaining effective working relationships.

To create a learning community, positive interdependence must be structured in relations: a) within the classroom, b) between the college and its larger community, c) between students and parents, and d) between members of the college community including students, faculty and administrators.

Cooperative Learning

The cooperative community begins with cooperative learning. Cooperative learning is the instructional use of small groups so that students work together to maximize their own and each others' learning (Johnson, Johnson, & Smith, 1998). According to Johnson & Johnson (1989), there are three types of cooperative learning. Formal cooperative learning consists of students working together, for one class period to several weeks, to jointly complete specific assignments, lessons, projects, and instructional units. In formal cooperative learning groups, instructors: a) make a number of preinstructional decisions such as specifying academic and social skills objectives, and deciding on size and composition of groups; b) explain the task and the positive interdependence; c) monitor students' learning and intervene within the groups to provide task assistance or to increase students' interpersonal and group skills; and d) assess students' learning and help them process how well their groups functioned.

Informal cooperative learning consists of having students work together to achieve a joint learning goal in temporary, adhoc groups that last from a few minutes to one class period. Informal cooperative learning groups are often organized so students engage in three-to-five minute focused discussions before and after a direct teaching session, and two-to-three minute turn-to-your-partner discussions interspersed throughout a lecture. Cooperative base groups are long-term, heterogeneous learning groups with stable membership that give the support, help, encouragement, and assistance each member needs to make academic progress and develop cognitively and socially in healthy ways. Base groups often meet at the beginning and ending of a class session or week.

Other Levels of Positive Interdependence

In the 21st Century it will be important to carefully structure positive interdependence at all levels of college life. Lip service to a learning community will no longer be sufficient. To "walk the talk" about learning communities, colleges and universities will have to structure positive interdependence at all levels of the college experience (Johnson & Johnson, 1989; Johnson, Johnson, & Smith, 1998). Class, departmental, college, and university cooperative goals may be established, such as: a) academic criteria for students, departments, and colleges to reach; b) academic improvement goals for each student, class, department, and college; c) rewards or celebrations when benchmarks are reached; d) clearer involvement in student governance and campus activities for each student; e) greater student responsibility for campus maintenance and upkeep; and f) greater communal responsibility and interaction within campus housing. A growing trend in colleges and universities is the use of cohorts. To maximize the effectiveness of a cohort of students, positive interdependence has to be carefully structured in their classes and other activities. In addition, a common college identity should be nurtured.

The Second C: Constructive Conflict Resolution

Conflict is the moment of truth in which the community is either strengthened or weakened. A conflict is constructive when all parties are satisfied with the outcomes, the relationship among the parties has been improved (or at least not damaged), and the participants' ability to resolve conflicts in the future has increased. Constructively managing conflicts depends largely on: a) disputants having clear procedures for managing conflicts, b) disputants being skilled in the use of the procedures, and c) the norms and values of the community encouraging and supporting the use of such procedures. The three essential procedures for constructively managing conflict are: academic controversy, problem-solving negotiation, and peer mediation (Johnson & Johnson, 1995a, 1995b). These procedures need to be taught to all members of the learning community, used frequently enough so that members become skilled in their use, and institutionalized within the ebb-and-flow of daily life within the community.

Constructive Controversy

An important aspect of college life is challenging others' conclusions and reasoning, and responding with curiosity and open-mindedness when one's own conclusions and reasoning are challenged. The procedure for doing so is Constructive Controversy (Johnson & Johnson, 1979, 1989, 1995b) which exists when one person's ideas, opinions, information, theories, or conclusions are incompatible with those of another and the two seek to reach an agreement. For example, students are randomly assigned to heterogeneous cooperative learning groups of four members. The groups are given an issue on which to write a report and pass a test. Each cooperative group is divided into two pairs. One pair is given the con-position on the issue and the other pair is given the pro-position. The cooperative goals of reaching a consensus on the issue (by synthesizing the best reasoning from both sides), writing a quality group report, and ensuring all members pass the test are highlighted. In Constructive Controversy, students: a) research, learn, and prepare their positions; b) present and advocate their positions to the opposing pairs; c) engage in an open discussion in which there is spirited disagreement in which they continue to advocate their positions, attempt to refute the others' positions, and rebut opposing pairs' attempts to refute their positions; d) reverse perspectives and present the best case possible for the opposing positions; and e) create a synthesis or integration of both sides on which all team members can agree.

Such intellectual "disputed passages" create higher achievement, longer retention, more frequent use of higher-level reasoning and metacognitive thought, more critical thinking, greater creativity, and continuing motivation to learn (Johnson & Johnson, 1979, 1989, 1995b). In addition, more positive interpersonal relationships develop and participants' self-esteem and liking for the experience improves. Learning how to engage in critical analysis and higher-level reasoning are important skills for living in the 21st century.

The controversy procedure is a primary means for doing so.

One of the responsibilities of U.S. colleges and universities is to prepare students to be participating citizens in a democracy (Johnson & Johnson, 2000a). This involves ensuring that students develop a commitment to democracy and a belief that they have a moral bond with fellow citizens to engage in political discourse to enhance the common good and shape the destiny of the society. There is evidence, however, of a growing political and civic passivity and detachment among college students. Political participation in the United States has been declining. One of the reasons given for this passivity is the lack of knowledge of how to engage in polite, constructive arguments. Many students seem to see intellectual disagreements as being laced with rage, profanity, cruelty, put-downs, and violence; opponents are not only wrong, but "bad." Consequently, instead of engaging in spirited arguments about today's great topics, many students withdraw from such discussions. Apathy and cynicism about political processes have increased, more and more citizens have come to believe that politicians' self-interests eclipse their public interest, and apathy and ignorance have grown about the issues decided in elections. For many students, materialist aspirations have become stronger than commitment to the welfare of society. Ironically, this withdrawal from intellectual and political discourse and civic responsibility has taken place while democratic forms of government have been spreading throughout the world where there is growing excitement about, and faith in, democracy.

Our democracy and societal well-being depend on the renewing energy of young people who have the commitment and vision to help create a better world. When political elections and decisions are characterized by misleading statements, image management, and ad hominem arguments, children, adolescents, and young adults may not learn how to engage in political discourse and may develop negative attitudes toward participating in the political process.

Conflict Resolution Training

Conflicts of interest arise between roommates, among study group members, between students and faculty, and in many other social settings. The quality of college life depends largely on how such conflicts are resolved. Students need to be taught how to resolve conflicts constructively by engaging in problem-solving negotiations and peer mediation (Johnson & Johnson, 1995a, 1996).

There are two types of negotiations: distributive or "win-lose" (where one person benefits only if the opponent agrees to make a concession) and integrative or problem solving (where disputants work together to create an agreement that benefits everyone involved). In ongoing relationships within a community, distributive negotiations result in destructive outcomes and integrative negotiations lead to constructive outcomes. Teaching students how to engage in integrative negotiations and peer mediation is the focus in the Peacemaker Program (Johnson & Johnson, 1995a). The steps in using problem solving negotiations are: a) describing what you want; b) describing how you feel; c) describing the reasons for your wants and feelings; d) taking the other's perspective and summarizing your understanding of what the other person wants, how the other person feels, and the reasons underlying both; e) inventing three optional plans that maximize joint benefits to resolve a conflict; and f) choosing one and formalizing the agreement with a hand shake. According to Johnson & Johnson (1995a), mediation consists of four steps: a) ending hostilities, b) ensuring disputants are committed to the mediation process, c) helping disputants successfully negotiate with each other, and d) formalizing the agreement. Ideally, the role of mediator is rotated so that all students serve as mediators equal amounts of time.

The research on the Peacemaker Program (Johnson & Johnson, 2000b) indicates that students and faculty quickly learn the negotiation and mediation procedures, retain their knowledge throughout the school year and into the following year, apply the procedures in conflicts, transfer the procedures to nonclassroom and nonschool settings, engage (when given the option) in problem-solving rather than win-lose negotiations, and develop more positive attitudes toward conflict. When integrated into academic units, the Peacemaker Program increases academic achievement and long-term retention of the academic material. Academic units, especially in subject areas such as literature and history, provide a setting to understand conflicts, practice how to resolve them, and use them to gain insight into the material being studied.

Cooperation and Conflict

It should be noted that conflicts cannot be resolved constructively when they occur in competitive and individualistic conditions. In a competitive context, individuals strive to win rather than solve the problem. In an individualistic context, people tend to care only about their own interests and ignore the interests of others. It is only in a cooperative context that conflicts are resolved constructively.

The Third C: Civic Values

For a community to exist and sustain itself, members must share common goals and values aimed at increasing the quality of life within the community (Johnson & Johnson, 1999a). A learning community cannot exist in schools dominated by competition or individualistic efforts. Rather, students need to internalize values in situations dominated by cooperation, controversy, and integrative negotiations (Johnson & Johnson, 1996b, 1999b). Whenever students engage in competitive efforts, for example, they learn such values as: a) life is about being smarter, faster, stronger, more competent, and more successful than others; and b) what is important is beating and defeating others, not mastery or excellence. The values implicitly taught by individualistic experiences are: a) life is about maximizing self-interest, and b) the pleasure of succeeding is personal and relevant to only oneself. Whenever students engage in cooperative efforts they learn such values as commitment to the common good and to the well being of other students, a sense of responsibility to contribute one's fair share of the work, respect for the efforts of others, behaving with integrity, caring for other people, compassion when others are in need, commitment to equal rights and social justice, and appreciation of diversity. When students engage in constructive controversies they learn to appreciate different points of view and are able to test their conclusions and reasoning through intellectual challenge. The values inherent in integrative negotiations and mediation include being committed to the other's well-being as well as to one's own, being honest and accurate in describing one's position and interests, seeking to maximize joint outcomes, and being responsive and compassionate when others are in need.

Positive Interdependence in College Life

Carefully structuring positive interdependence into all aspects of college and university life is especially important to deal with a series of critical issues that are facing colleges and universities in the 21st century.

Social and Academic Integration

The social and academic integration of students will remian two important issues for colleges and universities. Doing so largely depends on involving them in cooperative experiences on academic and campus issues, ensuring conflicts are managed constructively, and building a set of values that unites all members of the campus community. Attrition, based on alienation and lack of integration into academic and social aspects of school, will continue to be a major concern for colleges and universities. All the *Three Cs* are helpful in increasing retention and graduation rates. Social and academic integration, however, may especially benefit from: a) personalizing large classes through the use of informal cooperative learning, b) increasing the depth of relationships through the use of cooperative base groups, c) promoting networking and relationships through the use of formal cooperative learning, d) demonstrating the value of diversity through engaging students in academic controversies, and e) enhancing the quality of relationships through training in how to resolve conflicts constructively.

Remediation and Preparatory Courses

As more and more individuals seek higher education, there will be more and more need for remediation and preparatory courses. Since traditional lecture and whole class discussion methods have failed with these students in the past, there will be a greater need for cooperative learning.

Changes in Instructional Methods

The use of instructional procedures such as problem-based, inquiry, and case-based learning will increase. They require formal cooperative learning strategies. As other instructional innovations are implemented, formal cooperative learning will probably be an essential ingredient.

Diversity of Student Population

More and more people all over the world will seek a college education. The ease of transportation will enable them to attend colleges anywhere in the world, including the United States. More and more minority and foreign students will be attending colleges and universities in the United States. In addition, more and more students may commute, live off campus, be older, and attend part-time. As student diversity increases, it becomes increasingly important that instructional methods promote positive interactions among these students. One of the major benefits of cooperation is that it builds positive relationships among diverse individuals. In addition, having diverse friends increases a wide variety of other important outcomes of college, such as sophistication, global orientation, ability to view issues from a variety of perspectives, less prejudice and stereotyping, and more open-mindedness.

Technology and Face-to-Face Interaction

The technology revolution will change the nature of many parts of education. Electronic communication, for example, is growing exponentially. Online universities are now competing with traditional universities, and this trend will continue to grow. Within traditional colleges and universities, courses will increasingly be offered online as well as face-to-face. Telephones, video-conferencing, e-mail, chat rooms, and other technological innovations, however, all share a similar problem—they tend not to produce intense human relationships. In the competition for students, traditional universities and face-to-face classes will have one major advantage—face-to-face interaction can produce intense human relationships. This intensity, however, can be positive or negative. If the climate of traditional universities is competitive and individualistic, what face-to-face interaction that takes place may push students towards electronic universities. If the traditional university creates a learning community in which cooperative relationships dominate both in and outside of class, then intense positive relationships will tend to develop. Business and industry, for example, are increasingly recognizing the advantages of face-to-face relationships. Pfizer Incorporated (a pharmaceutical company) recently built a new research facility that organizes scientists in "families" of five to seven members and each family has its own open conference area called a "huddle zone." The families are grouped into "tribes" of 70. This program is expected to result in a 10 percent increase in productivity. Colleges and universities also need to capitalize on the power of cooperation.

Interpersonal and Small Group Skills

As technology, mobility, and other aspects of life that make relationships more impersonal and transitory increase, the need for interpersonal and small group skills will increase. The catch-phrase, "high tech, high touch," will become more and more relevant. College and university life, therefore, will increasingly emphasize interpersonal and small group skills. Cooperative learning and conflict training are essential in the development of these skills.

Student Incivility and Violence

During the 21st Century overall changes in society will be reflected in the behavior of college and university students. One trend is increased violence among students. While infrequent, the possibility of students planning a Columbine-style attack or violence against specific faculty members may increase in the next few years. At the very least, incivility among students and between students and professors may increase. Some incivility, such as being uninterested or disengaged in class, may be minor. Other forms of incivility, such as disrespectful, disruptive, and defiant behavior in class can be major problems for faculty. Bullying and scapegoating among students, which seems to be increasing in elementary and secondary schools, could increase dramatically on campuses. Faculty and students have largely been left to find their own solutions in addressing incivility, but as incivility increases more "whole campus" approaches will be sought. Problems with violence and incivility may be prevented and treated by involving students in cooperative (as opposed to competitive and individualistic) experiences, teaching all students and faculty how to resolve conflicts constructively, having peer mediators available, and inculcating civic values. When students work together cooperatively, for example, positive relationships are formed, social support results, and group members tend to intervene to stop someone from bullying a group member. Mastering the integrative negotiation and peer mediation procedures described earlier tends to provide a way to deal with conflicts when they first begin and to establish guidelines about acceptable and unacceptable behavior in conflict situations. The values underlying cooperation and constructive conflict resolution tend to prevent bullying from taking place.

The Most Important Outcomes of a College Education
While colleges and universities do need to be training grounds for careers, increasingly in the 21st Century the emphasis will shift toward more important outcomes of higher education. Those outcomes include increased ability to see issues from a variety of perspectives, decreased stereotyping and prejudice, increased valuing of diversity, greater sophistication and cosmopolitanism, greater global orientation, increased ability to work in teams and resolve conflicts constructively (especially with diverse groups), greater civic virtue and commitment to contribute to the common good, and increased ability to work effectively in a variety of cultures and countries. These outcomes and the achievement gains noted earlier directly result from the *Three Cs*.

Future Issues

Conceptual vs. Direct Methods

Cooperative learning procedures may be placed on a continuum from *direct* to *conceptual*. Many direct cooperative learning procedures consist of very specific and well-defined techniques that instructors can learn in a few minutes and apply immediately. Some instructors use direct procedures in a lock-step way that is the same in all situations. Many conceptual cooperative learning procedures consist of conceptual frameworks instructors use as templates to create cooperative lessons and activities to fit their specific circumstances. The conceptual end of the continuum is represented by the view of cooperative learning and conflict resolution presented in this chapter (Johnson & Johnson, 1989, 1995a, 1995b; Johnson, Johnson, & Smith, 1998). Direct methods tend to be easy to learn and require less training time, tend to be easily implemented, are often focused on specific subject areas and academic levels, are easy to discontinue as interest wanes, and are not easily adapted to changing conditions. Conceptual methods tend to be difficult to learn and use initially, may be used in any lesson and in any subject area for any level of student, and become internalized and routinely used and thus difficult to discontinue, and are highly adaptable to changing conditions. Once they are mastered, they may be integrated into instructors' teaching repertoires and used throughout their careers.

The exact changes that will take place in instruction in colleges and universities are unclear. We can predict greater use of cohorts and increasing emphasis on learning communities. But we can also predict greater use of online support for classes. What is clear is that to be effective, cooperative (and conflict resolution) procedures will need to meet two criteria:
1. Fidelity: Each cooperative experience will have to be structured to contain the five basic elements.
2. Flexibility: Each cooperative experience will have to be structured specifically to take into account the characteristics of the students and the circumstances within which the experience is taking place.

What we do know about college and university life in the 21st Century is that the nature of students will change, the needs of society and the world will change, and the ways in which cooperative learning will be used will change. Thus, in the long run, it is important that faculty internalize conceptual frameworks that allow them to create cooperative situations with fidelity and flexibility as they adapt to changes in college and university life and as the nature of the student body, the curriculum, the courses, the technology, and other aspects of higher education change.

Practice Based on Theory Validated by Research

The future of cooperative learning and constructive conflict resolution depends on advances in social interdependence theory and continued research on the variables that mediate the effectiveness of cooperative and competitive efforts. The results of such theorizing and research will need to be operationalized into revised cooperative learning procedures. The implementation of the revised procedures should lead to new insights that require modification in the theory and new research. This cycle, which has contributed so much to Johnson and Johnson's work in the last half of the 20th Century, should continue indefinitely through the 21st Century.

Appropriate Use of Competition

While the emphasis of the past several decades has primarily been on implementing cooperative learning, there has been a steady examination of the conditions under which competition may be effective (Johnson & Johnson, 1978, 1989, 1999a; Stanne, Johnson, & Johnson, 1999). Following the specified conditions, the use of constructive competition may increasingly supplement the use of cooperative learning in future college and university classes as a "change of pace."

Summary

In order to create and maintain an effective learning community and to maximize the effectiveness of higher education, colleges and universities need to: a) structure cooperative experiences in courses and throughout campus life, b) emphasize academic controversy in courses, c) ensure all students and staff are skilled in resolving conflicts constructively, and d) promote civic values and active citizen participation. Doing so will help institutions of higher education face the challenges of increasing social and academic integration of students, provide effective remedial and preparatory courses for under/prepared students, and adapt to changes in instructional procedures. Implementing the *Three Cs* will ensure increased diversity among students as a valued resource rather than a problem, create the personal relationships that cannot be found through technology, and improve students' interpersonal and small group skills. The *Three Cs* will maximize such important outcomes as becoming more globally sophisticated, more committed to being an active citizen in a democracy, and more committed to contributing to the well-being of the world. Future issues facing the *Three Cs* include the need to: a) maintain the fidelity of implementation of cooperative learning and constructive conflict training while adapting procedures to changing students and circumstances; b) maintain the cycle of theorizing, validating research, operationalizing results into practical procedures, implementing the procedures, and revising the theory; and c) integrate the use of some appropriate competition into a predominantly cooperative instructional program.

This chapter represents an optimistic vision for the future of cooperation and constructive conflict in higher education. It should be clear that cooperative learning and constructive conflict resolution will not go away. They are based on theory, confirmed by large bodies of research, operationalized in a variety of procedures, and widely implemented. The theory becomes more refined and the research evidence grows stronger each year. New applications are being identified and widely implemented. College and university life in the 21st Century will increasingly be based on the *Three Cs*.

References

Deutsch, M. (1962). Cooperation and trust: Some theoretical notes. In M. Jones (Ed.), *Nebraska symposium on motivation* (pp. 275-319). Lincoln, NE: University of Nebraska Press.

Johnson, D. W., & Johnson, R. (1978). Social interdependence within instruction. *Journal of Research and Development in Education, 12*(1), 3-15.

Johnson, D. W., & Johnson, R. (1979). Conflict in the classroom: Controversy and learning. *Review of Educational Research, 49*, 51-61.

Johnson, D. W., & Johnson, R. (1989). *Cooperation and competition: Theory and research*. Edina, MN: Interaction Book Company.

Johnson, D. W., & Johnson, R. (1995a). *Teaching students to be peacemakers* (3rd ed.). Edina, MN: Interaction Book Company.

Johnson, D. W., & Johnson, R. (1995b). *Creative controversy: Intellectual challenge in the classroom* (3rd. ed.). Edina, MN: Interaction Book Company.

Johnson, D. W., & Johnson, R. (1996). Cooperative learning and traditional American values. *NASSP Bulletin, 80*(579), 11-18.

Johnson, D. W., & Johnson, R. (1999a). *Learning together and alone: Cooperative, competitive, and individualistic learning* (5th. ed.). Boston: Allyn & Bacon (1st ed. 1975).

Johnson, D. W., & Johnson, R. (1999b). Cooperative learning, values, and culturally plural classrooms. In Leicester, M., Modgill, C., & Modgill,

S. (Eds.), *Values, the Classroom, and Cultural Diversity.* London: Cassell PLC.

Johnson, D. W., & Johnson, R. (2000a). Civil political discourse in a democracy: The contribution of psychology. *Peace and Conflict: Journal of Peace Psychology, 6*(4), 291- 317.

Johnson, D. W., & Johnson, R. (2000b, June). *Teaching Students To Be Peacemakers: Results of Twelve Years Of Research.* Paper presented at the Society for the Psychological Study of Social Issues Convention. Minneapolis, MN. Submitted for publication.

Johnson, D. W., Johnson, R., & Smith, K. (1998). *Active learning: Cooperation in the college classroom* (2nd ed.). Edina, MN: Interaction Book Company.

Stanne, M., Johnson, D. W., & Johnson, R. (1999). Does competition enhance or inhibit motor performance: A meta-analysis. *Psychological Bulletin, 125*(1), 133-154.

Cooperative Learning and Service Learning: Soul-mates for Reflection in Higher Education

James Mitchell

> *"All genuine education comes through experience."*
> John Dewey (1997)

Imagine a world in which all teaching was based on the development of citizenship skills through direct experience, one in which students were actively engaged by how their learning activities were structured and where those activities took place. Cooperative learning and service learning foster such citizenship-skill development through direct experience and active engagement. Both learning approaches possess common elements such as caring for others and understanding that true success means "success for all." The one component of each that is most easily identifiable and measurable is the element of reflection.

The Need for Citizenship and School-to-Career Skills Development

Oxfam International is a confederation of 12 non-governmental organizations working together in more than 80 countries to find lasting solutions to poverty, suffering and injustice.

According to Oxfam, effective Global Citizens:
- are aware of the wider world and have a sense of their roles as world citizens,
- respect and value diversity, and
- are willing to act to make the world a more equitable and sustainable place.

The key elements for developing responsible Global Citizenship are identified as: 1) knowledge and understanding, 2) skills, and 3) values and attitudes.

These key elements for responsible Global Citizenship are broken down as follows:

Knowledge and understanding
- Social justice and equity
- Diversity
- Globalization and interdependence
- Sustainable development
- Peace and conflict

Skills
- Critical thinking
- Ability to argue effectively
- Ability to challenge injustice and inequalities
- Respect for people and things
- Cooperation and conflict resolution

Values and attitudes
- Sense of identity and self-esteem
- Empathy
- Commitment to social justice and equity
- Value and respect for diversity
- Concern for the environment and commitment to sustainable development
- Belief that people can make a difference

(Oxfam, n.d.)

Both cooperative learning and service learning promote the development of these global citizenship skills. Likewise, both are very school-to-career oriented. The U.S. Department of Labor (2002) reports that employers look for the following:

1. Learning-to-learn abilities;
2. Listening and communication skills;

3. Adaptability: creative thinking, and problem solving, especially in response to barriers/obstacles;
4. Personal management: self-esteem, goal-setting/self-motivation, personal career development/goals, and pride in work accomplished;
5. Group effectiveness: interpersonal skills, negotiation, and teamwork; and
6. Organizational effectiveness and leadership: making a contribution.

Cooperative learning is well known for its focus on development of citizenship and school-to-career skills, such as listening and communication, critical thinking, ability to argue effectively, advocating respectfully, group effectiveness and making an effective contribution when part of a group. Cooperative learning has many forms and definitions, but most cooperative approaches involve small, heterogeneous teams, usually of four or five members, working together on a group task in which each member is individually accountable for part of an outcome that cannot be completed unless the members work together; in other words, the group members are positively interdependent. For cooperative groups to be effective, members should engage in teambuilding activities and other tasks that deal explicitly with the development of social skills needed for effective teamwork (Johnson & Johnson, 1995).

Over the past several years, cooperative learning has emerged as a viable and popular approach to classroom instruction. One important reason for this is that numerous research studies in K-12 classrooms, in very diverse school settings and across a wide range of content areas, have revealed that students completing cooperative learning group tasks tend to have higher academic test scores, higher self-esteem, greater numbers of positive social skills, fewer stereotypes of individuals of other races or ethnic groups, and greater comprehension of the content and skills that they are studying (Johnson, Johnson, & Holubec, 1993; Slavin, 1991; Stahl & VanSickle, 1992). Furthermore, the perspective of students working as academic loners in classrooms is very different from that of students working collaboratively in cooperative learning academic teams (Stahl & VanSickle, 1992). This emphasis on academic learning success for all members of the group is one feature that separates cooperative learning groups from other group tasks (Slavin, 1991).

The element of cooperative learning most clearly identified as reflective is that of *group processing*. Group members participate in processing activities in which they discuss the interpersonal skills that influence their effectiveness in working together. In truly cooperative groups, students spend time after the cooperative group tasks have been completed to systematically reflect upon how they worked together as teams. Discussion is usually related to the following areas: how well they achieved their group goals, how they helped each other comprehend the content, resources, and task procedures, how they used positive behaviors and attitudes to enable team members to be successful, and what they need to do next time to make their groups even more successful (Johnson & Johnson, 1995).

Service learning is another approach to classroom instruction that provides many citizenship and school-to-career skills development opportunities. Service learning has a positive effect on students' personal development, such as sense of personal efficacy, personal identity, spiritual growth, and moral development (Eyler, Giles, & Gray, 1999). The philosophical antecedent and academic parent of service learning is experiential learning. As in all types of experiential learning, such as cooperative education, internships, and field placements, service learning directly engages the learner in the phenomena being studied with the hope that richer learning will result. The distinguishing characteristic of service learning is its two-fold emphasis on both enriching learning and revitalizing the community. It is often confused with volunteering and internship, but is distinctly different from each. While volunteering is an experience that provides the opportunity to give time and energy to a worthwhile cause, it is for those who believe that they can make a difference in the lives of others through the application of their special talents and efforts. Service learning takes volunteering one step further. It involves meeting the same needs that volunteering does, but it is combined with conscious educational growth as an external part of an academic course of study. Service learning is a chance to learn and earn some credit, while helping to better the community. Internship is often considered an internal part of a program or course, a requirement that should be satisfied on the way to achieving certification toward a job-training skill. Service learning is an external component to a course, usually a component specifically designed to meet the needs of the community it serves. Edward Zlotkowski points out that, "experience has shown that there is probably no disciplinary area–from Architecture to Zoology–where service learning cannot be fruitfully employed to strengthen students' ability to become active learners as well as responsible citizens" (Marchese, p. 1., 1997).

Service Learning in Higher Education

In higher education, service learning is as an integral part of the college/university learning experience. For example, the Chancellor's Office of the California State University (CSU) system has an Office for Service Learning that oversees all 23 CSU campuses. Accordingly, every campus of the CSU system has a service learning program and offers extensive service learning opportunities for its population. Students on these campuses may participate in programs such as a biology course at CSU Bakersfield in which they learn nutritional basics, the latest information on a healthy diet, and how to prevent cancer with dietary selections. Students then provide nutritional seminars, demonstrating how to make various healthy meals and providing samples to communities in need. They may also be a part of a public relations course that provides assistance in community organizations and agencies, applying their public relations skills and knowledge in writing, organizing, budgeting, and planning.

CSU Dominguez Hills offers a liberal studies course that provides academic enrichment to children in after-school settings through the development of service learning projects for the children, one-to-one tutoring, and small group instruction. At CSU Fresno, students in a marketing course provide marketing services to a wide variety of nonprofit agencies. Example activities include assistance with promoting events, designing educational materials and brochures, database development or redesign, and working with the media. CSU Fullerton students, in an advanced biology course, partner with science teachers to provide needed help with school children doing hands-on science inquiry. Students write research papers about how learners develop complex ideas in science, and they develop action plans to resolve inequity and other science education issues. CSU Hayward students, who are preparing to become teachers, participate in a course on service learning as an educational practice. Students learn the theoretical and pedagogical underpinnings of service learning and then implement a service learning project in K-12 classrooms.

CSU Los Angeles students, in a psychological development course, work at a variety of local agencies and community programs, including College Smart, a mentoring program that connects university students with elementary and middle school children. The California Maritime Academy students who are in a course on death and dying perform hospice community service by working with terminally ill patients or interacting with their grieving families through a local hospice program. CSU Monterey Bay students, in a computer science course, work with public schools and advocacy groups to help rehabilitate old computers, train people on computer usage, and help set up computer networks. At the same time they discuss the impact of technology on people's lives and the effects of the digital divide. At CSU Northridge, students in a community health education course assemble and coordinate an interdisciplinary team of students and faculty to put on a series of health fairs at local elementary schools over two semesters.

Students at California State Polytechnic University, Pomona in a human development, learning and language acquisition course, work with elementary school students in the local school district as they learn to read. CSU Sacramento students, in a course on assistive technology and biomedical engineering, work with people through local nonprofit agencies who have physical disabilities. Students reflect on and evaluate each person's assistive devices for ease of use, effectiveness, and compatibility with his/her lifestyle. Students research alternatives and make recommendations for changes that they believe would benefit users in the performance of their daily activities. CSU San Bernardino students, in an environmental health course, work with faculty and community experts to identify and analyze key indicators to measure the regions' overall environmental quality. The work is used to generate an environmental report card for the region, which will be available to the general public. San Diego State University business students work in teams to implement social change programs within businesses. Projects range from instituting a recycling program at a community business to convincing local hotel management to make excess room capacity available to the homeless. They are involved in establishing a program for a major toy retailer to donate toys to a home for abused children. San Francisco State University students, in both marketing and communication arts departments, work collaboratively in an interdisciplinary course to develop and produce public service announcements for area nonprofit agencies, which then air on a local cable television station. Students in San Jose State University health professions classes provide services to persons with serious mental illness who reside in two licensed board and care homes near the university and in one local independent housing arrangement, through the Transdisciplinary Health Project.

California Polytechnic State University, San Luis Obispo students, in a course on nutrition and aging, expand their understanding of senior citizens and their nutritional needs through direct service to seniors in a day center for Alzheimer's patients, a retirement community of low income seniors, and private homes where seniors receive daily Meals on Wheels provided by the Senior Nutrition Program. CSU San Marcos students, in an interdisciplinary health course, study the ethics and politics of health care and spend time weekly volunteering in one of a wide range of health-related settings. They consider alternative health careers and plan their pre-health academic careers. Sonoma State University students, in a gerontology interdisciplinary seminar course focusing on connections across generations, meet weekly with adults at various senior centers in order to learn the skills and dynamics of group work with older adults. CSU Stanislaus students, in a public administration course, provide community service to a local citizen's group or to a community agency that works with citizens to understand their roles in public service as citizen advocates. (California State University, 2002).

These are just some examples of how service learning can be implemented on college and university campuses. Toward the end of this chapter two different approaches that blend cooperative learning and service learning will be presented.

The Importance of Reflection in Service Learning

To be truly effective, both service learning programs and cooperative learning experiences should incorporate time for reflection. Any service learning experience is enhanced when reflected upon, both during the experience and after it has been completed. In service learning, reflection is an essential component that affords participants the opportunity to think, write, and talk about their service; how it relates to the classroom; how it benefits them personally; and how it benefits others. Receiving feedback from those community members served and their peers provides participants the opportunity to share their thoughts with others while considering different perspectives on service. Reflection can happen through writing, speaking, listening, and reading about the service experiences. This further promotes the "learning" aspect of service learning by helping participants analyze the broad array of skills and knowledge that they have gained from their experiences. In their research Astin, Vogelgesang, Ikeda and Yee (2000) determined that "both qualitative and quantitative results underscore, once again, the power of reflection as a means of connecting the service experience to the academic course material" (p. 35).

Criticisms

Both cooperative learning and service learning can be meaningful, pointless, or harmful. Criticisms abound for each when they are not properly implemented. Cooperative learning is often condemned when students are simply placed into groups without any structure or guidance. David and Roger Johnson have worked extensively documenting cooperative learning's impact on achievement, interpersonal relationships and psychosocial well being. The teacher who simply places students in groups will often hear the complaints of students, parents and administrators who resent one student doing all the work or fellow teachers who are forced to deal with the resulting management problems. These situations are not cooperative. Instead, what results are consequences from a teacher not implementing each of the cooperative elements: positive interdependence, individual accountability, group processing, social skill development in a forum of face-to-face promotive interaction. It is essential that these elements be incorporated into a cooperative learning experience, including time for group processing (Johnson & Johnson, 1995).

Even with its increasing popularity, a large majority of the group tasks that teachers use, even teachers who claim to be using *cooperative learning*, continue to be cooperative group tasks–not cooperative learning group tasks. For instance, nearly all *jigsaw* activities are not cooperative learning activities. Merely because students work in small groups does not mean that they are cooperating to ensure their own learning and the learning of all others in their group. Teachers who fail to include the essential elements of cooperative learning into their group lessons report far more difficulties with their students and their group activities, and far less student academic achievement gains than do teachers who include them (Johnson, Johnson, & Smith, 1991). As a general rule, unless a well-researched strategy is used that allows for an alternative to one or more of these elements, teachers serious about implementing effective cooperative learning activities may encounter difficulties. They need to ensure that these requirements are met for each cooperative learning strategy they use. More importantly, unless these elements are used frequently and correctly, teachers should not expect the many positive long-term results of cooperative learning that can be achieved (Johnson, Johnson, & Holubec, 1993).

Likewise, service learning has its critics when it is not implemented and managed properly. If students are placed at a service learning site with no management or supervision, questions such as "What are we supposed to do?" and "Why are these people here?" are often heard. It is important that a service learning experience be based on planning, implementation and follow-up. Reflection is the key to getting meaning from one's cooperative and service experience (Eyler & Giles, 1999). Reflection allows students to learn from themselves and each other. Most viable and sustainable service learning programs contain a component for structured reflection. This reflection becomes central to overall program success. Studies that have examined the impact of quality differences in service learning, have found that programs with more opportunity for reflection, substantive links between coursework and service, and ethnic and cultural diversity have a stronger impact than programs without these elements (Eyler & Giles, 1999; Mabry, 1998).

The Power of Reflection

It is reasonable to conclude, therefore, that reflection plays a vital role in both cooperative learning and service learning. In both approaches, student reflection–either through the feedback of intragroup cooperative learning processing or the journals and discussions associated with service learning–is a tool used to help them become more responsible for their own educational growth. In addition, students' reflections provide feedback on classroom practices. The guiding principle of data-driven instruction is the notion of using quality information to provide useful feedback for improving learning. Too often students are left out of this effective educational process. They are tested and assessed, graded and rated, judged and prejudged without being asked to help interpret results. Reflection in both cooperative learning and service learning honors the spirit of standards-based instruction because it promotes student involvement in self-assessing progress and direction. Just as educators feel it is essential for teachers to reflect and share the successes and failures of their practices with colleagues, it is equally important for teachers and students to have a dialogue that creates the spirit of a learning partnership.

As mentioned, effective standards-based instruction requires educators to use reflection for both their students and themselves at different classroom junctures to establish equity in the assessment process. The Minnesota Graduation Standards requires educators and their students to analyze results and to plan for the future in three interrelated ways:

1) Building a Better Body of Evidence–Making Sure the Results are Right

One way standards-based instruction utilizes student reflection is to check the validity of the results teachers compile through their assessment methods. In performance-based class instruction, results sometimes can be masked by the type of performance used for assessment. Student reflection can provide clues into other aspects of students' lives that may affect their school performance. Although this evidence does not excuse students from meeting standards, it helps teachers provide accommodations for the students' learning.

2) Building Better Learners–Making Results Speak to Students

Students are often harsh self-critics. Teachers can use reflection to transform this criticism into effective plans for improvement. Perhaps more important, students examine their successes so they can build better understandings of themselves as learners. Reflective writing is a good way for students to analyze their skills and growth. Ongoing reflection provides both students and teachers with a basis to comment on their development as writers. Reflection helps sort and cement, in students' minds, reasons for both their successes and their failures. By giving students the chance to vent, teachers open the communication channels so both can more closely examine ways of improving their performances.

3) Building Better Classrooms–Making Results the Basis for Student/Teacher Conversations

The use of reflective teaching practices has been well documented (Cohen, 1992; Eyler & Giles, 1999). Including students in the professional practice of self-analysis and personal dialogue adds the client's voice to this process. Student reflection helps teachers determine how clearly the purpose and direction of the learning were communicated. It also models the reflective process for students: they are more likely to engage in quality reflection if they see their teachers doing so, and if they witness changes in their classrooms as a result of what has been suggested. Quality reflection takes practice and time. Students cannot be expected to produce meaningful reflection without understanding its goals and methods. Student responses also confirm effective teaching techniques (Department of Children, Families and Learning, 1997).

Quality reflective practices and processes lead teachers toward the goal of making students more responsible for their own learning. Reflection plays a critical role in student success. This reflective component is essential for both cooperative learning and service learning. It becomes incumbent upon educators to offer strategies like cooperative learning within the framework of approaches like service learning in order to meet this demand for promoting sustainable citizenship-skill development. Reflection must also be a viable part of that framework.

Two Models

Two models in higher education that reflect the partnership of cooperative learning and service learning will be described in this section. The first involves university teacher education candidates who become part of a pre-service service learning program as part of their field experience requirements in K-12 classrooms.

The University of Minnesota committed 57 undergraduates to teach a cooperative learning, conflict resolution curriculum to inner-city public school students from September 1998 to June 1999. Students were part of the Office for Special Learning Opportunities College of Liberal Arts service learning program, and most had expressed a desire to eventually become classroom teachers. The University established partnerships with three inner-city schools: one high school, and two elementary schools. The University of Minnesota students gave 932 K-12 students the treatment curriculum, while 436 of their counterparts did not receive the treatment.

The students attended an on-campus class each week, before going into the inner-city classrooms to teach the public school students. Undergraduates learned to specify the objectives for learning social skills, as well as make a number of decisions before beginning the process. An instructor from the Department of Curriculum and Instruction taught the undergraduates how to explain and orchestrate the academic task and curriculum procedure, monitor the public school students as they engaged in the curriculum, intervene when necessary to improve individual and team work, and to evaluate academic achievement. Undergraduates then visited their assigned public school classrooms to teach their lessons. In pairs, the public school students argued for one imaginary character or the other in a story that they constructed. Then as a group of four, they developed a synthesized decision by choosing a character, or making up a different imaginary counterpart, based on their structured argument. Both the university and public school students demonstrated the essential elements of cooperative learning as they participated in this program. Reflections consisted of group processing on the part of both university and public school students with follow-up written responses at the conclusion of each exercise.

Results of the program demonstrated that Minneapolis public school students who received the curriculum clearly outperformed their non-participating public school counterparts in: 1) cooperation and conflict resolution skills, and 2) liking for and willingness to participate in classroom cooperation.

The university students also demonstrated strong cooperation and conflict resolution skills and stated that they felt the program was beneficial. These students remarked about how glad they were to have had the opportunity to investigate the teaching profession before being required to invest the time and financial resources required by a full degree track (Mitchell & Quan, 2001).

A similar initiative was implemented in the Language, Literacy and Cultures Program at CSU San Bernardino during 2000-2001. Similar citizenship-development centered results were observed (Mitchell & Torrez, 2002).

Another example of a cooperative learning and service learning program in higher education was implemented on the campus of CSU Dominguez Hills during 2002-03. Students in the Teacher Education Department credential program study a cooperative learning AIDS education curriculum published by the National Institute of Health. They then teach the same curriculum in a cooperative learning format to a cadre of K-12 peer leaders in after-school programs at the sites they are performing their student teaching duties. The desired outcome is for the selected peer leaders to bring the gained knowledge to their respective classrooms and extra-curricular program activities.

Conclusion

Today's students face a world that is vastly different from the world of their parents and grandparents. The uncertainty of youth has added a completely new dimension since September 11, 2001. The word *safety* has been redefined in terms of physical and emotional security. The partnership between cooperative learning and service learning exists like a seed to be watered and a flower to be cultivated so that the seed may grow and the flower may bloom in order to meet the needs of today's future adults. The principles of both approaches are closely tied to one another. The benefits of developing better citizens, more employable workforce members, and fostering a stronger overall world community are waiting to be realized.

References

Astin, A., Vogelgesang, L., Ikeda, E., & Yee, J. (2001). *Combining service learning in higher education.* Santa Monica, CA: Rand, UCLA Higher Education Research Institute.

California State University (2002). *Service-learning courses across the California. State University.* Retrieved January 12, 2002 from the World Wide Web: http://www.calstate.edu/CSL/sl-courses.shtml

Cohen, E. G. (1992). Restructuring the classroom: Conditions for productive small groups. *Review of Educational Research, 64,* 1-35

Department of Children, Families and Learning. (1997). *Profile of learning.* St. Paul, MN: Department of Children, Families and Learning.

Dewey, J. (1997). *Experience and education.* New York: Harcourt Brace.

Eyler, J., & Giles, D. E., Jr. (1999). *Where's the learning in service-learning?* San Francisco: Jossey-Bass.

Eyler, J., Giles, D. E., & Gray, C. J. (1999). *At a glance: What we know about service learning on students, faculty, institutions, and communities, 1993-99.* Minneapolis, MN: National Service Learning Clearinghouse.

Johnson, D. W., & Johnson, R. T. (1995). *Learning together and alone: Cooperation, competition, and individualization* (4th ed.). Englewood Cliffs, NJ: Prentice Hall.

Johnson, D. W., Johnson, R. T., & Holubec, E. J. (1993). *Circles of learning: Cooperation in the classroom* (4th ed.). Edina, MN: Interaction Book Company.

Johnson, D. W., Johnson, R. T., & Smith, K. A. (1991). *Cooperative learning: Increasing college faculty instructional productivity.* (ASHE-ERIC Higher Education Report No. 4). Washington, DC: The George Washington University.

Marchese, T. (1997, March). Service learning in the disciplines: An interview with monograph series editors Robert Bringle and Edward Zlotkowski. *AAHE Bulletin, 49(7), 3-6.*
Mitchell, J., & Quan K. (2001, Summer). Service learning and conflict resolution education. *Online Journal of Peace and Conflict Resolution. 4.1.* Retrieved January 11, 2002 from the World Wide Web: http://www.trinstitute.org/ojpcr/toc4_1.htm
Mitchell J., & Torrez, N. (2002). *Service learning and language, literacy and culture.* Unpublished manuscript. Oxfam. (n.d.). *A curriculum for global citizenship.* Retrieved January 11, 2002 from the World Wide Web: http://www.oxfam.org.uk/coolplanet/teachers/globciti/globciti.htm
Slavin, R. E. (1991). *Student team learning: A practical guide to cooperative learning.* Washington, DC: National Education Association.
Stahl, R. J., & VanSickle, R. L. (1992). *Cooperative learning in the social studies classroom: An invitation to social study.* Washington, DC: National Council for the Social Studies.
U.S. Department of Labor. (2002). *Occupational outlook handbook: 2002-03 edition.* Washington DC: U.S. Department of Labor.

Small-group Learning in Higher Education: A Status Report and an Agenda for the Future

James L. Cooper, David Ball and Pamela Robinson

In 1996, Jim and Pamela, as editors of the *Cooperative Learning and College Teaching* newsletter, conducted a survey of national leaders in cooperative/collaborative learning. Their purpose was to assess the state of small-group instruction in higher education and to project what the interesting issues and challenges would be for the future. One issue that was identified in 1996 as a challenge to small-group instruction for the next 5-10 years was incorporating cooperative techniques with technology. As one examines the technology research literature in higher education for this time period, attempts to make distance learning and other applications of technology more interactive have certainly played a major role. Leaders of this movement included Steve Gilbert of the Technology Roundtable of the American Association for Higher Education (AAHE). However, Steve and many others, including respondents to the current survey whose answers are summarized below, still believe that pedagogy lags far behind technology in the appropriate design and delivery of distance learning and other forms of technology-based instruction.

A second area, which was identified as a challenge by respondents in 1996, dealt with the importance of *dissemination* of small-group techniques to greater numbers of colleagues and more careful implementation of the procedures within college classrooms. As we noted in the Interactive Lecture chapter of this volume (pages 336-348), in 1985 Jim expected that team-learning techniques would be widely implemented within 5-10 years. And, yearly analyses of ERIC citations under such descriptors as cooperative learning and collaborative learning do show significant growth from 1985 to the present. For example, in 1996, Jim reported that the number of ERIC "hits" using the descriptors "cooperative learning and higher education" went from 20 in 1985 to 80 in 1990 to 813 in 1996 (Cooper, 1996a). Thus, those *publishing* in higher education appear to view group learning as a powerful pedagogy, deserving of attention.

Still, many of the leaders in group learning, as we will report below, regard the absolute number of *practitioners* in higher education to be disappointingly low. Philip Abrami of Concordia University believes that this relative lack of implementation may be explained by expectancy theory. That is, for practitioners to change their reliance on more traditional instructional formats, they have to: 1) value the new techniques and/or the outcomes they produce, 2) have positive expectations of successful implementation, and 3) believe the physical and psychological costs of change are acceptable. We concur in this analysis. That is why in recent years we have focused on such informal techniques as cognitive scaffolding and Quick-thinks (see Interactive Lecture chapter). It is our hope that, if faculty have success using these relatively low-risk, low-effort procedures within their existing lectures and discussions, that they may ultimately develop more formal (and effortful) active-learning and small-group procedures, such as cooperative learning base groups that last for the entire semester.

In the spring of 2001 we e-mailed a survey to a number of leaders in college teaching research and practice. We received responses from Phil Abrami (Concordia University), Donald Bligh (University of Exeter), Joe Cuseo (Marymount College), Richard Hake (University of Indiana), Roger and David Johnson (University of Minnesota), Mark Maier (Glendale College), Jean MacGregor (Evergreen State College), Barbara Millis (Air Force Academy), Susan Prescott Johnston (California State University) and Maryellen Weimer (Penn State).

The 2001 survey consisted of six items similar to the ones used in the 1996 survey. Respondents were asked to speak to as many or as few items as they wished, in whatever length they preferred.

Item 1 asked how strong the research base for cooperative learning was, either in an absolute sense or relative to other educational interventions. In general, respondents replied that the research base was significant. Donald Bligh indicated that, depending on how one defines cooperative learning, the research base was "enormous." Jean MacGregor indicated that it "continues to expand and strengthen," citing the work of Alexander Astin, Richard Light, Vincent Tinto and Patrick Terenzini. Barbara Millis responded that the research is "reassuringly convergent," citing Chickering and Gamson's *Seven Principles of Good Practice in Undergraduate Education* and the work in Europe, Australia and Britain on deep learning. She also noted the recent work supporting cooperative learning by John Bransford and others addressing the biological bases of learning. The Johnsons reported that hundreds of studies have been conducted on cooperative procedures and that the research base was "very strong." Several respondents referred to the meta-analysis of cooperative learning in higher education relating to mathematics, science and technology conducted by Len Springer and his associates for the National Institute for Science Education and subsequently published in the *Review of Educational Research* (Springer, Stanne & Donavan, 1999). Springer and his associates reviewed 383 studies of small-group research and identified 39 that met their criteria of empirical rigor. Data from several thousand students were included in their analyses. They reported that the effect size was "robust," on the three outcomes studied: academic achievement, more favorable attitudes toward learning, and course persistence. Their article, in conjunction with meta-analyses reported by Johnson and Johnson (1989), and Johnson, Johnson and Stanne (2000), represents the best quantitative support for small-group, cooperative procedures in higher education.

Other respondents were somewhat more cautious in their assessments. Richard Hake views the research as "very weak" for all instructional methods in higher education, due to a variety of methodological flaws. At the same time he reports that his review of "Cooperative Peer Instruction" in physics yields an effect size of 2.4, an enormous effect virtually unheard of in higher education interventions. Maryellen Weimer reports that empirical justification for cooperative group procedures is still largely based on K-12 literature.

We concur that the greatest empirical support for group work is at the K-12 level. However, the meta-analysis of Springer et al. (1999) and the meta-analyses by the Johnsons in 1989 and 2000 are impressive. So too are the large number of reports of cooperative and collaborative learning in higher education identified in our ERIC searches. In our review of these ERIC studies (for example, Cooper, 1996b; Cooper & Robinson, 1998), we found that most are *applications* of group work within disciplinary areas. When empirical results *are* reported, findings are generally in favor of group work. Rarely do results produce significant differences favoring more traditional instructional formats such as the lecture. We acknowledge that these findings have some biases built in, such as the tendency for journals and other publication outlets to prefer positive findings supporting experimental techniques (as opposed to more traditional "comparison" approaches such as the lecture). However, not only do the empirical findings support the power of group work, but the literature on such outcomes as critical thinking/deep processing, attention, motivation and memory all tend to support the use of cooperative group work. Thus there is a kind of "convergent validity" surrounding carefully structured small-group work.

Responses to our current survey indicate that there are still issues of definition that concern many people. Despite attempts (Mathews, Cooper, Davidson, & Hawkes, 1995; see Article 2, pages 6-17) to reconcile such concepts as cooperative learning, collaborative learning, team learning, and group learning, some faculty and some researchers are more comfortable with specific terminologies and associated research traditions and traditions of practices (such as the distinction between cooperative learning and collaborative learning). This chapter will not address that issue, since the discussion has been reviewed by Matthews et al. (1995) and others.

Our second survey item asked what questions remained as interesting issues on the research agenda for the next 5-10 years. Many respondents identified issues relating to the specific *mechanisms* associated with the powerful overall effects of cooperative group techniques demonstrated in reports such as the Springer, Stanne, and Donavan, and the Johnson and Johnson meta-analyses. For example, the Johnsons reported that they were interested in the internal dynamics of cooperative groups, including the relative amounts of interdependence among group members and the amount of group processing or reflection structured within the groups.

Donald Bligh thought that task design was an interesting issue requiring more detailed analysis. Susan Prescott Johnston suggested that more careful analysis of the relationship between the learning outcomes and task design was needed and that work should focus on which strategies would (and would not) work in large classes as particular issues requiring attention. Mark Maier indicated that more attention to assessment of group work was needed. Jean MacGregor also identified assessment as an important issue for future researchers and practitioners, and noted the importance of linking group work with learning communities and problem-based and case-based learning. Joe Cuseo expressed interest in the mechanisms that might account for the power of group learning, including the relative impact of intentional group formation, positive interdependence, individual accountability and processing/reflection.

We agree with the respondents that researchers and practitioners need to examine more closely the learning outcomes they are attempting to foster before designing group tasks. Teaching strategies should be driven by a clear understanding of the *learning objectives* to be fostered. This issue is of particular importance and concern since most faculty have not had courses in pedagogy in their graduate experiences. Similarly, most faculty are not familiar with the research and theory associated with small-group instruction.

The third item on our survey asked respondents to offer advice for those beginning to apply cooperative learning in their classrooms. Several respondents urged teachers to start small. They suggested that faculty familiarize themselves with group procedures by reading the literature of the field and attending workshops addressing teaching strategies. Susan Prescott Johnston advised faculty to identify important and difficult concepts within a single course and develop group techniques to address those learning outcomes. Donald Bligh agreed saying, "Start with simple tasks in small groups for short periods of time, and gradually increase their respective complexity, size and duration." Jean MacGregor concurred with these sentiments and suggested that faculty find partners to work with and perhaps team teach a course. Research by Joyce and Showers (1988) supports the view that working with one or more colleagues is the best way to sustain teaching innovations over time. Richard Hake advised studying the "lore of interactive engagement, not just the narrow segment of 'cooperative technique.'" He also advised joining professional organizations interested in interactive pedagogies and to use the Internet to "promote interdisciplinary synergy." We agree with Hake's emphasis on going beyond the literature of cooperative learning so that faculty can be grounded in larger issues of teaching and learning, including the work in critical thinking, information processing, motivation and developmental issues such as William Perry's work in cognitive development among college students and the Womens' Ways of Knowing literature.

The source most recommended by respondents for information concerning group learning was *Cooperative Learning for Higher Education Faculty* (Millis & Cottell, 1997) a book that Maryellen Weimer characterized as "a well organized compendium of techniques and advice." She noted that it was "great." The work of the Johnsons and Karl Smith was also widely cited.

We second these recommendations. The Johnsons and Karl Smith have published several volumes, which provide brief descriptions of research and theory accessible to a general academic readership but which primarily focus on applications of group procedures (Johnson, Johnson & Smith, 1991; 1998). The Millis and Cottell book is a detailed description of these same issues and is very well written. No library of work concerning college teaching and learning issues is complete without one of the Johnson volumes and the Millis and Cottell text. We would also suggest that readers explore web sites such as Ted Panitz's (http://home.capecod.net/~tpanitz/) and our own (http://www.csudh.edu/SOE/cl_network/). These sites provide descriptions of good practice, summaries of research and theory, and links to other sites.

The fourth survey item asked respondents to assess the current status of cooperative techniques in higher education. It asked if: 1) the strategies were being implemented at the level they expected at the time of the last survey in 1996, and 2) what possible impediments they see regarding implementation. The Johnsons reported that "... there is definitely more activity now than five years ago..." although "... the use of *carefully crafted* cooperative groups is still rare." They also described significant interest in the techniques internationally. Maryellen Weimer noted that the use of group work has "truly penetrated educational practice at the grassroots." However, she reported that most faculty still do not understand the distinctions between the various types of group work. Barbara Millis believes that group work is generally well accepted. Joe Cuseo added that national surveys indicate that there is a surge of interest in collaborative techniques. However, he is not sure whether "this involves anything more than unstructured group work." Jean MacGregor believes that there is a large buy-in conceptually but stated that systematic applications of group work are disappointingly small. This concern with the poor implementation of group work is a constant among almost all respondents.

We believe that this should not be surprising since, as previously noted, few faculty have formal training in instructional design and issues of teaching and learning. However, we worry that poorly implemented group work will have adverse effects on both students and teachers, thus limiting the growth of well-crafted group procedures. Barbara Millis reported greater interest in group work among junior faculty. Needless to say, we would like to see greater attention paid to pedagogy in graduate programs, and there is some reason to believe such training is taking place (Lewis, 1997). However, this training is still disappointingly infrequent and superficial, in our view. Valuing the scholarship of teaching in promotion and tenure decisions would also send a signal to faculty that careful attention to research and other creative activity relating to pedagogies of engagement can provide an avenue to a successful academic career, just as more traditional forms of scholarship have historically.

We like Phil Abrami's expectancy approach to resistance to change, noted earlier, as an explanation of the still limited use of group work in higher education. Another impediment to greater implementation for group work, as one respondent reported, is that there is not a major champion of cooperative/collaborative learning in higher education such as John Gardner in the freshmen experience area, and Jean MacGregor and Barbara Leigh Smith for learning communities.

The fifth survey item asked if the cooperative learning movement had developed synergistic relationships with folks working in technology, service learning, learning communities and other fields at the forefront of the higher education agenda. Jean MacGregor responded, "Not enough. We need to continue to work on this." The Johnsons reported, "We have not noticed any particular relationships with the programs mentioned above." They went on to say that there is wider acceptance of group work at the community colleges, where they have seen a greater interest in teaching and a greater need to address issues of diversity relative to four-year institutions. Joe Cuseo reported that in applications of cooperative techniques in instructional technology, it is the technology that is driving implementation rather than pedagogy. Maryellen Weimer reported that she couldn't think of examples of synergistic relationships. She noted that cooperative learning, "...continues to be a method of change used individually, one faculty by one faculty and hence its impact is less visible..." relative to such innovations as learning communities. In general, although relationships between group work and the innovations described above seem natural allies to most, synergistic relations seem to be lacking. In our view, problem-based learning and case-based learning often to use groups, but not always with the intentional design that is characteristic of well-crafted cooperative learning.

The final item on the survey asked respondents if there was additional information, not covered in the previous survey items, that they would like readers of this chapter to know. Susan Prescott Johnston suggested the potential power of cooperative techniques in distance learning, such as having e-mail buddies and critiquing projects by group members. Additionally, Susan is concerned about the lack of structure and unfair evaluation procedures which characterize much group work. She also worries about excessive amounts of time spent in groups (versus teacher-led direct instruction). Phil Abrami concurred, indicating that many students come to college classes with prior histories of poorly-designed team learning, leading to low expectations for positive group experiences in their college classes. Mark Maier called for more research, particularly of a qualitative nature, which includes videotaping of groups in action and examinations of student writing and self assessment. The Johnsons reported that it would be best if students know in advance that classes are to be taught in cooperative groups (presumably so that those actively opposed to group work can select classes using other instructional formats). Donald Bligh noted that, "... there needs to be a planned sequence of methods each one extending their [instructors], and their students' cooperative skills." Jean MacGregor reported that it is important to go beyond thinking of cooperative learning as a procedure or technique and view it as a way of, "...conceiving and re-conceiving the entire teaching and learning enterprise..." for both teachers and students. She believes that we all need to join together to become "...community organizers on behalf of cooperative learning."

In summary, the concerns expressed in the 1996 survey of group work in higher education that continue to challenge us are: 1) the appropriate use of group work principles as applied to technology-based education, and 2) the relative low incidence of *carefully-designed* group work in college classrooms. The amount of interest in group-work among researchers and higher education leaders is still significant, as reflected in the number of ERIC citations and other publications, and the recommendations endorsing group work appearing in national reports and disciplinary commissions. Although group work seems to be one of the three or four topics that are of most interest in higher education, it does feel to the chapter authors as if limited progress has been made since our 1996 survey. Perhaps this is due, in part, to the lack of champions such as John Gardner, Jean MacGregor and Barbara Leigh Smith, who have institutionalized national research and training efforts relating to specific educational reforms over the last two decades.

References

Cooper, J. (1996a) Cooperative learning in higher education: 1996. *Cooperative Learning and College Teaching, 6*(2), 1-2.

Cooper, J. (1996b). Research in cooperative learning in the 1990s: What the experts say. *Cooperative Learning and College Teaching, 6*(2), 2-3.

Cooper, J., & Robinson, P. (1998). Small-group instruction in science, mathematics, engineering and technology (SMET) disciplines: A status report and an agenda for the future. *Journal of College Science Teaching, 27*(6), 383-388.

Gilbert, S. W. (1995). Technology and the changing academy: Symptoms,

questions and suggestions. *Change, 27*(5), 58-61.
Johnson, D. W., & Johnson, R. T. (1989) *Cooperation and competition: Theory and research.* Edina, MN: Interaction Book Company.
Johnson, D. W., Johnson, R. T., & Smith, K. A. (1991*). Cooperative learning: Increasing college faculty instructional productivity.* ASHE-ERIC Higher Education Report No. 4. Washington, DC: The George Washington University.
Johnson, D. W., Johnson, R. T., & Smith, K. A. (1998). *Active learning: Cooperation in the classroom* (2nd ed.). Edina, MN: Interaction Book Company.
Johnson, D. W., Johnson, R. T., & Stanne M. B. (2000, May). *Cooperative learning methods: A meta-analysis.* Retrieved December 14, 2001, from: http://www.clcrc.com/pages/cl-methods.html
Joyce, B., & Showers, B. (1988). *Student achievement through staff development.* New York: Longman.
Lewis, K. G. (1997). Faculty development in the United States: A brief history. *The International Journal for Academic Development, 1*(2), 26-33.
Matthews, R. S., Cooper J. L., Davidson, N., & Hawkes, P. (1995). *Building bridges between cooperative and collaborative learning. Change 27*(4), 35-40.
Millis, B. J., & Cottell, P. G., Jr. (1997). *Cooperative learning for higher education faculty.* Phoenix, AZ: American Council on Education and The Oryx Press.
Springer, L., Stanne, M. E., & Donovan, S. S. (1999). Effects of small-group learning on undergraduates in science, mathematics, engineering and technology: A meta analysis. *Review of Educational Research, 69*(1), 21 – 51.

Cooperative-learning Structures for Brain-compatible Instruction

Spencer Kagan

> ...*teaching is generally a delightful experience when we focus on activities that students' brains enjoy doing and do well, such as exploring concepts, creating metaphors, estimating and predicting, cooperating on group tasks, and discussing moral or ethical issues. Conversely, teaching loses much of its luster when we force students to do things their brains don't enjoy doing and do poorly, such as reading textbooks that compress content, writing and rewriting reports, completing repetitive worksheets, and memorizing facts that they consider irrelevant.* Robert Sylwester (1995, pp. 119-120)

There is an explosion of recent research and theory which is dramatically increasing our understanding of the brain. Active brain imaging techniques give us windows through which we can view the brain in action. Sophisticated physiological methods, undreamed of but a decade ago, are allowing us to watch the reactions of single neurons as learners react to different kinds of stimuli.

Clearly, teaching will be more effective if it uses methods that are aligned with how the brain best attends to, processes, and retains information. The search is on: Can we identify teaching methods that are brain-compatible? Although some have warned against basing teaching methods on the new findings from brain science, many are making the attempt to build bridges from theory to practice. Educators are being urged through books and workshops to make classrooms "brain-compatible."

A number of principles of Brain-compatible Learning have been derived, and educators are attempting to align practice with these principles. Systematic use of Kagan Structures implements some of the most important principles of Brain-compatible Learning. Without going into a detailed analysis of the underlying brain structures and functions, this chapter overviews how Kagan Structures are aligned with five important principles of Brain-compatible Learning. It also gives an overview of the range of teaching methods that are brain-compatible. It does not explore ways in which curriculum can be aligned with the principles of Brain-compatible Learning. The very best of brain-compatible instructional strategies are of little worth if the curriculum is not meaningful, relevant, challenging, and developmentally appropriate. Discussion of how to apply the principles derived from brain research to improving curriculum, while terribly important, is beyond the scope of this chapter.

What are Kagan Structures?

Kagan Structures are instructional strategies carefully crafted to structure the interaction of students with each other, the curriculum, and the instructor in ways that promote positive educational outcomes. Not all Kagan Structures involve cooperative learning. For example, *Journal Reflections* is a simple structure to promote making meaning of content. The instructor simply asks students on a regular basis to make entries in their journals to note their most significant learnings, their questions, what they most want to better understand, and so on. *Journal Reflections* is a brain-compatible structure because it helps the brain do two things the brain needs to do to learn: process information and construct meaning. While *Journal Reflections* is a structure—it structures the interaction of students with the curriculum—it is not a cooperative-learning structure—it does not structure the interaction of students with each other.

Most Kagan Structures, though, are cooperative-learning structures. They are carefully crafted to structure the interaction of students in ways that align with the four basic principles of cooperative learning (Kagan, 1994). This makes most Kagan Structures brain-compatible, because, as we will see, brains are social organs and are most engaged when in social interaction.

To understand Kagan Cooperative-learning Structures, it is necessary to understand four basic principles of cooperative learning, symbolized by the acronym PIES. PIES stands for Positive Interdependence, Individual Accountability, Equal Participation, and Simultaneous Interaction.

The PIES principles in the Kagan model are a set of lenses through which to view the interaction in an instructional setting. They provide a way to evaluate interactive-instructional strategies to determine if they align with the basic principles of cooperative learning. In the Kagan model, interactive-learning strategies that do not respect all four PIES principles are called "group work," rather than "cooperative learning." To qualify as true cooperative learning in the Kagan model, all four of the PIES principles must be in place. Putting all four PIES principles in place increases dramatically the probability of a high level of learning for all students. If any of the PIES principles is not implemented, there is a strong probability that a high level of learning will not occur for all students.

To understand the power of PIES, let's contrast two apparently similar structures, one (Timed Pair Share) a strong Kagan Structure, and the other (Turn to a Partner), a structure which does not respect all four PIES principles.

Turn to a Partner vs. Timed Pair Share

An instructor has been lecturing and wants students to interact for a few minutes over a topic in the lecture. The lecture and subsequent discussion might be on any topic (conflicting motiva-

Table 1
PIES Present in Timed Pair Share

Positive Interdependence:	+	Positive correlation of outcomes: The ideas of one student enrich the thinking of the other
	+	Interdependence: No student alone can complete the task
Individual Accountability:	+	Each student is required to perform in front of a peer
Equal Participation:	+	Each student performs for about the same amount of time
Simultaneous Interaction:	+	50% of the class is verbalizing ideas at any one moment

tions of a historical, contemporary, or literary character; alternative explanations of a puzzling science experiment; the pros and cons of two alternative computer programs; advantages of an alternative approach to data analysis; or the assumptions underlying an economic theory). Applying the Kagan model, the instructor might have the students interact using Timed Pair Share. In Timed Pair Share, students pair off so there is a Student A and a Student B. "A" in each pair speaks for a specified time, receives feedback from his/her partner, and then "B" does the same. Timed Pair Share, like all of the Kagan Structures is carefully designed to include the PIES principles (see Table 1).

When using Timed Pair Share, the teacher can be confident that good cooperative learning (as defined by the Kagan model) has occurred; the PIES principles are "built into" Kagan Structures. Without knowledge of the Kagan model, a teacher might say, "Turn to a partner, and talk it over." The teacher is using unstructured interaction or group work; Pair Discussion is not crafted to contain all of the PIES principles (see Table 2).

For years my colleagues and I have been developing structures which are carefully crafted to maximize learning. We have developed some structures explicitly designed to implement the basic principles of cooperative learning (Kagan, 1994) and other struc-

Table 2

PIES Missing in Turn to a Partner

Positive Interdependence:	+	Positive correlation of outcomes: The ideas of one student enrich the thinking of the other
	−	Interdependence: One student alone can do all the talking
Individual Accountability:	−	Students are not all individually accountable for talking
Equal Participation:	−	One student may do most or even all of the talking
Simultaneous Interaction:	+	50% the class is verbalizing ideas at any one moment

tures to engage each of the multiple intelligences (Kagan & Kagan, 1998). There are now close to 150 carefully constructed Kagan Structures.

How are Kagan Structures Brain Compatible?

Brains Need Nourishment

Brains are small—they weigh about three pounds and are approximately the size of two fists put together. Although they account for only about 2% of our body weight, they consume almost 25% of the body's oxygen and blood glucose. When brain oxygen and glucose levels drop, so does brain functioning. Increasing the supply of oxygen and blood to the brain of students in a classroom increases student alertness, sense of well being, and learning.

In the Kagan approach, we encourage instructors to use an active structure about every ten to fifteen minutes. Instructors following that advice do not experience low energy-level dips among students, dips that are inevitable if students sit quietly for prolonged periods. Kagan Structures include movement, interaction among students, and hands-on manipulatives (Kagan, 1994). The classbuilding structures all have students get out of their seats and move in the classroom (Kagan, Robertson, & Kagan, 1995). There are a host of brain-breaks and energizers that take only a few minutes and dramatically increase the energy level among students (Kagan, 2000). The movement and interaction which are characteristic of Kagan Structures increase breathing rate and volume as well as heart rate, which in turn increase blood supply to the brain. Increased blood supply to the brain increases the delivery of both oxygen and glucose, the primary nourishment that fuels cognitive activity.

Take Off, Touch Down is one of the simplest of all Kagan Structures. In this structure, students stand when the instructor says something true of them and sit if it is not true. For example an instructor wishes to poll the class to see how many agree with four alternative actions our country can take in response to terrorism. Traditionally, we would simply have students raise their hands to indicate agreement. Using *Take Off, Touch Down* the instructor would announce each action and students would stand to express their agreement. Everything is exactly the same except the students are using a total physical response rather than just raising their hands. Why bother with something as apparently silly as *Take Off, Touch Down*? My physiology friends say there is approximately 15% more blood and oxygen in the brain after standing and sitting twice compared to raising one's hand twice! There are many Kagan Structures that engage the whole body. Thus Kagan Structures actually nourish the brain!

Brains Are Social Organs

In a remarkable book, *Friday's Footprint: How Society Shapes the Human Mind,* Leslie Brothers (1997) makes the case that our brains have evolved to selectively attend to social stimuli. For example, babies at nine minutes of age are much more likely to turn their heads and eyes to follow a black and white picture, if the parts are arranged to resemble a human face than if the same parts are arranged randomly. Single neurons of primates respond selectively and preferentially to social stimuli. Some neurons do not respond to an inanimate object moving, but do respond to a person moving; others do not respond to a geometric form, but do respond to a form resembling a hand—and the more the form resembles a hand, the more they respond! In *Mapping the Mind*, Rita Carter (1999) displays results of active brain imaging studies which show that brains are dramatically more active when people are learning in interaction with others than when learning alone, reading or listening to a lecture. Opiate-like substances are released in mammalian brains during care giving and play, explaining why these activities are so rewarding. Our brains, to a remarkable extent, are social organisms.

If we naturally attend far more to social stimuli, and our brains are more active during social interaction, it makes sense to have students interact regularly over academic content—having them discuss, debate, and work together. Kagan Structures do exactly that.

For example, if rather than answering questions alone, the instructor uses *Numbered Heads Together* to have students respond to a question, they are far more engaged. In *Numbered Heads Together* students usually sit in teams of four, each with a separate number from one to four. The instructor asks a question, has students think and write their individual responses, discuss their responses in their teams, and signal when they are ready to respond. The instructor then randomly calls a number and the student with that number responds. There are many possible response modes. The instructor can have students with the called number write answers on slates or dry-erase boards, go to the chalkboard to write their answers, indicate their answers by holding up their fingers on their hands, or even move to other teams to share their answers. Because most Kagan Structures involve a great deal of social interaction, they provide the kind of stimuli which increases learning.

Brains Seek Psychological Safety

Our brains have evolved to help us survive. When we are frightened, our primitive "fight or flight" defense alarm system kicks in. The brain's limbic system becomes highly activated and we prepare for, or engage in, primitive modes of survival-related functioning. Although these responses are very adaptive in the face of an actual physical threat, when the threat is imagined or only a psychological threat, the responses can be quite non-adaptive. During a fight or flight defense alarm reaction, the cortex is less efficient, diminishing the ability of students to engage in higher-order cerebral functioning. If we hear fire engine sirens blaring outside, see people running in panic, hear people screaming "fire," and smell smoke, we are not going to be very successful in solving a series of mental math problems! Higher-level thinking occurs best when we are in a state of relaxed alertness—when we feel psychologically safe. When fight or flight defense alarm reactions are not activated, our cerebral cortex is freer to function optimally. Anything that creates anxiety or threat decreases the probability of learning.

Kagan teambuilding (Kagan, Kagan, & Kagan, 1997) and classbuilding structures (Kagan, Robertson, & Kagan, 1995) are explicitly designed to create social safety. The classbuilding and teambuilding structures allow students to know and support each other and to accept individual differences. Because of the teambuilding and classbuilding structures, students drop their fear of social rejection and their worry about social acceptance—they are free to focus more on the academic content. Kagan communication building structures also create a safe context for learning. These structures teach students to express understanding and concern for each other's ideas. No longer fearing rejection of their ideas, students are freer to share and get feedback; the communication building structures create a safe context in which to think and learn.

For example, during a team or class discussion the instructor might use *Paraphrase Passport*. The rule is simple: The right to speak is earned by accurately paraphrasing the opinion of the person who spoke just beforehand. Because of this structure, every student knows his/her ideas will be listened to and validated, creating a caring, safe context for the exchange of ideas. *Paraphrase Passport* reduces the risk students experience because it creates a psychologically safe environment within which to share opinions. Each student knows his/her ideas will meet a sympathetic paraphrase rather than an argument or put-down. This reduction of fear frees the brain for higher-level cerebral functioning. Safe students think more clearly and more deeply.

Brains Are Emotional

Brains are exquisitely designed to respond to stimuli that elicit emotions. There are receptors on the cell walls of neurons that respond to chemicals that are released as we experience emotions. Each receptor is a single very large, complex amino acid chain molecule—some approach 3,000 times the size of a water molecule. Seventy types of receptors have been identified to date, and each responds to only one type of chemical. For example, some receptors respond to endorphins (which make us feel euphoric), and others respond to cortisol (which makes us feel stressed and anxious). A neuron may have millions of receptors on its surface, different numbers of different types—perhaps 10,000 of one type of receptor and 100,000 of another. Thus a particular neuron may be quite sensitive to one type of chemical, but relatively insensitive to another. Just as our eyes and ears sense different types of stimuli in the external world, our receptors sense different types of stimuli in the internal world of our bodies—emotional stimuli. Candace Pert (1997) aptly calls these receptors "Molecules of Emotions."

Why is sensitivity to emotions so crucial to brain functioning? Emotions are the primitive signals that keep us alive by motivating us to flee from being bitten or eaten, care for and protect our progeny, and hunt for a tasty morsel. It is elegantly argued by Antonio Damasio (1999) that the very origin of consciousness resides in the brain's capacity for emotion. The brain is exquisitely designed to become aware of and remember stimuli associated with emotions and the ability to respond to and remember what produces pain, fear, and pleasure keeps us alive. As a nation we pay huge sums to keep our emotional reactions in tune, if only by exercising them vicariously through spectator movies, sports, and drama.

Our brains are structured so that which makes us feel is remembered. You can prove this to yourself with the following experiment: Close your eyes and remember an incident from your childhood. The probability is very high that you remembered an incident linked to emotions!

A brain-compatible classroom is one in which emotions are not avoided, but rather elicited in the service of learning. Various Kagan Structures help instructors link emotions to the academic content and help students understand and deal effectively with their own emotions and those of others.

In *Agree-Disagree Line Ups*, for example, students learn to take a stance depending on their feelings about an issue, and to listen with respect to the opinions of other students who hold different feelings about the issue. The instructor simply states an opinion and the students line up to indicate the degree of their agreement with the opinion, strongly agree at one end of the line and strongly disagree at the other. Students then talk to those nearest them in the line to reinforce their position and to gain fresh arguments in favor of the their opinion. The line is then folded so the strongly agree and strongly disagree students interact, often using *Paraphrase Passport*. In the constructive controversy which results, students find the content more memorable, and also learn to better understand their own emotions and those of others. Anything which elicits and lets students deal effectively with their own emotions and those of others promotes emotional literacy and emotional intelligence while making the academic content more memorable. Many Kagan Structures elicit and help students deal with the emotional component of curriculum and so are compatible with the finding that brains selectively respond to and remember any stimuli associated with emotion.

Brains Process Information

Brains are exquisitely designed to process information—especially information relevant for survival. They seek novel stimuli, attempt to make meaning of stimuli, and seek feedback. Further, they are capable of processing a great deal of stimuli simultaneously—they are parallel processors and store many types of content differently. A brain-compatible approach to instruction must account for the way brains attend to and process information. Finally, a brain-compatible approach to instruction must allow time for processing if the information we present is not to be more water poured into a glass already full!

Brains Seek Novelty

The attention systems in the brain are activated when novel or unexpected stimuli appear; we become more alert and attend more carefully. The evolutionary basis for this is obvious: Those animals that did not become more alert when novel or unexpected stimuli appeared, did not survive to pass along their genes! One of the greatest sources of novelty is other people. When we interact with others there is always new and unexpected stimuli. Part of the reason we find interaction with others so rewarding is because we become more alert and engaged in the novel stimuli they present.

When computer learning programs were first introduced, students showed a great deal of initial interest. Each time they got a problem right a little man bounced along the bottom of the screen, as a reward, holding up a sign saying "Great job!" Soon though, students tired of these programs and did not want to play them any more. What was the problem? Predictable programmed stimuli became boring. Modern games capture our interest in part because they have been designed to constantly adjust the challenge level to the player, and so constantly present novel stimuli.

The feedback of a peer is often unpredictable and so is unlikely to wear out as a source of novel stimulation. Kagan Structures have students interact with others on a regular basis. They have students share ideas, respond to each other's ideas, and give each other feedback and coaching. Students are encouraged to use new and unexpected praise, and to use different gambits as they interact to keep the stimulation high. The stimulation which students provide each other is always fresh. It is in contrast to the stimulation provided by early computer learning systems.

The Kagan Structures are compatible with the brain's need for novelty in two ways. First, an instructor using a range of structures is always creating novel stimuli in her/his classroom, quite in contrast to the instructor who always lectures or uses any other single mode of instruction. Second, most of the Kagan Structures involve interaction, and social interaction is a primary source of novel stimuli. Students in classrooms in which Kagan Structures are used regularly report the classes to be more "fun."

One of many Kagan Structures that increase novelty for students is *One Stray*. Students are working in teams of four and each is assigned a number; one through four. The instructor randomly calls a number. If number three is called, student Three on each team stands. The other three students remain seated but raise their hands, calling for a new Three. Threes stray to new teams, sit down, and the discussion is continued. The visiting Threes bring fresh, novel ideas to teams, energizing discussions.

Brains Seek Patterns and Construct Meaning

Brains seek predictable patterns. Seeking patterns is one way we make sense of the world; it is related to our need for safety. For some students, a classroom is not safe unless there are predictable routines.

A number of Kagan Structures are explicitly designed to help students discover patterns in stimuli. Seeking patterns is but one of the many ways our brains seek to construct meaning. Facts learned in isolation are soon forgotten; facts that are part of a coherent whole, which have meaning, are retained. Making meaning goes beyond seeking patterns; it involves examining relationships, relating stimuli to other stimuli and categories of stimuli, and constructing conceptual models.

One of the many Kagan Structures designed explicitly to help students make meaning of the academic content is *Team Mind Mapping*. There are many forms of *Team Mind Mapping*, but a very simple form is to have students in teams, each working with a different colored marker, create one large Mind Map of the content. They begin by putting the main idea in the center of a piece of chart paper. They draw lines out from the main idea and write or symbolize core concepts. Supporting details extend out from the core concepts. Use of colors, pictures, symbols, arrows and other graphic elements offer more ways of organizing information and creating meaning than traditional outlines. Further, in the process of negotiating agreement on how to construct the Mind Map, the students are more likely to discover patterns and construct meaning than if they were to work alone. Having constructed meaning of the content, it becomes part of a memorable schema. This, in part, is why structures improve academic achievement. The structures are brain-compatible because they assist the brain in its natural search to construct meaning.

Brains Seek Feedback

The 100 billion neurons in the brain each fire not only as a simple function of the amount of input they receive, but also as a function of how other neurons in the past have responded when they fired! There are feedback loops even at the neuronal level. Our brains are feedback hungry. If what we do does not make a difference, we stop doing it. The search for feedback is biologically rooted in our need to be an effective organism, to satisfy our needs, and to make a difference. A brain-compatible classroom is feedback rich.

The search for feedback is also related to the search for meaning. In our search for meaning, we try something and then check to see if it worked. All of us are scientists from birth, conducting mini experiments to see which behavior produces which consequences.

Traditional individual worksheets or individual assignments are feedback poor. Students do not get feedback until the next day, or until after the instructor has graded the papers. But the brain seeks immediate feedback. Kagan mastery structures like *RallyCoach* provide immediate peer feedback and are brain-compatible; they are aligned with the brain's need to receive frequent and immediate feedback.

RallyCoach is simple. Students work in pairs solving a series of problems or answering a series of questions. Student A in the pair solves or answers the first question, talking through the solution while writing it. Student B, watches and listens, and then either praises (if the answer is correct) or coaches (if A needs help). Then the students reverse roles. Student B solves or answers the second problem while Student A watches and listens, and then either coaches or praises. Students continue alternating roles as they work through the series of problems.

There are many advantages to *RallyCoach* over individual worksheet work, including immediate rather than delayed feedback, frequent rather than infrequent feedback, peer-based feedback, immediate and frequent reinforcement, and peer support and coaching. Students who might otherwise practice a whole worksheet wrong get immediate correction opportunities and have the opportunity to immediately practice the correct skill. *RallyCoach* meets the basic need of all humans to have what they do make a difference—we all need positive feedback.

Brains Are Differentiated, Simultaneous Information Processors

Brains Are Parallel Processors: Brains do lots of things at the same time. While they process the instructor's words they have energy left over to process a range of additional information. In determining the reaction of a student to a classroom, it turns out that almost everything counts. Students respond to the instructor's tone of voice, facial expressions, dress, make-up, hairstyle, other students' attitudes, seating arrangements, wall decorations and wall color, background music, class context, temperature of the room, and distracting noises. The brain is a multimodal input processor, simultaneously responding to a great range of content.

The need for mulitmodal input is greater among today's youth than it was a generation ago, because they have become accustomed to a steady diet of mulitmodal input including MTV, DVD's, video arcades and the Internet. Whereas yesterday's instructors could hold the attention of students with straight instructor talk (because that was the most stimulating game in town), today's instructors rarely can.

Because there is a strong need for mulitmodal input, if the academic content is presented through only one channel, a substantial amount of students' processing will be on non-academic content. For example, if an instructor is lecturing, the brain is capable of processing those words plus attending to other stimuli. This explains why, during a lecture, students doodle, attend to memories, fantasize, and flirt! The more the content is presented mulitmodally, the more it will occupy the attention of students, and the more it will be retained.

That is one reason Kagan Structures are so powerful: They are mulitmodal events. They can involve interacting, drawing, writing, discussing, constructing, using a variety of hands-on manipulatives, moving, and responding to music. Structures create brain shifts. For example, there may be a quiet think time followed by a rapid-paced pair interaction, followed by a structure which creates a total physical response, engaging the kinesthetic intelligence. With each structure, and often with each step within a structure, different parts of the brain are engaged, so there is more stimulation, the content is approached in more ways, and the brain is allowed to function as it is designed to function—as a multimodal parallel processor.

Brains Have Multiple Intelligences: Multiple intelligences theorist, Howard Gardner (1983) originally identified seven types of intelligences, with an eighth intelligence (the Naturalist) added later. Each of the intelligences corresponds to a different type of stimuli and each to some extent, is processed by different parts of the brain or at least different processing modes. A brain-compatible classroom includes experiences that stimulate and develop each of these intelligences. In our own work in this area (Kagan & Kagan, 1998), we have developed 84 Multiple Intelligences (MI) Structures so an instructor may make any lesson a multiple intelligences lesson, engaging and developing each of the eight intelligences. Kagan MI Structures are brain-compatible because they engage and develop different parts of the brain and different types of brain functioning.

Brains Have Multiple Memory Systems: The brain stores different types of information differently. For example, learning to ride a bike (procedural memory), remembering a scene from a funny movie (episodic memory), and remembering a list of unfamiliar vocabulary words (semantic memory) involve quite different memory systems. Procedures are usually learned by trial and error, with plenty of practice. Episodes are often remembered effortlessly, with little or no conscious intent, especially if they have emotional components. Formal memory systems such as peg systems and other mnemonics can facilitate semantic memory. Semantic memory that is not related to a meaningful context can be quite difficult, but if semantic memory can be embedded within memorable episodes, it can become effortless.

Just as the brain processes different information differently, individuals process the same information differently and have preferences for how best to remember information. One student may remember information easily by using a memorable visual image, a second student might be more comfortable with a peg system, a third may need to draw the content, and yet another student may find making kinesthetic movements to be the most helpful. Because students have different preferred ways of processing information, using a range of structures is the approach most likely to reach the most students.

In multiple intelligences workshops I often use a variety of Kagan Structures to have participants learn the eight intelligences. One method is *Chunking*. I have participants think about the intelligences as four groups with two intelligences in each group, as follows:

- The two intelligences we have traditionally emphasized in school as we stress reading, writing, and arithmetic: Verbal Linguistic and Logical Mathematical
- The two intelligences we emphasize when we talk about the

importance of instruction in art and music: Visual Spatial and Musical Rhythmic
- The two intelligences that are most often engaged outdoors: Bodily Kinesthetic and Naturalist
- The two personal intelligences: Interpersonal and Intrapersonal

It is far easier to remember just four categories, and then remember the two items in each category, than it is to remember a string of eight items. *Chunking* is a powerful, brain-compatible structure because it helps students work within the brain's processing capacity, and helps create meaning as well.

I also approach remembering the intelligences using *Kinesthetic Symbols*. I have workshop participants use their hands to create a symbol for a stimulus in order to help them recall each intelligence independently from each of the others. For example, they might put their two hands together, palms facing them at a slight angle to symbolize an open book for the Verbal Linguistic intelligence. For the Logical Mathematical intelligence they might cross their two index fingers to form an addition sign. After creating a symbol for each intelligence, they practice them as a team, sharing their team symbols with another team.

The second day of the workshop, when I quiz participants on the eight intelligences, something very interesting happens. Some participants use their hands to remember, going through the kinesthetic symbols they had created and practiced. Others don't use their hands at all but rather think back to the four groups of intelligences we created via chunking. Although each person has all the intelligences, some people remember best logically, forming logical groups, while others remember best kinesthetically.

Chunking and *Kinesthetic Symbols* are only two of the many Multiple Intelligences Structures. The most powerful thing about these structures is that they can be used to aid memory and understanding of any content. All structures are content-free and can be used as part of any lesson. Presenting structures for each of the intelligences is beyond the scope of this chapter, and has been done elsewhere (Kagan & Kagan, 1998). Suffice it to say there are some students who prefer presentations in each of the different intelligences. For example, when we make up a tune or jingle to remember the eight intelligences or any other content, there are students who prefer that approach to any other. They are strong in the Musical Rhythmic intelligence. The instructor who only lectures is biasing outcomes to favor only those strong in the Verbal Linguistic intelligence.

The more ways we present content, the greater the probability we will reach each student through his or her preferred intelligence. Because there are different brains in each classroom, we need a range of instructional strategies.

Brains Need Processing Time

Perhaps the most powerful way any instructor can make his/her presentations more brain-compatible is to allow frequent processing time. The brain can take in only so much information before it must withdraw to process that information. Information overload begins after about ten minutes of lecturing. For most students, additional information after that time without a break for processing is like more water being poured into a glass already full.

An analogy to the desktop is helpful in understanding the need for processing. When either my brain or my computer gets overcrowded, my attention gets diffused and I cannot give any single task full attention. If I take some time to file things away so there are no distractions, I return to the task at hand more fully able to concentrate. Processing time is the brain's filing time. We can only hold a certain amount of information in intermediate-term storage; if it is not to be replaced by the next information to come in, it must be filed in a more permanent way. To do that we must relate it to personal experience, file it with related information, express it in our own words, or in short, process the information.

The need for processing occurs at many levels. During the day we take in information, as the day wears on, we become fatigued. Finally, we withdraw into sleep. During sleep, with no need to process new stimuli we are free to process the old stimuli. Having done so, we are fresh and alert, ready to take in new information. One major function of dreaming is information processing. If dreaming is consistently interrupted, the mind becomes confused. We need to process information. But this need for processing occurs on shorter-term cycles than the day-night cycle. Various biorhythms have been identified. During the day at regular intervals we oscillate between alert attention to outside stimuli and withdrawal into fantasy and dream-like states, replicating all day what we do on a larger scale in the day-night cycle. In the shorter term, for a lesson to be brain-compatible, it too must oscillate so students have a chance to take in, then respond to and put out their thoughts and feelings.

I am reminded of something Einstein did on a regular basis. During discussions while working with others on complex problems, he would suddenly have everyone be silent or leave. He would simply say, "I need to think."

If students are allowed to process the information, alone, in pairs, or in small groups, they quickly become ready to take in more information. Processing can be as simple as stopping and having students write one sentence that expresses the essence of an idea, list applications, or share their reactions to the content with partners. Active brain-imaging technology reveals, however, that the most powerful processing techniques involve social interaction; the brain is more engaged during social interaction than in any other way (Carter, 1999). When sharing with a partner, though, it is important to use cooperative learning rather than group work.

References

Brothers, L. (1997). *Friday's footprint: How society shapes the human mind.* New York: Oxford University Press.

Carter, R. (1999). *Mapping the mind.* Berkeley, CA: University of California Press.

Damasio, A. (1999). The feeling of what happens: Body and emotion in the making of consciousness. New York: Harcourt Brace

Gardner, H. (1983). *Frames of mind: The theory of multiple intelligence.* New York, NY: Basic Books.

Kagan, S. (1994). *Cooperative learning.* San Clemente, CA: Kagan Publishing.

Kagan, S. (2000). *Silly sports and goofy games.* San Clemente, CA: Kagan Publishing.

Kagan, S., & Kagan, M. (1998). *Multiple intelligences: The complete book.* San Clemente, CA: Kagan Publishing.

Kagan, L., Kagan, M., & Kagan, S. (1997). *Cooperative learning structures for teambuilding.* San Clemente, CA: Kagan Publishing.

Kagan, M., Robertson, L., & Kagan, S. (1995). *Cooperative learning structures for classbuilding.* San Clemente, CA: Kagan Publishing.

Pert, C. B., & Chopra, D. (1997). *Molecules of emotions: Why you feel the way you feel.* New York: Scribner.

Sylwester, R. (1995). *A celebration of neurons: An educators guide to the human brain.* Alexandria, VA: Association for supervision and curriculum development.

Surveys and Cooperative Learning: Using Student Experiences as the Basis for Small-group Work

Mark H. Maier

In my experience as a college instructor, I find that cooperative learning can be combined effectively with surveys in which students analyze data gathered from each other. I use the term "survey" broadly to encompass many types of empirical and descriptive information collected from students either prior to class or as part of an in-class activity. Possibilities include analyses of students' poem interpretations in English courses, interviews of students' cultures in ESL courses, and analyses of household incomes in economics courses. The unifying element in these examples is that small groups work with information drawn from students' experiences.

Why Use Surveys?

Because students often are eager to examine information that comes from themselves and their peers, surveys provide rich classroom content for small-group activities. In addition, group process may improve because surveys turn student attention away from the instructor and toward other group members. When data are collected within the small group itself, success by the group requires participation from every student. This promotes positive interdependence, a key feature of cooperative learning. Also, because each small group has different information for analysis, students are less likely to sandbag, that is, wait for the instructor to solve the problem. Even when data are collected from the class as a whole and each group is working with the same information, the problem has inherent appeal because it is specific to those class members, and not "cooked up" by the instructor.

Providing examples related to student experience is common practice in college lectures. However, surveys allow instructors to collect fresh material quickly so that the examples can form the basis of small-group activities. Michael Dulay, a psychology instructor at Glendale Community College suggested the following class activity in which the instructor identifies the implicit view of human behavior used by students when they analyze an event on campus.

> *Psychology.* The instructor notes that fights have become a common occurrence in school parking lots. Students are asked to respond individually to: "Why do you think they occur?" These student reflections are used later in class for a small-group activity in which students correlate their responses with different theories of human behavior (biological, learning theory, psychodynamic, cognitive, sociocultural).

In the next examples, instructors use surveys to find out what students learned prior to class, a technique readily applicable to other disciplines.

> *English.* Richard Dry, an English instructor at Las Positas College, asks students to identify three sentences in the reading assignment: one that conveys an important idea, one that conveys an incorrect or weak idea, and one that is confusing. In small groups, students assess those incorrect and confusing sentences and rewrite them.

> *Plant systematics.* The instructor surveys students about which three plants that they have the most trouble identifying. In small groups, students develop methods for correctly identifying these plants.

Surveys also can help instructors address misperceptions, contradictions and ambiguities in student thinking. In the following example, a political science instructor determines the bias students bring to their study of Marxism. Later, after course work on Marxism, students revisit their initial understanding to see if it has changed.

Political science. Before a section on the ideas of Karl Marx, the instructor asks students for words or phrases they would use to characterize Marxism. After students have completed a reading and listened to a lecture, small groups evaluate the appropriateness of their words and phrases.

Four Strategies for Implementing Surveys

As with other cooperative learning techniques, surveys raise the issue of time constraints. How is it possible to collect information and analyze it within a typical class meeting? Unless the subject matter itself focuses on data collection, as in a survey methods course, instructors will want to minimize the information collection process. The following section describes four classroom-tested methods for quickly gathering survey results. The first method listed below, Whole-class, In-class Anonymous Survey is, in my experience, the easiest method for gathering data quickly. The Whole-class, In-class Non-anonymous Survey allows instructors to query students about their responses. The In-class Small-group Survey requires students to collect their own data. Finally, the Before Class Electronic Survey utilizes Internet classroom management tools in the survey process.

I. Whole-class, In-class Anonymous Survey

1. Provide a clearly stated question that students will answer. Ask if there are uncertainties about the question. If personal information is involved, state that students may decline to participate by simply not turning in their responses.

2. Ask students to write their answers either on a form provided, or on blank pieces of paper. Remind students not to add their names.

3. Collect all answers.

4. Redistribute answers at random. Tell students that if they receive their own answers not to say anything.

5. Gather survey data by asking students to respond, perhaps by raising their hands, using the answers redistributed to them, *not*

the answers they wrote. This step preserves confidentiality and allows survey results to be compiled quickly.
    6. Proceed with the appropriate small-group activity.

    Following are two appropriate activities.

    Sociology. In a lecture class with more than 100 students, the instructor wants to show that most individuals consider themselves to be "middle class." Using the Whole-class, In-class Anonymous Survey the instructor obtains confidential data on students' self-described class status. The survey is administered and data compiled in less than five minutes.

    Economics. Data on household income have been collected anonymously from the entire class. Working in small groups, students organize the data as a Lorenz Curve, measure its Gini coefficient and compare the equality of the classroom income distribution with the equality of U.S. income distribution (Keenan & Maier, 1999).

II. Whole-class, In-class Non-anonymous Survey

    1. The instructor poses a clearly stated question and provides three to six possible answers based on different solutions or strengths of feelings. These answers are then written on the board.
    2. Students work in pairs to choose solutions. These choices and students' names are written on post-it notes, or on 3x5 cards if explanations are required.
    3. Students stick their post-it notes next to the matching answer on the blackboard (or place them in piles under the matching answers if 3x5 cards are used). If the class is large, student volunteers may place the answers in appropriate piles.
    4. The instructor chooses individual Post-its or cards to ask for additional explanation for a particular answer, if needed.
    5. Students begin the appropriate small-group activity based on the results. They may be given the opportunity to change their answers.

The two samples activities below illustrate the use of the Whole-class, In-class Non-anonymous Survey.

Journalism. Posted in front of the room are possible lead sentences for one newspaper story. Student pairs indicate which lead sentence is preferable and explain why on a 3x5 card. In a follow-up activity, students work in small groups to write a better lead sentence (Aschettino, 1993).

Economics. Todd Easton, an economics professor at the University of Portland, has his students study the private benefits and external costs of studded tires. Policy choices are all posted in the front of the room: status quo, new tax, and abolition of studded tires. Student pairs select a policy by sticking a Post-it on the policy array. During subsequent discussion, students may change their minds and move their Post-its.

III. In-class Small-group Survey

1. Working in small groups, students conduct surveys based on their own groups. In this step, students develop and practice the survey question, adjusting its wording so that the survey will succeed.

2. Students collect survey information from another group or groups using the question developed in step 1. The information may be collected from one other group so that the sample includes two groups, or each individual may collect data from a different group so that the sample includes several groups.

3. Proceed with the appropriate small-group activity.

For example, the following is an activity for a history class.

History. Students survey one another about their high school experiences to test the hypothesis that social class is a concept avoided in secondary school history courses.

IV. Before Class Electronic Survey

1. Pose a question to students using Internet classroom management software such as Blackboard or WebCT (Novak, Patterson, Gavrin, & Christian, 1999).
2. Require that the answers be submitted prior to the beginning of class with enough time for the instructor to analyze them.
3. Distribute student answers for an appropriate small-group activity, such as the three below.

> *Music history.* Before class, ask students to list the influences they hear in a musical piece. For each influence listed, students must provide a short explanation.

> *History.* Peggy Renner, a history instructor at Glendale Community College, has team members read different interpretations of Virginia colony's 1675 Bacon's rebellion. Then each team member gives a short summary of that interpretation and the team explores causes of the rebellion.

> *Art history.* Before class, students have viewed two versions of a painting, one original and one copy. Students must select the original and explain why they made this choice.

Determining the Instructional Goal

Surveys have the potential to fulfill several possible instructional goals: they can help students learn to write good questions, they can help students evaluate the responses of other students, they can help students to determine the diversity of student viewpoints, and they can help students organize and interpret information. Typically, instructors will choose only one of these goals as the focus for group work. For example, in the following activity for a physics class, students explain why a rewinding tape spins faster at the end than at the beginning. The instructor designs the question, collects the information, and chooses which responses will be analyzed by other students. This cooperative learning activity requires students to evaluate other students' answers. The instructor completes the more mundane steps so that students can focus on the most rewarding task.

Goal: To help students to evaluate the responses by other students.
   Physics. Prior to class, students submit answers to a question about the rewind speed of video or audiotapes. Responses are chosen by the instructor and distributed to small groups. Working with a rubric, students evaluate the accuracy, clarity and completeness of the answers (Novak, Patterson, Gavrin, & Christian, 1999).

Goal: To help students to write good questions.
   Statistics. Working as an entire class, students agree on a problem-free survey question regarding a non-intrusive characteristic such as family size or number of CDs owned. Small groups administer the survey with at least one group member responsible for recording measurement problems in this ideal survey.

Goal: To help students to determine the diversity or homogeneity of student viewpoints.
   English. Working in small groups, students survey classmates on their responses to a poem with an ambiguous ending. The different meanings students find in the ending of the poem are identified.

Goal: To help students organize and interpret information.
   Social work. Working in small groups, students examine information they have collected about boards of directors at their practicum locations.

Putting Surveys in a Cooperative Learning Format

It may be a challenge to use student responses—often voluminous and disorganized—as the basis for small-group activities. One major contribution of the cooperative learning literature is that it provides structures that help students work together in a focused and efficient manner (Millis & Cottell, 1998; MacGregor, Cooper, Smith, & Robinson, 2000). Cooperative learning structures that work effectively with survey data are Paired Critique, Small Group Analysis, and Group Survey.

I. Paired Critique

Variation one. Each student pair receives a copy of one student response. Using a rubric distributed by the instructor, pairs analyze the response.

Variation two. All responses are distributed randomly to student pairs (two responses per pair). Student pairs critique responses and return them to the original authors.

> *Math.* Prior to class, students solve a problem and provide a careful step-by-step explanation of their solutions. The instructor selects one or more student answers for analysis. Working in pairs, students evaluate the step-by-step explanations for accuracy and clarity.

> *Geology.* Prior to class, students are asked to explain plate tectonics as if they are speaking to their 80 year-old uncles. These answers are distributed randomly to pairs of students who must judge the explanations for accuracy, clarity and originality.

II. Small Group Analysis

Patti Lynn O'Brien, a member of the education faculty at Central Connecticut State University, suggests that students work in small groups to consider a controversial issue for which a number of possible answers have been posted on the board. If consensus in a group is reached, students choose that answer, write an explanation on a 3x5 card, and place it under the answer chosen. If there is no consensus, more than one card may be submitted. The instructor tabulates the responses and selects competing answers for elaboration.

> *Education.* Groups are asked: "When is it appropriate to introduce a discussion of homosexuality to students?" Listed answers include: never, in college, in high school, in middle school, or in grade school.

III. Group Survey

Working in small groups, students collect data from other students using the fast In-class Small-group Survey method described previously. In the ESL example below, students learn language skills in constructing, administering, and reporting the results of a survey, a technique that could be easily applied in foreign language study. The example from economics is a classroom experiment in which student behavior is used to illustrate an economic concept.

> *ESL.* Working in small groups, ESL students write questions for surveys to be administered to non-ESL students on campus regarding their attitudes toward immigrant students. After collecting the data, students write summaries of the survey results (Leki, 1999).

> *Economics.* Students interview one another to find out their willingness to supply their labor at various wages. Small groups use the data to draw and analyze a labor supply curve (Keenan & Maier 1999).

The techniques presented in this chapter are intended to encourage the use of surveys in disciplines in which they are not often considered. It is not necessary to collect empirical data, nor is it necessary to analyze survey data with the high level of rigor that might be expected in a statistics course. By using one of the quick survey methods listed above, it is possible in nearly any discipline to generate data in the classroom. In combination with cooperative learning, these survey techniques effectively engage students with analyses of data drawn from their own experiences.

References

Aschettino, E. M. (1993). Cooperative learning structures to foster student involvement. *Cooperative Learning and College Teaching.* 4(1), 12–14.

Keenan, D., & Maier, M. (1999). *Economics live! Learning economics the collaborative way.* New York: McGraw-Hill.

Leki, I. (1999) *Academic writing: Exploring processes and strategies.* New York: St. Martin's Press.

MacGregor, J., Cooper, J. L., Smith K. A., & Robinson, P. (Eds.) (2000). *Strategies for energizing large classes: From small groups to learning communities.* San Francisco: Jossey-Bass.

Millis, B., & Cottell, P. G. (1998). *Cooperative learning for higher education faculty.* Phoenix: Oryx Press.

Novak, G., Patterson, E., Gavrin, A., & Christian, W. (1999). *Just-in-time teaching: Blending active learning with web technology.* Upper Saddle River, New Jersey: Prentice-Hall.

Using Cooperative Games for Learning and Assessment

Barbara J. Millis

Games have a long human history. According to Costello (1991) the earliest known game board, probably dating back to between 4000-3500 BC, was found in a predynastic cemetery in El-Mehasna, Egypt. Measuring just seven by three inches, it appears to be an early version of Senet, a backgammon-type game based on the underworld, that was popular in Egypt for over a thousand years. Tomb paintings depict players eagerly engrossed in play. Games, including variations of the popular African strategy game, Mancala, have been found in East and West Africa, southern India and Sri Lanka. Some games, such as the North American Native Americans' games of dexterity and chance, were typically played by adults for recreation, but others, for example Mayan and Aztec ball court games, suggest darker elements.

In general, however, games typically appeal to the human love of play and tend to engage one's entire attention. Their learning value was quickly put to use in the early U.S. colonies. Didactic games assuaged the early settlers' fear of frivolity and emphasized moral development. Love (1979) declares that the first board game produced, in what later became the United States, sought to teach children the difference between right and wrong.

El-Shamy (2001) defines a game as a "competitive activity played according to rules within a given context, where players meet a challenge in their attempt to accomplish a goal and win" (p. 21). She distinguishes a game from a simulation in that the latter often deliberately sets up an uneven playing field where players begin unequally or receive unequal treatment as the simulation progresses. Furthermore, unlike the fantasy worlds prevalent in some games, simulations often mirror real-life situations and encourage players to gain insights and/or to build their professional skills by making informed decisions. In classroom settings the distinctions between games and simulations often blur, so the term "game" will be used to describe all of the goal-based activities discussed in this chapter.

The Solid Educational Basis of Games

Games are effective learning tools for a number of reasons. They mesh with many theories of educational development, including adult learning theory with its emphasis on self-directed, goal-oriented learning. Games also appeal to a variety of senses, particularly the visual, auditory, and kinesthetic, making them attractive to different types of learners. New developments in cognitive psychology emphasize the role of emotions in learning: games create positive associations and also allow for the repetition and deeper processing that strengthens neural pathways. As Thiagarajan (1999) reminds us: "Learners cannot master skills without repeated practice and feedback" (p. vii).

Games can become even more effective, when cooperative elements are introduced. Students who work in teams or pairs have significant advantages over individuals who compete against other individuals. The anxiety level lessens when more than one head is involved and the social context heightens team motivation. Furthermore, the dialogue and discussion that occurs within the teams as members respond to questions encourages higher order thinking such as analysis and evaluation. Feedback is enhanced by the immediate responses of peers, leading to reflection and reinforcement. In developing cooperative games to be used as learning tools, instructors need to keep in mind the key principles behind cooperative learning, including individual accountability, positive interdependence (vested reasons to work together), and the need for group processing and feedback (Millis & Cottell, 1998).

Teachers will want to place games in the context of sequenced learning. Students should be responsible for learning material on their own so that class time can be used beneficially for student-student interactions and active learning techniques that provide feedback on how well the material has been mastered. This approach fosters a deep, rather than a surface learning approach. The research on deep learning has been ongoing, systematic, and convergent. A project, Improving Student Learning, sponsored by the Council for National Academic Awards in Britain, was initiated not to generate new research about student learning, but rather to encourage faculty to use the existing research and tools to strengthen their courses. The project is predicated on research indicating that:

> The students' approach to learning—whether they take a surface or a deep approach—[is] the crucial factor determining the quality of learning outcomes. Those who take a deep approach understand more, produce better written work containing logical structures and conclusions rather than lists, remember longer, and obtain better marks and degrees than those students who take a surface approach. (Cited in Rhem, "Deep Learning, Surface Learning," 1995, p. 14)

Rhem (1995) cites three international scholars, Ference Marton of Sweden, Noel Entwistle of Scotland, and Paul Ramsden of Australia, whom have identified the same emergent patterns in deep learning. This research suggests that although specific implementations will vary, four key components characterize a deep approach to learning. These four components—motivational context, learner activity, interaction with others, and a well-structured knowledge base—are evident when students are motivated to master content outside of class for an upcoming game that is structured cooperatively.

One way to measure the efficacy of games as a learning tool is to place them in the context of Chickering and Gamson's (1987) highly respected, *Seven Principles for Good Practice in Undergraduate Education*. These principles were compiled by a team of scholars and educational researchers in a study supported by the American Association of Higher Education, the Education Commission of the States, and the Johnson Foundation, and will be discussed below.

Good Practice Encourages Student-Faculty Contact

As academic games progress, the faculty member/facilitator constantly observes the students to assess their progress. When teachers function as game show hosts or hostesses, they encourage students to perceive them as likeable and approachable. Games often require student input to an instructor, which increases the communication channels, particularly through e-mail exchanges or submissions. As Chickering and Gamson (1987) emphasize, "frequent student-faculty contact in and out of classes is the most important factor in student motivation and involvement."

Good Practice Encourages Cooperation Among Students

Healthy competition between teams promotes interest and involvement. However, it is essential for students to see the value of working together. Thus, games should be designed to promote the peer coaching and sharing of information that leads to increased learning and camaraderie. Chickering and Gamson (1987) point out that "sharing one's own ideas and responding to others' reactions improves thinking and deepens understanding."

Good Practice Encourages Active Learning

Games definitely promote active learning and can increase student commitment to learning. Games often involve physical as well as mental activity; "High fives" and cheers are as much a part of the process as the rules of the game. Chickering and Gamson (1987) succinctly remind us that "learning is not a spectator sport."

Good Practice Gives Prompt Feedback

Numerous scholars, including Angelo and Cross (1993) emphasize the tremendous impact that feedback has on learning. "Knowing what you know and don't know focuses learning," according to Chickering and Gamson (1987). Cooperative games offer immediate feedback from peers during the discussion period. When an answer is given, feedback is further refined. Finally, teachers can understand how well students have mastered their content by monitoring their performance level during play and by reviewing their worksheets after the game has concluded.

Good Practice Emphasizes Time on Task

As Chickering and Gamson (1987) put it, "Time plus energy equals learning." During cooperative games students are totally focused on the game, thereby increasing learning. Games typically progress rapidly and energetically to maximize learning within a short period of time because of the intense focus.

Good Practice Communicates High Expectations

Using cooperative games suggests to students that teachers not only care about their learning, but that they are also willing to let learning occur in an atmosphere of fun and cooperative competition. Chickering and Gamson (1987) remind us that "high expectations are important for everyone—for the poorly prepared, for those unwilling to exert themselves, and for the bright and well motivated." Because many games introduce an element of luck, such as the roll of a die or the pick of a card, all students—regardless of their relative skill levels—have opportunities to succeed.

Good Practice Respects Diverse Talents and Ways of Learning

Chickering and Gamson (1987) state that "there are many roads to learning. People bring different talents and styles of learning to college. Students need the opportunity to show their talents and learn in ways that work for them. Then they can be pushed to learning in new ways that do not come so easily."

Cooperative games offer an exhilarating, motivating alternative to traditional lectures or discussions. They allow many students to excel and to become well-respected team members.

Principles Underlying Effective Game Use

Typically, instructors will assign students specific material to master prior to the game and then use the in-class game activity as a means of processing the information and providing feedback on whether or not it has been mastered. Occasionally, a game will precede formal instruction. Popular in corporations and training settings, games and simulations can also play an important place in the classroom, if the following six key principles to optimize learning are applied.

1.) Students must understand the relevance of games to the course objectives. Adult learners, in particular, may find games a waste of their time and money if they perceive them to be frivolous. Thus, any game activity must be preceded by clear explanations, including a careful rationale linked to course goals.

2.) One way to ensure the educational value of games is to match the level of challenge to students' skills. Thus, games should offer challenges to all students, but the material should not be so complex that students feel overwhelmed—and thus will give up; or so simple that they lose interest in participating.

3.) To ensure continuing interest, games should be designed so that they are predicated on a combination of knowledge and luck. This premise is extremely important because otherwise one or two dominant teams will discourage other teams from contributing their best efforts. If only knowledge is involved, then the same teams will repeatedly win, a disincentive for other teams to master the material prior to play or to continue trying to score if they fall behind. If the game is predicated only on luck, then obviously students have no incentive to study the material prior to play. Because the luck of the draw determines the placement of markers games like BINGO incorporate this combination of knowledge and luck.

4.) To maximize learning, games should be structured cooperatively. There can be competition between teams, but optimum learning will take place during the independent learning accomplished prior to the game and with the peer coaching that occurs as team players agree on responses. Peer consultations reinforce learning or provide instantaneous feedback that learning was nonexistent, incomplete, or misguided.

5.) Games must emphasize learning. Both instructors and students must recognize that the greatest learning occurs during "processing" periods, either as the game unfolds or at the end. A post-game debriefing by the instructor helps students learn what they have mastered or should have mastered. Too often, instructors may gloss over these critical "teachable moments" in the spirit of fun. This is a serious mistake—however unconscious—because the game then loses its relevance. As Sugar (1998) advises: "Know what you want your audience to learn or demonstrate during and after the game" (p. 8). Keen, dean of the faculty of Antioch College, states that the research on whether games promote learning is still mixed: "It depends on whether you're savvy about why you are doing it and if you take the time to work up to it and to debrief. The rule is to spend at least as much time debriefing as you spend playing the game; otherwise, what did you do it for?" (Quoted in Rhem, 1996).

6.) Classroom games must be well organized and well structured so that class time is not wasted on vague instructions and confusion. Obviously, the game playing period must be appropriate for the length of the class, and the physical environment must allow teams to work together.

Examples of Effective Educational Games

An educational game should be an intriguing blend of novelty and familiarity. That is why well-known formats such as BINGO or Jeopardy are particularly effective. Instructors can add their own creative touches by using seasonal items for BINGO markers such as candy hearts or Halloween candy.

BINGO

BINGO is a game format which is adaptable to virtually all disciplines. For example, in foreign language or English as a Second Language (ESL) classrooms, word or sentence translations provide the content for rapid scoring. BINGO sheets can be created using the "Table" option on most word processing packages. Alternatively, Sugar (1994) has developed a set of reusable materials for a variation of BINGO called QUIZO. Many instructors use it as a viable, engaging review for a midterm or final examination.

As students study prior to play, they e-mail their instructors two or more questions that include factual and higher order thinking items. In a composition class with a research paper requirement a factual question could be: "Define 'search engine' "; and an open-ended question might ask classmates to provide three examples of plagiarism. In a literature class, questions could include "What is the name of Antigone's sister?" (Factual) and "Why did Antigone insist on burying her brother?" (Open-ended or interpretive). Students need to be coached on question writing. Their most common problem is making them overly complex. They need to learn to quantify answers (e.g., "List three of the six steps in contract negotiation."). Students typically receive credit for their questions, such as points applied toward a criterion referenced final grade. They must indicate the type of question, provide the answer, and identify where the answer can be found for later reference. A typical entry would look like this:

Factual Question
Define mitosis.
Student: John Doe

Answer: A process that takes place in the nucleus of a dividing cell that results in the formation of two new nuclei each having the same number of chromosomes as the parent nucleus.
Source: *Learning Biology* by Adams and Smith, p. 57.

Learning to write viable, cogent questions is a valuable skill in and of itself. For example, a Nobel prize-winning physicist, Isidor Rabi, credits his mother with prompting him to value the questions he asked above the answers he gave. When he returned from school, she never asked him what he learned that day. Instead, she asked him, what good *questions* he asked that day (Barell as cited in Costa & O'Leary, 1992).

Instructors play critical roles in evaluating and categorizing the student-submitted questions. They eliminate weak and inaccurate questions, perhaps returning them to the students for revisions or replacements. They also add significant questions that will help students learn critical material. They rank order the questions within the two categories (factual and open-ended) so that the most valuable questions will occur early in the play. They "cut and paste" the questions to a document that will later be given to students—in hard copy, via e-mail, or on a web page—as a study guide.

To use the questions during play, instructors enlarge the fonts to prepare transparencies. There needs to be a space between the student's name and the answer, so that the answer can be easily covered when the question is posed. Instructors purchase needed supplies: Skittles or M&Ms for the markers, and candy bars—large and snack sizes—for the prizes. Healthier prize alternatives can be bags of pretzels, cocoa packets, or Kleenex packs.

To play the game, the instructor often purposefully pairs weak students with strong students for coaching and teaching. Although most students know the object of BINGO (five markers in a row in any direction) and the rules of play, it is important to explain the procedures so that those who don't know BINGO are not compromised or made to feel inept. Each pair receives markers and two colored work sheets (green for the factual; gold for the higher level questions) where they record their answers and if they were right or wrong. A work sheet [abbreviated] looks like this:

Factual Questions		
Student Pair or Trio:		
Answer	Rt or Wrong?	Space
1. Cro Magnon	Rt	B2
2.		

The instructor then poses the questions in sequence within each category, giving sufficient time based on their complexity. To make the game student-centered and to allow students to receive feedback on the viability and fairness of their questions, the student who submitted the question is the expert/arbitrator who decides what alternative answers are acceptable.

Pairs with correct answers place a marker on the designated square (e.g., B2 or G4). The square is determined by having the pairs in turn draw a scrabble tile or a homemade variation (B,I,N,G,O) and roll a die (they roll again if a six emerges). Instructors can purchase a ten-sided die with only five numbers at novelty shops.

Pacing is very important. The factual questions speed up play and the higher order thinking questions lead to valuable class discussion/teaching. The first pair (often there will be ties) to cover five contiguous squares in any direction declares "BINGO." They then clear their boards and continue playing until the period ends. In a 50-minute period, it is possible for every pair to become "winners." The winners select their prizes: those "BINGOing" first invariably choose the large candy bars, leaving the mini-bars for the ones who finish later. After the games, as a study aid, students receive copies of the questions and answers or they are posted to a class web page.

Besides the active involvement with learning, the assessment value of BINGO is phenomenal. Because the students submit the questions, the instructor gets an immediate sense of their knowledge. Students often receive immediate feedback from the instructor on the value of their questions, and later during play, they get vocal, often vehement feedback from their fellow classmates on the quality and fairness of their questions. As question experts, students teach the material, making the class student-centered. By reviewing the work sheets with the recorded answers, instructors get a sense of which questions students did well on or missed.

Students are actively engaged with the material, thus increasing the likelihood of their remembering it. Enthusiastic and energetic students often "high-five" each other when they get a correct answer. They listen attentively to the answers and suddenly care about the material, even where the commas go in an MLA bibliographic entry.

Jeopardy

As a review prior to examinations Gibsen (1991) divides the material into six categories or topic areas, as is done on the TV show. The students are divided into teams. During the day of the review, the instructor, serving as the emcee, provides the teams with answers of increasing difficulty, and allows them to accumulate points as they confer on the proper responses. As in the TV show, the game includes Daily Doubles and a Final Jeopardy.

Gray-Shellberg (1994) devised an ingenious ongoing Jeopardy game combining the well-known quiz-show format with the cooperative jigsaw technique. Students submitted ten Jeopardy questions on index cards for each chapter of the text, rated on five levels of difficulty. Each team assigned one student to a particular subtopic in the chapter. The students then met in expert teams where they discussed the topic in depth, ensuring that all experts not only mastered the materials, but were also capable of teaching it in the same depth to their other team members prior to the Jeopardy competition. In preparation for the game, the home teams reassembled and team members coached the other members on their portions of the chapter. Meanwhile, the instructor selected student-generated questions of various difficulty levels from each section of the chapter. During play, designated players, rotating systematically, responded from each team, ensuring that no one student could dominate. The teams indicated their readiness to respond with a noisemaker and the instructor, serving as the game show host, assigned points based on the question difficulty level. To facilitate play, a student assistant, dubbed "Vanna" or "Danna," distributed point/money cards to the teams providing correct responses.

Course grades were not based on student performance during the Jeopardy game. To emphasize individual accountability, the following percentages were used for course grades:

- Quality and quantity of the Jeopardy questions: 25%
- Scores on three class examinations 55%
- Attendance 10%
- Participation 10%

Although Gray-Shellberg conceded that this ongoing class format was time-consuming, she felt that students' positive attitudes toward the course and their enthusiasm about learning the course material made the effort worthwhile.

Reaction Course

Revak and Kline (1998) and their colleagues developed a dynamic, engaging game that gets students physically as well as academically involved. The activity, called a Reaction Course, is appropriate for any topic for which practice or review is needed. In this game, groups of students progress through five stations, working on different problems or questions at each station. The goal is for the students to complete each station of the course in the allotted time, gaining as many points as possible.

To prepare, instructors create problems or questions in the desired topic area that should be of similar difficulty level so that an equal amount of time can be allotted for each station. Instructors write out detailed solutions for each problem or question. They create a scoring rubric with point values to be awarded for each problem or question that goes on the solution sheet. Each team receives a blank Reaction Course scorecard with members' names and the team's sequence of stations. Each team starts at a different station but all teams rotate through all the other stations. The correct solutions and point values can be on the back of problem/question sheets, or they can be kept at the instructor's desk. More time will be needed if instructors opt to check the solutions themselves.

Before class starts, instructors post station signs and problems around the classroom (chalkboard ledges work well—students can write their solutions on the boards). To begin play, they announce the time limit for each station (all need to be equal) and distribute a scorecard to each team. Student teams then proceed to their designated stations and start the clock. When time runs out, students check their answers against the approved solutions and record the number of points earned. If students finish working at their stations before time runs out, they may check their solutions early. However, once they see the correct answers, they may not make changes to their work. When all solutions have been checked and the points recorded, the teams progress to the next stations. Play continues until all teams have visited all stations. At that point, the instructor collects the scorecards and determines which team won. Scores may be used to award prizes (points, candy, or privileges) or as quiz or participation grades.

As with all cooperative activities, instructors monitor students' progress. They circle their classrooms to make sure that all students are actively involved, asking questions and giving hints as needed. Little or no learning will occur if students are unable to even begin a proposed solution. The instructor can add props such as a whistle and a ringmaster's circus hat to highlight the Reaction Course theme.

Go Fish

This game, also developed by Revak and Kline (1998) and their colleagues in the Department of Mathematics, is modeled after the children's card game Go Fish with modified rules. It offers a useful way to help students make connections between different aspects of a topic. The instructor prepares a special deck of cards with sets of three cards to four cards, all having some relationship to one another. The game may be used in any subject area requiring matching of facts or concepts. Sets of cards for English literature might have an author card (Shakespeare), a title card (*Hamlet*), and a famous passage card ("To be or not to be"). A fourth card in this set might be a speaker card (Hamlet). Sets of cards for a chemistry class might have a chemical name card (sodium chloride), a formula card (NaCl), and a common name card (table salt). Sets of cards for a mathematics class might have a polynomial card ($x^2 - 7x + 10$), its factorization card ($[x - 2][x - 5]$), and a zeros card (2, 5).

To involve students in the preparation process and to help their learning, instructors, as in BINGO, can require them to contribute possible sets. These sets are used not only to develop decks of cards, but they are also made available, usually on a web page, as a study aid prior to play.

Example of an English Literature Class Using "Go Fish" to Learn the Plays of Shakespeare

To play, the instructor divides the class into groups of three or four students and gives each group a deck of cards. A dealer in each group deals four cards to each player, and places the remaining cards facedown on the table. The dealer begins game play by identifying another player and requesting a specific card: "John, do you have the speaker, 'Hamlet'?" If the player has the requested card, he must relinquish it. Otherwise, the player responds with "go fish," and the requesting player draws a card from the table. Play proceeds around the group. Players who acquire complete sets of three or four cards place the cards face-up on the table during their turn. The other players then check the cards and offer challenges if the set is erroneous. If a set is inaccurate, the player producing it must continue play with those cards. Play proceeds until all players are out of cards. The player with the most accurate sets on the table at the end of the game wins designated prizes, such as candy bars.

Instructors can prepare different decks of cards that are used simultaneously by different groups. That way, if groups finish a game with their original deck, they can then swap with another team that has also reached the end of play. Thus, each group will remain on task and will now face a new set of concepts. Learning is enhanced through the repetition involved in asking for cards in a set and through the reinforced associations.

Conclusion

The word "game" carries with it a certain amount of baggage for many educators who may echo Ms. Trunchbull's credo in the movie *Matilda*: "If you are having fun, you are not learning." Many instructors, on the contrary, have found that students become engaged in learning through carefully structured, highly interactive game formats. In cases where students design games, such as "Who Wants to Be a Millionaire" for their classmates to play, they add wonderfully creative touches that enhance academic learning. Making the games cooperative enhances both student involvement and learning.

References

Angelo, T. A., & Cross, K. P. (1993). *Classroom assessment techniques: A handbook for college teachers.* San Francisco: Jossey-Bass.

Barell, J. (Ed.). (1988, April). *Cogitare, 3*(1). Alexandria, VA: Association for Supervision and Curriculum Development

Chickering, A. W., & Gamson, A. F. (1987). Seven principles for good practice in undergraduate education. Racine, WI: The Johnson Foundation, Inc./ Wingspread. [Available by contacting the Seven Principles Resources Center, P.O. Box 5838, Winona State University, Winona, MN 55987-5838; (507) 457-5020]

Costello, M. J. (1991). The greatest games of all times. New York: John Wiley and Sons.

El-Shamy, S. (2001). Training games: Everything you need to know about using games to reinforce learning. New York: Sage.

Gibson, B. (1991). Research methods Jeopardy: A tool for involving students and organizing the study session. *Teaching of Psychology, 18* (3), 176-177.

Gray-Shellberg, L. (1994). Jeopardy 305: A cooperative learning method for teaching history and systems of psychology. *Cooperative Learning and College Teaching, 5* (1), pp. 12-14.

Love, B. (1979). *Great board games.* New York: McMillan.

Millis, B. & Cottell, P. (1998). *Cooperative learning for higher education faculty.* Phoenix: Oryx Press (Now available through Greenwood Press).

Revak, M., & Kline, B. (1998). *Teaching toolbox II.* Faculty development workshop offered at the United States Air Force Academy, Colorado Springs, CO.

Rhem, J. (1995). Deep/surface approaches to learning: An introduction. *The National Teaching & Learning Forum, 5* (1), 1-3.

Sugar, S. (1994). *Games that teach.* Faculty Development Workshop offered at the University of Maryland, College Park, MD.

Sugar, S. (1998). Games that teach: Experiential activities for reinforcing learning. San Francisco: Jossey-Bass.

Thiagarajan, S. & Parker, G. M. (1999). *Teamwork and teamplay: Games and activities for building and training teams.* San Francisco: Jossey-Bass.

The Interactive Lecture: Reconciling Group and Active-learning Strategies with Traditional Instructional Formats

James L. Cooper, Pamela Robinson, and David Ball

When Jim first began using cooperative learning in 1985, he assumed that it would be a matter of a few years before most teachers in higher education would be using small-group instruction. He thought that the research foundation for small-group instruction was among the largest of any educational intervention since it was based on several hundred research studies (Johnson & Johnson, 1989; Ellis & Fouts, 1994). Over the last 15 years researchers and theorists including Wilbert McKeachie, Robert Slavin, Alexander Astin, Donald Bligh and Kenneth Bruffee have added their voices to the national reports of disciplinary groups and professional organizations calling for the use of small groups to engage students. Although many today in higher education are using some form of group work, it has not taken hold in ways that Jim had predicted.

In considering reasons for this, Jim examined what professors were saying who seemed resistant to considering a movement from a lecture format to one that involved more student involvement. Their reasons for not changing to a more student-centered, group approach focused on: 1) problems in assigning grades for group work; 2) concerns about sacrificing content which could be covered with the lecture, but which could not be covered if significant amounts of class time were spent in group activities; and 3) the amount of time and risk involved in redesigning existing courses which, if not exceptional, were perceived as satisfactory by the teacher. Perhaps implicit in some of the resistance was a fear of change. And some of that fear seemed to come from the impression that those of us in favor of active and cooperative learning sent the message that those tied to lectures are Luddites, fearful of taking even the smallest of risks in their classrooms.

Pamela joined Jim at California State University, Dominguez Hills (CSUDH) in 1991; shortly thereafter, she began teaching the class that Jim has been teaching since 1974, Research Methods and Statistics in Education. They began exchanging ideas relating to teaching strategies appropriate to this content-dense class required of (and feared by many) students in all M.A. Education programs at CSUDH. About 70% of our students are minority, with great differences in prior academic achievement and in levels of math anxiety. Ultimately, Jim and Pamela came up with the Interactive Lecture notion, which is described below.

Jim and Pamela note that 50% of their class time still utilizes a teacher-focused format. They acknowledge that the lecture is still an effective way to present information designed for the particular audience taking their classes and that lectures allow them to model a form of academic discourse that they want their students to ultimately use. Thus, they implicitly believe that the lecture serves useful purposes, as Cuseo (1996), Johnson and Johnson (1989) and McKeachie (2001) have long noted.

Jim and Pamela are not radical constructivists who believe that an entire class period should be spent having students construct their own meaning in groups and in other active-learning environments. Neither do they believe that all learning comes from the teacher explicitly modeling all the information to be mastered for later student assessment on tests. Rather, they believe that some portion of the class should be spent having the teacher model appropriate ways of thinking about the subject matter, then stopping the class every 15-30 minutes in order to have the students practice or otherwise reflect on previous content (either individually or in pairs). After leading the class through several iterations of this Model-Practice-Feedback loop, both Jim and Pamela break students into formal groups of four to engage in more formal and elaborate team problem-solving work.

It has taken Jim and Pamela several years to come to this set of teaching strategies, blending teacher-led instruction with cooperative group work. Jim and Pamela have had the advice and support of Susan Prescott Johnston, Joe Cuseo and a number of other collaborators in developing and implementing this strategy. How realistic is it to expect a single faculty member without this kind of support, to move from the lecture format that has guided his/her professional life, to more student-centered teaching strategies?

Sample Interactive Lecture Narrative

In order to succinctly describe the Interactive Lecture, we would like to describe a hypothetical scenario in which a second-year faculty member incorporates the Interactive Lecture and cooperative learning in her class.

Dr. Paula Paxton, a second-year teacher in the graduate education program at CSUDH, enters her class in Research Methods and Statistics in Education with a sense of anticipation. She has taught this class for two semesters and the student reception of her lectures has been muted at best. Lecturing on this topic has proven to be difficult, particularly because the content is dense for most students and the class is almost three hours in length. Her graduate students, most of whom work in inner-city schools, often fail to see the benefit of the course content and frequently arrive at the weekly 7:00 PM class exhausted from eight- to ten-hour workdays. Also, many have taken another graduate class from 4:00-6:45 PM.

This semester however, Dr. Paula has the advantage of a weeklong workshop on interactive lecturing, provided by the Center for Teaching and Learning. She begins this class (Week 7 in the semester) by briefly reviewing the material covered in the previous class meeting and previewing this evening's content. By doing this, she gives students an overall structure for the day's activities and gets them to start relating the new content to information that they have been exposed to previously. This encourages *meta-cognitive* activity in which new content is related to prior course content. At the end of last week's class, Dr. Paula gave her students a Quickthink task called a Minute Paper, in which she asked them to describe the most important thing they learned in the class that meeting and what concept(s) was least clear in their minds. Quick-thinks are brief, active-learning exercises that can be inserted in lectures or other instructional formats and require students to process information individually and/or collaboratively.

Based on a quick scan of these Minute Papers, which she completed right after last week's class, Paula now spends five minutes reviewing content presented last time that was unclear to students. In this case, the muddiest point is the kind of information presented in a frequency distribution. After briefly reviewing this topic, she draws two frequency distributions on the board and discusses each. Once this modeling of appropriate behavior is completed, she draws a third distribution on the board and labels the X- and Y-axes. She then asks students to complete the figure in this problem (using data showing the number of students scoring in the 50s, 60s, 70s and 80s on the SAT-9 achievement test).

Last year she would have just asked the students to do the drawing from scratch, without labeling the axes for them. By *Partially Working the Problem* (a cognitive scaffolding technique) most students are able to draw the correct figures working individually. Cognitive scaffolds are forms of support provided by the teacher (or another student) to help students bridge the gap between their current abilities and the intended instructional goal (this concept will be developed in later sections of the chapter).

After students complete their drawings, they are asked to turn to their neighbors to compare drawings (a Quick-think known as *Comprehension Check*). Those who completed their drawings incorrectly receive feedback from their neighbors and correct their drawings. Then Dr. Paula briefly goes over the correct answer, completing a Model-Practice-Feedback loop that is known to have a powerful impact in the teaching effectiveness literature (Rosenshine & Meister, 1995).

The previous class meeting addressed the issue of descriptive statistics and included presentations of central tendency, dispersion and frequency distributions. Tonight's content addresses the issue of correlation. Based on last year's classes, Dr. Paula knows that students often confuse drawings of frequency polygons with drawings of correlation scatterplots. This semester, she is trying to address this confusion by having students focus on the kind of information presented in a frequency polygon (the number of people scoring in certain intervals of scores, such as the number of students scoring in the 50s, 60s, etc. on the SAT-9 achievement test). Last week she had her students draw frequency polygons in their cooperative-learning base groups of four. These base groups meet following the lecture/presentation that consumes about the first 50% of every class meeting. As noted above Dr. Paula reviewed this concept of frequency polygons at the start of tonight's class. As part of this presentation, she indicated that later in the class she would be presenting a *similar* figure called a correlation scatterplot. She also explained that the correlation scatterplot presents very different information than the frequency polygon. As previously noted, these figures are commonly confused by students, which is why she wants students to be clear on this point *prior* to beginning her presentation on correlation. This technique, known as *Anticipating Student Errors*, will now be put to the test. Dr. Paula begins her lecture on correlation. When she gets to the part where she models how to draw a correlation scatterplot, she draws the X- and Y-axes. Before labeling the X- and Y-axes, she asks the class, "If this was a frequency polygon, what kind of information would I be putting on the X-axis? on the Y-axis?" Put another way, what does each dot represent in the frequency polygon picture? Many of the students can now correctly answer this question, so Dr. Paula solicits their answers and confirms this information, a brief review designed to firm up understanding among students who are still fuzzy on this concept.

After 15-20 minutes of lecturing on correlation and drawing two correlation scatterplots, she says:

> Let's consider when we might want to use correlation in your classroom. Suppose that you have noticed that students in your class who you perceive as having high levels of self-esteem also seem to do well in school. You want to test that anecdotal observation. So you rank your students (high, medium, or low) on their self-esteem. You try to think of some quantitative measure of achievement and decide to

use SAT-9 achievement scores since you just got that information from the district testing office. You want to draw a picture, to see if those who are high in self-esteem are also high in standardized achievement scores and those who are low in self-esteem are also low in achievement. Which of the two pictures or figures (a frequency polygon or a correlation scatterplot) would best illustrate that relationship? Well, we know that frequency polygons tell you how many people score in certain intervals of scores. And, we have just established that correlations tell us the strength of the relationship between two variables. Since I am trying to see if the variable of self-esteem is related to the achievement variable, I think that the correlation scatterplot figure is my best bet to visually represent that relationship.

Dr. Paula has used the cognitive scaffolding technique *Thinking Aloud* (in which an expert in the field verbalizes her thoughts as she addresses an issue or problem). After engaging in two or three examples of *Thinking Aloud* regarding frequency polygons and correlation scatterplots, she poses a Quick-think problem for her students. She asks them to think of how the two pictures are similar and how they are different, the *Compare/Contrast* technique identified by Johnston and Cooper (1997). Recent meta-analysis research by Marzano and his colleagues has ranked *identifying similarities and differences* as the single best predictor of high academic achievement (Marzano, Pickering, & Pollock, 2001).

After students consider this *Compare/Contrast* problem, working independently and writing their answers on pieces of scrap paper, she asks them to turn to their neighbors and exchange answers. Then she solicits answers from the class. This task is initially difficult for students since it doesn't just call for a relatively rote skill such as labeling the axes of the two figures. It forces students to conceptually distinguish similarities and differences in a personal way. Thus, although it is a difficult task for many students, once it has been mastered, they are likely to retain this distinction long after they have finished the class. Dr. Paula provides some reteaching of this skill once she has solicited answers from the full class.

Later that same class meeting, she provides pictures of both figures for sample data and asks cooperative base groups of four to take each figure and, taking turns in their groups, explain the information each picture depicts. This task is an example of a Quick-think called *Paraphrase the Idea*, in which students put the essence of concepts presented in class in their own words. Often it is helpful to ask the students to explain the idea for a specific audience, such as parents or other grad students. This forces students to engage in *cognitive elaboration*, in which technical content material is related to their own background knowledge and experiences. Such activities have been shown to foster higher-level thinking and long-term retention of information going far beyond the duration of the class (Rosenshine & Meister, 1995).

If time permits, Dr. Paula introduces some sample problems in correlation to the class. After showing students how to compute the Spearman rank-order correlation by working two or three examples, she gives the class a sample problem to work. She sometimes sets the problem up *partially working* the first half of the problem, and then has the students, working individually or in pairs, complete the second half of the problem.

After about 75 minutes of interactive instruction, Dr. Paula gives the students a 15-minute break. After the break, she conducts some minor reteaching of difficult or unclear concepts that she identified by observation or by having students complete a Minute Paper, either individually or in pairs. The last 75 minutes are spent having students work problems in their teams of four. Included in the problem sets are more exemplars of the Quick-thinks described in the teaching narrative just described or some problems like *Select the Best Response, Correct the Error, Reorder the Steps* or *Reach a Conclusion* (see the Quick-thinks section of this chapter and Johnston and Cooper, 1997, Article 14 of this volume). After an hour or so, she goes over the answers to the problems, identifying particularly difficult content and doing some reteaching if necessary.

Students appreciate the scaffolding of having their three teammates available to work these problems together. The better students often provide *Think Alouds* for the less-skilled students as they describe how they solved a problem or addressed an issue.

Another form of scaffolding occurs as Dr. Paula circulates around the room doing informal *Comprehension Checks* by listening to students' comments and spot-checking the problems. She often stops the students when several teams have difficulty with an issue and reteaches the concept for five minutes, a teachable moment difficult to identify in traditional lectures.

Rationale for Interactive Lectures

We like the Interactive Lecture for a number of reasons. Some reasons relate to our own use of the technique and some relate to persuading others to begin using active- and group-learning strategies, particularly others who have historically been reluctant to move away from an overreliance on traditional lectures.

Interactive lecturing can be used in all disciplines. We have seen its application in a wide range of settings, from the humanities and the sciences, in undergraduate, graduate and professional schools. We know of no content area in which the procedures cannot be applied.

An interactive technique, such as a Quick-think, can be used at the beginning of class to provide an anticipatory set to interest students in the coming lecture. Spencer Kagan reports that he asks students to list their favorite TV shows and/or movies at the beginning of an English class and uses this list to introduce the concepts of comedy and tragedy. In this way, an otherwise dry topic can be made timely and relevant to today's students. Quick-thinks can be used in the middle of a class to provide *Comprehension Checks* regarding content covered in the previous 20-30 minutes. For example, Jim Cooper uses the procedure after he has presented three sampling techniques in his Research Methods class. Rather than continuing to present additional sampling procedures, he asks the students to answer a workbook problem relating to one of the three initially presented and to underline the part of the word problem that "tips off" the students. Students work individually for sixty seconds, then each student shares his/her answer with a neighbor for a minute or two. Jim then asks the class for the correct response. The cognitive load of learning three sampling procedures is manageable for his students and ensures that they are able to distinguish between the three concepts. After doing the *Comprehension Check* for the first three sampling procedures, Jim lectures on three more procedures, then does another Comprehension Check over all six procedures. By breaking this difficult and (for some students) boring content into manageable chunks, students perceive this as a doable task and don't slip into the passive aggressive mode that can follow when teachers pour difficult content upon difficult content, without allowing students time to reflect and assess their mastery as they move through the material.

What is an Interactive Lecture?

Interactive Lectures are lectures in which active- and group-learning exercises are embedded at frequent intervals in order to foster deeper processing of content. This term is not original to us, since it has been used in a formal sense by Johnson, Johnson and Smith (1998), and used informally by others for several decades. In the 1980s Graham Gibbs and David Jenkins (Gibbs & Jenkins, 1992) in England used the term Structured Lecturing to refer to a similar concept. In his classic text, *What's the Use of Lectures?* Donald Bligh (1972) made a case for a similar strategy. Dean Osterman and his colleagues at Oregon State University used the term Feedback Lecture to refer to a similar approach in the late 70s and early 80s (Osterman, 1985). We hope to re-energize interest in this concept. To do this, we would like to focus attention on two strategies (cognitive scaffolds and Quick-think assessment procedures) which may easily be embedded in the traditional lecture and which may yield powerful benefits to learners while still allowing faculty committed to the lecture to feel comfortable in the classroom. Interactive lecturing addresses the concerns about group work mentioned earlier for faculty strongly committed to the lecture. It is a way of getting faculty comfortable with group- and active-learning procedures without requiring the greater risks involved in more formal cooperative learning. We hope that success in using this format encourages experimentation with more comprehensive group strategies.

In the next two sections are descriptions of cognitive scaffolding and Quick-think assessments, which can make lecturing more engaging to students and can foster deeper processing of course content.

Cognitive Scaffolding

Scaffolds are forms of support provided by the teacher (or another student) to help students bridge the gap between their current abilities and the intended goal (Rosenshine & Meister, 1995). As noted by Brown and Palincsar, "The metaphor of a scaffold captures the idea of an adjustable and temporary support that can be removed when no longer necessary" (1989, p. 411). Jim and his CSUDH colleague, Susan Prescott Johnston have written about scaffolding in recent years (Cooper, 1997; Johnston & Cooper, 1999). Readers are encouraged to review (Article 15) for more detailed information concerning the research and theory that support this concept, as well as more detailed examples of scaffolding.

Among the scaffolds described more fully in the Johnston and Cooper reading are *Anticipate Student Errors*. In this technique, faculty call upon prior experience to identify difficulties students have had in the past, in order to "pre-correct" common misconceptions. For example, students in Research Methods in Education often confuse frequency polygons and correlation scatterplots, since both pictures have X- and Y-axes and both have dots depicting statistical information. As in the teaching narrative described earlier, Jim and Pamela draw this common misconception to students' attention *prior* to teaching both concepts, thus readying the students for something to focus on as the lecture unfolds.

A second cognitive scaffold is called *Partial Solutions*. In this technique, teachers provide students with answers to the first few steps of a problem to allow them to easily move to the aspect of the problem that is the focus of the current bit of instruction. Freed from the demands of working 3-10 minutes on prior technical content, students can focus their limited attention spans on the new, important content for the day. In the narrative example described earlier, our fictitious instructor worked the first half of a correlation problem so that students could focus on the issue most important in a presentation of the Spearman correlation (the *relative ranks* of scores in a distribution).

A third scaffold is termed *Think Alouds*. In this procedure, an expert practitioner addresses a relatively complicated problem, describing explicitly the thought process that she goes through in addressing the issue. Too often in traditionally-taught classes, the lecturer simply summarizes the important issues in the field without modeling how the lecturer got to that point of analysis. Small wonder that when higher-order thinking is required on a test or paper, students simply spit out the same predigested information presented in the lecture. They are unable to apply the concepts presented in a new or interesting way, which they might have been able to do if the instructor modeled such thinking, and then allowed students to practice with examples developed by the teacher.

Procedural Guidelines are a form of scaffolding, which are very useful to those in laboratory courses and professional- and trade-school settings. When using this scaffold, students are given a list of items or sequential steps to check off as they engage in a task, such as testing a patient's blood pressure, writing a research proposal or conducting a lab experiment.

The last of five scaffolds described in the Johnston and Cooper reading, though there are obviously many more which could be described (see Cooper, 1997), is *Comprehension Checks*. Examples of Comprehension Checks are described in the Quick-thinks section that follows.

Quick-thinks

Quick-thinks are brief active-learning exercises that can be inserted in lectures or other instructional formats and require students to process information individually and/or collaboratively. We will briefly introduce the eight Quick-thinks that Susan Prescott Johnston developed (Johnston & Cooper, 1999; Article 15). Research and theory relating to Quick-thinks can also be found in that reading.

The eight Quick-thinks described by Johnston and Cooper (1999) are: 1) *Select the Best Response*. This technique utilizes a multiple-choice test question. 2) *Correct the Error.* As suggested by the name, the instructor creates a test item containing an error and students must describe the error. 3) *Complete a Sentence Starter.* A sentence stem is provided for students to complete. 4) *Compare or Contrast.* Students are asked to compare or contrast concepts previously presented separately. 5) *Support a Statement.* The instructor provides a statement and students provide support, from their class notes, homework or personal experiences. 6) *Re-order the Steps.* Students are presented a series of randomly-ordered steps and are required to place the steps in the proper sequence. 7) *Reach a Conclusion.* This task requires students to make a logical inference about the implications of facts, concepts or principles they have just learned. For example, in a class in operant conditioning students might have to address the following, "If a consequence to a student's behavior *decreases* the likelihood of that behavior occurring in the future, the consequence can be considered " The correct response would be a "punisher." 8) *Paraphrase the Idea.* This task requires students to rephrase an idea in their own words. In an educational research methods class, one might ask a student to describe to a parent what norm-referenced testing is, and how her child's standardized test score can be interpreted normatively.

The research and theory, which support the Interactive Lecture principles (Article 14 and Article 15) provide a kind of convergent validity that implementing such strategies will have a significant impact on student learning, attitude towards the discipline being studied, and a number of other cognitive and attitudinal measures. And, such procedures involve little risk to the instructor and yet provide a substantial gain in student satisfaction. For Jim and Pamela, the best evidence is that it works on a daily basis in their classrooms.

References

Bligh, D. A. (1972). *What's the use of lectures?* Harmondsworth, England: Penguin Books Ltd.

Brown, A. L., & Palincsar, A. S. (1989). Guided cooperative learning and individual knowledge acquisition. In L. B. Resnick (Ed.). *Knowing, learning, and instruction: Essays in honor of Robert Glaser.* Hillsdale, NJ: Lawrence Erlbaum Associates.

Cooper, J. (1997). Teaching higher-order cognitive strategies. *Cooperative Learning and College Teaching, 8(1),* 6-7.

Cuseo, J. B. (1996). Cooperative learning: A pedagogy for addressing contemporary challenges & critical issues in higher education [Monograph]. *Cooperative Learning and College Teaching.*

Ellis, A. K., & Fouts, J. T. (1994). *Research on school restructuring.* Princeton Junction, NJ: Eye on Education.

Gibbs, G., & Jenkins, A. (1992) Teaching large classes in higher education: Maintaining quality with reduced resources. London: Kogan Page.

Johnson, D. W., & Johnson, R. T. (1989). *Cooperation and competition.* Edina, MN: Interaction Book Company.

Johnson, D. W., Johnson R. T., & Smith, K. A. (1998). *Active learning: Cooperation in the college classroom* (1st ed.). Edina, MN: Interaction Book Company.

Johnston, S., & Cooper, J. (1997). Quick thinks: Active-thinking in lecture classes and televised instruction. *Cooperative Learning and College Teaching, 8(1),* 2-6.

Johnston, S., & Cooper, J. (1999). Supporting student success through Scaffolding. *Cooperative Learning and College Teaching, 9(3),* 3-6.

Marzano, R. J., Pickering, D. J., & Pollock, J. E. (2001). *Classroom instruction that works.* Alexandria, VA: Association for Supervision and Curriculum Development.

McKeachie, W. J. (2001). *Teaching tips: Strategies, research, and theory for college and university teachers* (11th ed.). Boston: Houghton Mifflin Company.

Osterman, D. N. (1985). The feedback lecture. (Idea Paper No. 13). Manhattan, KS: Center for Faculty Development and Evaluation, Kansas State University.

Rosenshine, B. V., & Meister, C. (1995). Scaffolds for teaching higher-order cognitive strategies. In A. C. Ornstein (Ed.), *Teaching theory into practice* (pp. 134-153). Boston: Allyn & Bacon.

A Crisis of Clarity

Susan Johnston

The future of cooperative learning may depend more on returning to the basic principles of effective instruction rather than on any particular innovative strategy. Evaluations of faculty consistently indicate that when students are not clear on what they are to do and how they are to do it, active learning may cease to be an attractive instructional option from the perspective of both teacher and student. If we view the classroom experience through the eyes of the student, the mandate for clarity of both content and procedure becomes unavoidable.

Thinking clearly about curriculum is probably the greatest challenge faced by most instructors. The problem is not a lack of knowledge on the part of the teacher; it is often an inability to organize knowledge so that a novice learner can master it. Before faculty can plan effective cooperative tasks, they need to be clear on what it is that they want students to learn. When students demonstrate confusion caused by unclear content, it is usually because the content is perceived to be vague, overwhelming, or meaningless.

The problem of vague content might be the result of instructors identifying broad topics to be learned and neglecting to subject those topics to further scrutiny. The tendency to focus on broad topics for classroom tasks may be influenced by syllabi based mainly on chapter titles and textbook sub-headings. But topics are only a starting point, unsuitable for designing group activities. Clear cooperative tasks require the generation of essential content statements that specify what it is that students need to know about a topic. Following are examples of content that have been given a more precise focus so that students can work successfully together on a task.

In a literature course, the concept *characterization* might be refined to *"the author's use of actions, internal and external dialogue, and narrator perspective to create a character description for the reader."* In a basic mathematics course, the broad skill of *problem-solving* could be broken down into several steps, one of which could be *"to define in words the mathematical question embedded in a real-life scenario and set up the problem to be solved in symbolic language."* In a political science course, the *election process* might be narrowed down to several elements, one of which might be the *"role that media plays in influencing the public's image of a candidate."* This refining process requires the instructor to meet the challenge of having to decide what the essential content will be before the group work is planned. It is unfair to turn that responsibility over to students by default, as they struggle to make sense of a confusing task that is based on content that is too broad. It is to the instructor's advantage to take the planning time to explicitly fine tune the content selected to be learned, because the classroom explanations and demonstrations will then more closely match the desired learning outcome.

Clarity of content is enhanced when instructors design their courses with the end learning outcomes in mind. Within each major topic, specific concepts and skills that students should master need to be identified. This essential content then provides the selective framework for planning lectures, assignments, readings, assessments, and cooperative learning tasks. Both teacher and student can then be confident that the course content reflected in all these activities is focused and clear.

The problem of overwhelming content is the result of instructors trying to cover too much information in a single class session or in a cooperative learning task or project. The breadth of different ideas or pieces of information crammed into a lecture or assignment often confuses and overwhelms students; their learning becomes scattered and fragmented. It is impossible to teach everything about the topics on most course syllabi. Instructors might be able to claim that they covered it all through lectures and assigned readings, but covering is not teaching, and students know that exposure to mass amounts of information is certainly no guarantee of mastery. Some faculty believe that it is the students' obligation to create order out of chaos by sifting through vast amounts of information to distill the most essential ideas. But, by definition, students are novice learners and need expert guidance to identify the most significant concepts and principles in a course and text.

The painful process of eliminating content from a course of study can be made somewhat easier by having specific criteria in mind which serve as a kind of test that each piece of content must pass in order to be retained in the course syllabus. One criterion for inclusion is that the content under consideration is a prerequisite for understanding future course content or future courses in the degree program. A second criterion is that diagnostic assessment reveals that students have weaknesses that must be addressed. A third criterion is that an academic department within a school has identified certain content as non-negotiable. A fourth criterion is that the content represents the most fundamental concepts and core principles of a discipline and cannot be omitted without jeopardizing the integrity of the course. A fifth criterion is that the instructor has special knowledge and expertise that would greatly enrich students' knowledge.

Too often students are given tasks that focus on trivial or pointless content. Meaningful curriculum is powerful because it focuses on skills, concepts, and principles that can be used to make sense of the world. In order for content to be meaningful, it must have the potential for transfer to other settings. Content with this transfer potential enables students to apply newly learned information in order to explain phenomena, solve real problems, create something new, predict events or trends, and evaluate opinions, policy, or products. Meaningful curriculum relates to ideas or skills that are central to the course or discipline. When students are asked to focus exclusively on detailed factual information, they lose sight of the underlying fundamental concepts and principles. Because students are novice learners, they often have difficulty extrapolating important patterns, principles, or rules from lectures or texts that emphasize discrete pieces of factual information. The instructor plays an important role in guiding students to focus on the content that has the maximum transfer potential. Cooperative tasks are effective vehicles for having students engage in critical thinking about important content. Precisely because they are not facing difficult tasks alone, students are motivated to work on problems that require the application of previously learned skills and ideas.

In addition to clarity of *content*, another challenge faced by many instructors is clarity of *procedure*. Even when content is clear in all the ways described above, it is possible to confuse students with cooperative tasks that are not clear. Unclear tasks are most often caused by a failure to plan the method by which students will demonstrate their understanding of important content. The most effective group work requires a fair degree of structure. There is a temptation to take planning shortcuts and then have to rely on the students to provide their own direction, which usually results in a great deal of frustration on the part of both teacher and learner. Failure to plan the details of partner or group tasks in advance can cause resentment of this active learning strategy, when it is the implementation of the strategy that is in error. When students experience confusion from a procedural mishap, it is usually because the task is perceived to be unclear with respect to the assignment, interaction, or supporting materials.

The problem with unclear assignments is often the result of instructors failing to plan a specific task that will closely match the intended learning outcome. College faculty are often inexperienced in the design of student-centered learning activities. Because the act of translating content into an activity with an observable product can be a formidable challenge, instructors may resort to asking students to simply discuss a topic with no further requirements. When there is no clear end product required, student productivity is often adversely affected. Groups need specific goals and welcome the structure of working toward a concrete demonstration of their ideas. Options for generic tasks that work across a variety of disciplines include the following: summaries, explanations, inferences, predictions, critiques, diagrams, proposals, solutions, arguments, multiple perspectives, and dialogues. The possibilities are endless and can range from the simple to the complex and from those that take 1-2 minutes to those that take several class sessions. The course textbook is also a good source of creative task material. Captions for photos or illustrations can be written or supplemented using newly learned information. Graphs or diagrams lend themselves to interpretation. Conclusions can be provided by the instructor and then supported or refuted by students using statements from the text. Chapter sub-headings can be converted into review questions for each group.

The problem of interaction arises when instructors fail to give specific guidelines for how students are to work together to accomplish a task. When instructors ask students to *discuss* a topic, they assume that students will know what this means and will have a clear idea of how to proceed. Unfortunately, this overused directive is not helpful when giving directions for group work because it is vague and open to wide interpretation. It could mean to take turns sharing each person's thoughts and then record the reasons for any discrepancies among the group. Or, it could mean generating all possible interpretations followed by each member's personal choice. It might just mean that members of the group who want to, can give their opinions. As a preventive measure, teachers need to take a few minutes to demonstrate how group members might interact in order to successfully complete the work.

Options for interaction that engage each group member include the following. Each person records his own ideas silently and then shares in turn followed by an open discussion. Pairs split off to work together and then recombine to report results to other pairs. Each member takes a portion of the assignment and first works alone in order to later explain his part to teammates. Students can also contribute ideas in a random manner as they occur, using brainstorming techniques. College faculty often resist providing this kind of structure because they are convinced that adult learners do not need guidance and that they might even resent it. Student evaluations of faculty prove that both of these assumptions are false. The flames of student resentment are fanned by having to perform in a classroom environment with consistently unclear expectations. New faculty seem to be especially vulnerable to a belief system that ignores students' needs for clarity of both content and procedure. A most unfortunate consequence of this practice is that students who ask for clarification and structure are accused of immaturity and unwillingness to take responsibility for their own learning. In fact, it is the instructor who has abdicated the professional responsibility to create an environment that is most conducive to learning. The seasoned and successful cooperative learning practitioner avoids the temptation to *blame the victim* when group work fails because of a lack of clarity.

Problems with supporting materials result when instructors erroneously assume that college students need only verbal instructions in order to successfully complete a cooperative task. In fact, group members in both the work place and the classroom benefit greatly when they have worksheets with visual frameworks that help to organize their thinking and written responses. These graphic organizers help reduce wasted time spent figuring out how to start tasks. A blank paper will often stop groups in their tracks, causing them to get sidetracked debating procedure instead of content.

Types of graphic organizers include T-charts, column charts, spider maps, continuums, vertical or horizontal box chains, and sentence starters. These visual formats contain blank spaces with labels to guide responses. The selection of organizer depends on the specific content and requirements of the task. In a government course for example, a T-chart could be used for an assignment that requires students to create arguments for and against the Electoral College. Such a simple visual structure has the power to keep all members on task and meets the needs of those with a variety of learning styles. These worksheets can be handed out or copied by students from a projected image on a screen.

In addition to graphic organizers, students need materials that function as the stimulus for critical thinking. Possibilities include: news articles, scenarios, case studies, video segments, selections of texts, diagrams, data tables, graphs, or illustrations. For example, in the Electoral College task described above, students could be given a news article, could be shown a news video clip, or asked to review a relevant section of the text. Without this kind of concrete supporting material, students may be operating in a kind of abstract vacuum having to rely solely on their memories of lectures or readings. These supporting materials are powerful motivators that accelerate progress on the cooperative learning task.

Clear content and procedures allow students to be engaged in learning rather than squandering valuable classroom time trying to make sense of a confusing situation. Faculty report that clarity is the determining factor in successful cooperative learning sessions. While not every cooperative work session will proceed smoothly, instructors can ask themselves important questions during the planning process to increase that likelihood. The questions asked in advance by instructors in their offices are preferable to the questions raised by students once cooperative group work is underway in the classroom.

The Status of Small-group Instruction, 2008: What the Experts Say

Jim Cooper & Pamela Robinson

Small-group instruction has been identified as one of the most powerful interventions in education (Ellis, 2001; Johnson & Johnson, 1989; Johnson, Johnson & Stanne, 2000). This chapter is a status report on small-group instruction in higher education as of late summer, 2008. Small-group instruction, for the purposes of this chapter, includes such strategies as cooperative learning, collaborative learning and other approaches in which groups of two or more students work jointly to address issues and develop products. We will not attempt to make a distinction between the various forms of group learning since that has been addressed elsewhere (Cuseo, 2003; Matthews, Cooper, Davidson, & Hawkes, 1995).

In 1996 and 2003 we published comparable status reports (Cooper, 1996; Cooper, Ball, & Robinson, 2003). In the present report, as in the two previous publications, we used similar methodology, sending electronic surveys to educational leaders in teaching and learning, asking them to comment on a number of issues. For this 2008 assessment, we are grateful to David and Roger Johnson (University of Minnesota), Barbara Millis (University of Texas, San Antonio), Susan Prescott Johnston (CSU Dominguez Hills), Maryellen Weimer (Pennsylvania State University, Berks Campus and the *Teaching Professor*), Donald Bligh (University of Exeter), Philip Abrami (Concordia University), Richard Felder (North Carolina State University), Joseph Cuseo (Marymount College, Palos Verdes), Mark Maier (Glendale College), Kathleen McKinney (Illinois State University), George Jacobs (consultant, AF New Paradigms), Craig Nelson, (Indiana University) and Karl Smith (Purdue University and the University of Minnesota) for their thoughtful responses to the survey. Some of the respondents have historically done much of their work on small-group learning in higher education and others have focused on other issues relating to teaching and learning and other areas of higher education.

Research Base

The first survey item asked respondents to assess the research base for small-group instruction in higher education. Most respondents indicated that the base was significant. The Johnson brothers reported that "Cooperative learning may have more empirical support than any other instructional practice." Craig Nelson wrote "... the single most important intervention for most instructional goals." Richard Felder noted that the base was "Probably stronger than for any intervention I know of." Karl Smith noted that the research base "is vast" and that we know more about the efficacy of cooperative learning than the lecture, the fifty minute class period, the use of instructional technology or almost any other aspect of education. Barbara Millis wrote that research is "reassuringly convergent" and noted the Seven Principles work of Chickering and Gamson in the 1980s, the international deep learning research and the newer research on the biological basis of learning by Bransford, Brown and Cocking (2000), Jenson (2005), Leamnson (1999) and Zull (2002). Maryellen Weimer concurred that the base is strong, and indicated that in her review of two years of pedagogical journal publications she could find no journal without articles on this topic.

George Jacobs identified the base as "strong" and Phillip Abrami noted that the base is stronger at the K-12 level, but feels that there is no reason to believe that the work on younger students may not be applied to higher education. Donald Bligh reported that most topics in higher education are not well researched but that "small group teaching is an exception."

We feel that the research base is strong for well-structured group learning and point to the resources noted above and the meta-analyses of David and Roger Johnson (Johnson & Johnson, 1989; Johnson, Johnson & Smith, 2007), Richard Hake and Eric Mazur's work in college physics, and the meta-analysis in science, mathematics, engineering and technology performed by Springer, Stanne

& Donovan (1999). Robert Marzano's (1998) meta-analysis at the K-12 level found significant effect sizes for small-group work, and Arthur K. Ellis, in his review of the cooperative learning literature, concluded "Cooperative learning is one of the most durable, if not the most durable educational innovation of our time" and that "...cooperative learning has the best and largest empirical base" of any considered in his text assessing the research base for a number of educational innovations (Ellis, 2001).

Interesting Issues for Future Researchers

Item 2 on the survey asked what questions will remain as interesting issues for researchers in the next five to ten years. Philip Abrami responded that the use of "small-group instruction mediated by technology, especially distance learning" was an important issue, as did Barbara Millis. This seems to reflect a wider interest in small-group work as it relates to distance learning. Over 25% of ERIC citations in a recent review of work in collaborative or cooperative learning in higher education were applications to distance learning. Alexander Astin, in a presentation at CSU Dominguez Hills some years ago, noted that the factors that seemed important in "live" instruction (particularly student-student and student-faculty interaction) characterized effective distance learning. These same factors are prominent elements in small-group learning. The distance learning literature supports the importance of small-groups, including the work of Phillip Abrami (Bernard, et al., 2004; Lou, Bernard, & Abrami, 2006), the work of Steven Ehrmann and his Teaching, Learning and Technology group (http://www.tltgroup.org) and others. It is encouraging to note the increase in studies of distance learning in recent years that have gone beyond the focus on technological "bells and whistles" to a focus on underlying pedagogy as essential to the effective use of technology-mediated instruction.

Mark Maier noted the importance of context in assessing the impact of small-group work. Along the same lines, Joe Cuseo noted discipline-specific applications of group work as important issues to delineate, as did Richard Felder. Maryellen Weimer and Donald

Bligh called for more work that integrates what we already know. Kathleen McKinney called for more development of the theoretical underpinnings of group work. The number of issues addressed in response to this item was substantial, and included team composition, how to get more faculty to implement the procedures, issues of task design, and identifying the underlying mechanisms to explain the observed overall effects of well-designed group work. As we have noted elsewhere (Cooper, Ball & Robinson, 2003) the diversity of opinion regarding this issue may reflect the fact that higher education research on group work still lags behind K-12 research. The higher education work has not had pioneers like David and Roger Johnson, Robert Slavin and others who have done systematic work over many years dealing with mechanisms underlying the impact of group learning, the relative importance of cooperation and competition, issues relating to individual accountability and similar analytical studies using experimental and quasi-experimental designs. There seems to be general consensus concerning the power of well-crafted small-group work but relatively little work on moderator variables to delineate more subtle effects across task design, outcomes, students and other issues.

Advice to Practitioners

In his response to this third survey item, Donald Bligh suggested that practitioners "Start with simple tasks in small groups for short periods of time; and then gradually increase their respective complexity size and duration." Karl Smith echoed this advice and suggested that teachers ask students to reflect on what is working [and not working] and engage in conversations with other teachers concerning applications of group work to their classrooms. George Jacobs said to "Start small. Start simple. Monitor groups carefully." Barbara Millis also called for starting slowly and collaborating with like-minded colleagues. She noted that, current college-age students, sometimes called Millennials, "….are highly social and team oriented" and that experts have described these students as using group work in everything from "…Barney to youth soccer as this generation grew up and that their collaboration is both in-person and virtual so that when this generation is not engaging in group activities they are talking on their cell phones and text-messaging." In fact, she finds that the greatest divide between Millennials and adult learners occurs with their use of technology. However, they both like group activities where adult learners can share their experiences and Millennials can talk, if not text. We concur that faculty may want to start movement toward student-centered instruction with informal, turn to a neighbor strategies like Think-Pair-Share, then move to more formal team work as students (and instructors) see the value of group work.

Craig Nelson cautioned that student evaluations may initially go down as instructors first implement small-group learning (but he also noted that this is true of any intervention new to faculty). Joe Cuseo suggested that practitioners avoid giving undifferentiated group grades. Maryellen Weimer called for individual accountability in groups (versus undifferentiated group grading) and stressed the importance of careful task design before implementing group work. George Jacobs echoed this focus on well-structured tasks, as did Richard Felder, Susan Johnston and Phillip Abrami. The sense one gets reading these responses is that some students have had bad experiences in using poorly-designed group work and that group formation, task design and equitable grading emphasizing individual accountability are essential to successful small-group work. Together we have over 50 years of experience in group work and emphatically endorse the emphasis on clarity and organization in designing tasks.

Frequency of Small-group Work

This item also produced a range of responses. Maryellen Weimer reported "It's widespread...one of those innovations that has diffused widely..." Karl Smith reported that it has "been part of the landscape of engineering education for the past 30 years." Richard Felder wrote that over half of the science and engineering faculty participants in his workshops use some in-class group work. Barbara Millis indicated that group work is "generally well accepted" and that "virtually every new book on teaching and learning advocates learning-centered teaching." Mark Maier noted that small-group work is the most cited of new pedagogies in economics, but Becker and Watts' survey of college teaching (2008) identified "chalk and talk" lecturing to be the overwhelming instructional strategy used in economics. Joe Cuseo noted that he sensed a growth in small-group work during the 1990s but that it had leveled off in the new millennium.

Kathleen McKinney believes that growth of small-group work has grown but is still quite limited. It seems to us that the use of small-group work has increased substantially since our 1996 survey and much of this growth is in specific areas, including science, mathematics, engineering and technology. Such growth may be related to the work of Uri Triesman in mathematics, Eric Mazur in physics, and Karl Smith and Richard Felder in engineering, among others. Maryellen Weimer recommended that the wider higher education community needs to be aware of literature reviews of small-group work, such as Becker and Watts' (2008) piece on the frequency of groups used in economics. We feel that a systematic assessment of the frequency of using group work, perhaps including a discipline by discipline analysis, could be of value as we confront such issues as critical thinking, student persistence, appreciation of diversity and other outcomes known to be associated with small-group instruction. We feel that investment in this in-class pedagogy (as opposed to add-on programs like learning assistance and summer bridge programs), could be a cost-beneficial method available to academic and student affairs professionals concerned with fostering student success, particularly for at-risk students, in an era when funding for education is increasingly under scrutiny and accountability iniatives mandate programs document that they provide "bang for the buck."

Obstacles to wider use of group work noted by respondents were similar to comments made to our earlier surveys and include fear of change (McKinney), lack of information (Abrami), lack of training in graduate school (Cuseo), and lack of faculty reading outside of their own disciplines (Maier). Joe Cuseo pointed to the lack of a national champion for group work in recent years, such as the Evergreen State folks in learning communities and John Gardner and his group in the first-year experience.

Synergy with Other Interventions

Item 5 on the survey asked if small group work had developed synergistic relationships with other interventions, such as learning communities, service learning and educational technology. A wide range of responses were received for this item. Some folks indicated that such relationships existed. For example, Karl Smith reported that work on social network theory and communities of practice had been applied to cooperative learning. Richard Felder noted that group work "goes naturally with inductive methods such as inquiry, problem-based learning, project based learning, etc." Joe Cuseo indicated "Perhaps some synergy with technology and possibly supplemental instruction, but that's about all I've seen." Philip Abrami stated "Definitely with educational technology. There are whole areas devoted to it—e.g., computer-supported collaborative learning." (Abrami has done significant work in this area, for example Bernard et al., 2004; Lou, Bernard and Abrami, 2006). George Jacobs pointed to Problem Based Learning in affirming the synergy, and Mark Maier reported using group learning in his new work on Just in Time Teaching (JITT) in economics.

Donald Bligh responded that "It could, but I don't think is has, particularly in Europe." The Johnsons noted, "It is a requirement for most other innovations, but advocates of service learning, learning communities and so forth often ignore cooperative learning." Maryellen Weimer reflected that "groups are used a lot in learning communities and service learning but I am not sure I would describe the relationship as synergistic. I don't think use of groups has improved in these contexts or elsewhere."

Additional Information for Readers

Item 6 of the survey asked respondents to identify information they would like readers to know that had not been addressed in their responses to Items 1-5. Joe Cuseo noted that the issue of diversity had "huge potential for cooperative learning" in terms of its "implications and applications." It should be noted that the K-12 literature has identified appreciation/tolerance of diversity as one of the most consistently identified benefits of group learning (Johnson & Johnson, 1989). In their survey response, the Johnson brothers lamented that constructive controversy has been largely ignored in higher education. In constructive controversy, half the members of a team debate one side of an issue and the other half take a different position. Team members then switch positions and further discuss the issue, not to "win" the debate, but to adduce as much information on the topic as possible. The Johnsons have found that this technique develops more mature views on difficult and complex concepts than other instructional approaches. Karl Smith noted that "the National Survey of Student Engagement [NSSE] is an important player in this area." (for more on the engagement work by George Kuh and his associates, go to: http://nsse.iub.edu/index.cfm). Barbara Millis observes that the NSSE data emphasizes the value of interactive approaches with at-risk students. In fact, recent research from NSSE "found that student engagement had a 'compensatory effect' on grades and students' likelihood of returning for a second year of college, particularly among underserved minority populations and students entering college with lower levels of achievement" (Wasley, 2006, p. A39.) Donald Bligh declared that there is a large body of work in Group Dynamics that is not often used and may be useful in understanding discussions occurring within groups. He also decried pedagogies that focus on "didactic authoritarian methods of teaching" and getting a single "right answer" at the expense of John Stuart Mill's beliefs in the importance of discussion and freedom in the pursuit of ideas.

Resources

The final item on the survey asked respondents to identify resources for those wanting more information on the research, theory and/or practice relating to small-group instruction. Among the general works identified in response to this item were the 1997 book *Cooperative Learning for Higher Education Faculty* by Barbara Millis and Phillip Cottell, the 2004 book by Elizabeth Barkley, Pat Cross, and Claire Major, *Collaborative Learning Technique: A Handbook for College Faculty,* and Dee Finks' 2003 volume *Creating Significant Learning*. More discipline specific resources identified included Richard Felder's web site: www.ncsu.edu/felder-public/Student-Centered.html and the Science Education Resource Center http://serc.carlton.edu/sp/library/cooperative/index.html. Readers may also be interested in the short book by Johnson, Johnson and Smith (1991) and the first edition of the current book (Cooper, Robinson, & Ball, 2003). Donald Bligh's work on lecturing and discussion (Bligh, 2000; Bligh, 2004) offer very useful research and theory regarding underlying mechanisms associated with the impact of small-group work, as well as applied work. Ted Panitz's web site: http://home.capecod.net/~panitz/ offers an array of resources, including links to other websites (as does Richard Felder's site). Phillip Abrami has done significant work on research and theory relating to group work and of particular interest to readers may be his recent work on group learning in distance education noted above (Lou, Bernard & Abrami, 2006; Bernard et al., 2004). A recent article by Millis (2009) places cooperative learning at the heart of effective teaching, linking it to the research on deep learning and the biological basis of learning.

Final Thoughts

It seems to us that the theoretical and empirical evidence for the power of carefully-designed group work is significant. As Barbara Millis indicated and as we have noted elsewhere, there is a kind of convergence surrounding the power of group learning, coming not just from the direct work on cooperative/collaborative learning but also emerging from the work on student persistence, critical thinking/deep learning, problem-based learning, distance education, and appreciation of diversity. The work on discipline-based research in small-group instruction in science, mathematics, engineering and technology noted above is encouraging, and is consistent with the more generic work also described previously.

Once we look past the "main effect" of small-group learning on a variety of cognitive and attitudinal outcomes, the outlook is murkier. More analytical work on moderator variables, such as gender, task type, grading procedures, group size and formation, and other variables seems largely ignored. We are unaware of long-term, systematic attempts to analytically explore these outcomes in higher education that are comparable to work like the K-12 research of David and Roger Johnson, Robert Slavin and a few others.

The research base for well-designed small-group work is substantial. As the cost of education continues to increase, we feel that this approach may yield benefits for a wide array of student success measures, including persistence, critical thinking, appreciation of diversity, and addressing differing learning styles. The *cost* of using in-class pedagogy is relatively low when compared with other interventions available to administrators, especially those working at commuter campuses, where students are not available to attend out of class programs such as tutoring and summer bridge.

Distance learning researchers and practitioners are beginning to develop ways of incorporating pair and group work into their methods of delivering instruction in new and interesting ways, as the work of Abrami, Ehrmann and others demonstrates. Teachers in first-year experience programs can also benefit from systematic applications of small-group pedagogies.

In 2003 Jim Cooper wrote that, in 1985 when he began using group work, he believed most teachers in higher education would be using small-group instruction within a few years (Cooper, Robinson & Ball, 2003). Clearly, he was optimistic in his assessment. Having said that, it seems to us that group work is one of the most frequently used and powerful interventions in higher education, ranking along side such innovations as learning communities and the first-year experience. Jim underestimated the conservative nature of many practitioners and institutions in universities in turning more control of pedagogy to student-centered instruction. As he enters his 40th year in college teaching, he remains optimistic that colleagues like Pamela, starting her 17th year as a college teacher, and the respondents to this survey and their students will continue to see incrementally greater use of small-group instruction over the next decade.

References

Barkley, E. F., Cross, K. P., & Major, C. H. (2004). *Collaborative learning techniques: A handbook for college faculty.* San Francisco: Jossey-Bass.

Becker, W. E., & Watts, M. (2008). A little more than chalk and talk: Results from a third national survey of teaching methods in undergraduate economic courses. *Journal of Economic Education, 39*(3), 273-286.

Bernard, R. M., Abrami, P. C., Lou, Y., Borokhovski, E., Wade, A., Wozney, L., Wallet, P. A., Fiset, M., & Huang, B. (2004). How does distance education compare to classroom instruction? A meta-analysis of the empirical literature. *Review of Educational Research, 74*(3), 379-439.

Bligh, D. (2000). *What's the use of lectures?* San Francisco: Jossey-Bass.

Bligh, D. (2004). *What's the point in discussion?* Exeter: Intellect Books.

Bransford, J. D., Brown, A. L., & Cocking, R. R. (2000). *How people learn: Brain, mind, experience, and school.* (Expanded Version). Washington, DC: National Academy Press.

Cooper, J. (1996). Research in cooperative learning in the 1990's: What the experts say. *Cooperative Learning and College Teaching, 6*(2), 1-2.

Cooper, J., Ball, D., & Robinson, P. (2003). Small group learning in higher education: A status report and an agenda for the future. In Cooper, J., Robinson, P. & Ball, D. (Eds.) *Small group learning in higher education: Lessons for the past, visions of the future* (pp. 282-291). Oklahoma City: New Forums Press.

Cooper, J., Robinson, P., & Ball, D., (Eds.). (2003). *Small group learning in higher education: Lessons for the past, visions of the future.* Oklahoma City: New Forums Press.

Cuseo, J. (2003). Collaboration & cooperative learning in higher education: A proposed taxonomy. In J. Cooper, P. Robinson, & D. Ball (Eds.), *Small group learning in higher   education: Lessons for the past, visions of the future* (pp. 18-26). Stillwater, OK: New Forums Press.

Ellis, A. K. (2001). *Research on educational innovations.* Larchmont, NY: Eye on Education.

Fink, L. D. (2003). *Creating significant learning experiences: An integrated approach to designing college courses.* San Francisco: Jossey-Bass.

Jenson, E. (2005). *Teaching with the brain in mind.* Alexandria, VA: Association for Supervision & Curriculum.

Johnson, D. W., & Johnson, R. T. (1989). *Cooperation and competition: Theory and research.* Edina, MN: Interaction Book Company.

Johnson, D. W., Johnson, R. T., & Smith, K. A. (2007). The state of cooperative learning in postsecondary and professional settings. *Educational Psychology Review, 19*(1), 15-29.

Johnson, D. W., Johnson, R. T., & Smith, K. A. (1991). *Cooperative learning: Increasing college faculty instructional productivity.* ASHE-ERIC Higher Education Report No. 4. Washington, DC: The George Washington University.

Johnson, D. W., Johnson, R. T. & Stanne M. B. (2000). *Cooperative learning methods: A meta-analysis*. Retrieved November 24, 2008, from: http://www.co-operation.org/pages/cl-methods.html

Leamnson, R. N. (1999). *Thinking about teaching: Developing habits of learning with first year college and university students*. Sterling, VA: Stylus.

Lou, Y., Bernard, R. M., & Abrami, P. C. (2006). Media and pedagogy in undergraduate distance education: A theory-based meta-analysis of empirical literature. *Educational Technology Research & Development, 54*(2), 141-176.

Marzano, R. J. (1998). *A theory-based meta-analysis of research on instruction*. Aurora, CO: Mid-continent Research for Education and Learning.

Matthews, R. S., Cooper, J. L., Davidson, N., & Hawkes, P. (1995). Building bridges between cooperative and collaborative learning. *Change, 27*(4), 35-40.

Millis, B. J. (Spring 2009). Becoming an effective teacher using cooperative learning: A personal odyssey. *Peer Review, 11*(2), 17-21.

Millis, B. J., & Cottell, P. G., Jr. (1997). *Cooperative learning for higher education faculty*. Phoenix, AZ: American Council on Education and The Oryx Press.

Springer, L., Stanne, M. E., & Donovan, S. S. (1999). Effects of small-group learning on undergraduates in science, mathematics, engineering and technology: A meta analysis. *Review of Educational Research, 69*(1), 21-51.

Wasley, P. (Nov 17, 2006). Underprepared students benefit most from 'engagement.' *Chronicle of Higher Education*, pp. A39-A40.

Zull, J. E. (2002). *The art of changing the brain: Enriching teaching by exploring the biology of learning*. Sterling, VA: Stylus Press.

www.ingramcontent.com/pod-product-compliance
Lightning Source LLC
Chambersburg PA
CBHW070716160426
43192CB00009B/1210